BUSINESS MOVES

Eight Energies of Leadership

C. JOE ARUN

PARTRIDGE

Copyright © 2021 by C. Joe Arun.

ISBN:	Hardcover	978-1-5437-6707-0
	Softcover	978-1-5437-6705-6
	eBook	978-1-5437-6706-3

All rights reserved. No part of this book may be used or reproduced by any means, graphic, electronic, or mechanical, including photocopying, recording, taping or by any information storage retrieval system without the written permission of the author except in the case of brief quotations embodied in critical articles and reviews.

Because of the dynamic nature of the Internet, any web addresses or links contained in this book may have changed since publication and may no longer be valid. The views expressed in this work are solely those of the author and do not necessarily reflect the views of the publisher, and the publisher hereby disclaims any responsibility for them.

Print information available on the last page.

To order additional copies of this book, contact
Toll Free +65 3165 7531 (Singapore)
Toll Free +60 3 3099 4412 (Malaysia)
orders.singapore@partridgepublishing.com

www.partridgepublishing.com/singapore

To MP, for the great energy

CONTENTS

Preface ix
Acknowledgements xiii

Part 1: Introduction 1
    Competence and Energy 7
    Managing Persons Today 12
    Anthropos of Energy 18
    Dynamo of Energies 24
    Agility of Energy 27

Part 2: Moves and Energies 29
    Backward—Historical Consciousness 33
    Forward—Vision 46
    Rightward—Authority and Power 57
    Leftward—Affective Maturity 73
    Inward—Inner Attitude 87
    Outward—Expressions and Productivity 100
    Upward—Transcending Limitations 117
    Downward—Being Earthly 132

Part 3: Dynamics of Moves and Energies 149
    Organic Connect of Moves and Energies 150
    Deep Practice 152

Part 4: DINCO—a Mantra for Moves Leadership 155
    Discernment 156
    Innovation 163
    Networking 164
    Collaboration 166
    Conclusion 168

Appendix: Moves and Energies in the Great Speeches 171
References 183
Endnotes 187
Index 209

PREFACE

This book argues a case for a leadership that is guided by moves and energies. It looks at human resource development as a way of understanding movements and actualising energies within and without.

There are eight energies and eight movements. To become a competent leader, one should uncover and develop the eight energies in eight movements. Each move has an energy that powers a leader in an institution to achieve the goals and targets.

The fundamental idea of the book is that anthropologically, we are driven by the eight moves we make constantly, and in them, there are eight energies. Efficient and effective leadership lies in the ways one uses these energies by making the appropriate moves. Training of human resources must focus on the eight moves and eight energies to make a person competent for a job in an organisation.

When one is able to have proper energies and use them appropriately, he/she can lead the people and the organisation efficiently. The competency of a person does not develop by acquiring degrees and developing skills alone, but it remains mostly in the way one handles movements within, unearths the energies of the movements, and uses them effectively and efficiently. If an organisation wants to be successful in terms of achieving the end for which it was founded, more investments should be made in developing the needed competencies in personnel. This book attempts to provide a perspective and a model for this.

Let us have a preliminary look at the moves and energies. In every person's life, there are eight movements that have eight energies: *backward move, energy of historical consciousness*; *forward move, energy of sense of future*; *rightward move, energy of authority*; *leftward move, energy of flexibility*; *inward move, energy of attitude*; *outward move, energy of output*; *upward move, energy of transcendence*; and *downward move, energy of humility*. The energy in each movement moves the person to think, feel, and act, which creates a culture unique to that organisation, or what we call as company culture. A leader is not just a manager who handles a function but also one who manages the entire organisation by setting its vision and evolving strategies to achieve the goals set for the company. For this, one needs an integrated and comprehensive outlook that this book provides.

Backward move denotes the concept of understanding of one's history. Forward focuses on the vision and the mission one has. These two movements are closely interconnected. When you think of what you have been, immediately your mind moves you to think of what you want to be. The realisation of your past gives you an idea of your future. History is energy, in the sense that it provides you a consciousness that instructs you about what you should and should not do. Equally, the sense of future (futurology) is an energy that moves you to formulate what you should be and should do in the years to come.

The next two movements are rightward and leftward. Leftward movement talks about love (passion and emotions) that moves a person to act. Love melts rigidity. It makes one flexible and bends to the signs of time. This provides the capacity to adapt to new changes. Heart is tilted towards the left side of the chest. The left hand is always supportive of the activities of the right hand. That support is not complementary but fundamental as love is crucial to human lives. Rightward has the energy of power. This is about one's strengths, talents, skills, and capabilities. More sharply, this is about the way in which one uses her powers. The moves of leftward and rightward have to work together. If a person is more on the leftward move, she will be too fragile. In the same way, if a person is more on the rightward move, she will be autocratic, rigid, and domineering and the institution she manages would become monolithic. There should be a tactful blend of power and flexibility. This is a way of being strict with kindness.

Inward move indicates one's own attitude. Attitude is an energy that guides one's actions and determines one's behaviour. In managing people, we need to first understand one's attitude towards life and work. Even in an effort to effect changes in an institution, we must first focus on the attitudinal change of personnel towards the goals set for the change. Outward move has the energy of output, the expression of the ways in which the other five energies—such as historical consciousness, futuristic sense, power, love, and attitude—are used in order to produce results. These five energies are inner competencies. Outward move and output energy brings out concrete actions. The inner energies must be seen in outward actions and expressions. What is within will be seen without. In managing personnel, every theory or idea should be seen or shown ultimately in deeds. Thinking big is not sufficient. Big ideas should be translated into concrete actions and should produce intended results. The inward and outward moves and their two energies are interrelated: what you do outwardly speaks about what you are inward.

The last pair of moves is upward and downward. Upward means transcendence. Upward always denotes God. We look up to God when we are weak. We also look up to people who are stronger than us when we are in difficult times. But here, by transcendence I mean going beyond one's own preferences, one's own likes and dislikes and placing the common good as priority. It deals with going beyond selfish interests and embracing the interests of the institution in which one works, the advancement of the society, and the environment in which we live. Downward movement refers to the energy of being practical and being earthly. This means being relevant to the context (place and people). Ultimately, whatever we do should benefit the earth, in the sense of development of the country and enhancement of the individuals' personality and competence. A leader should be grounded on the earth while speaking of high ideals. This is what we mean by coming home. Managing people here directs attention to being real.

All these eight movements and eight energies are interconnected and interrelated. One does not have any meaning if isolated from the other. In managing human resources, all the movements and energies have to be considered equally. When you talk about being conscious of the past, immediately you need to place your future in sight. When you realise the energy of powerfulness, you need to soften it with love and emotional appropriateness. In the same way, your attitude should be seen on your actions. In a sense, we should have integrated outlook of developing human resourcefulness and managing personnel. No one-sided focus and no extreme position in managing human resources. There should be a balance. Often, conflict arises only when one gets obsessively attached to a single energy alone and one single move. An equal measure of eight energies makes a person competent, committed, and cultured, who in turn becomes productive.

Human resource development and management are all about understanding and actualising these movements and energies. This is what will make a person an effective, efficient, and productive leader, and the organisation one works for will stand above the rest. More importantly, this is what makes one's life and work meaningful. In a larger context, this helps a nation grow ethically. It is an integrated and balanced leadership that we need in times of extremes.

Writing this book has been a cathartic and formative experience as I tried my best to articulate a new kind of approach to leadership. During the years this book was in the making, I incurred many pleasant debts to people and institutions that provided help and support to ease the lonely hours of writing.

ACKNOWLEDGEMENTS

It has been a long process that involved my working with the help of a network of incredible people. I want to express my sincere gratitude to all, although mere words will fail to convey my sincere appreciation for their guidance and accompaniment in the process of writing this book.

First of all, I would like to acknowledge the contribution of my biological father, Mr V. Chockalingam. As a child, I learnt many valuable lessons of leadership from him. He is no more, but he lives in me now more than ever.

I am deeply grateful to Dr Danis Ponniah, SJ, provincial superior of Jesuit Madurai Province (MDU), who saw in me, early in 1982, capabilities as well as deficiencies and embraced me into his family. In my hard times, he carried me on his shoulders silently. He chose appropriate opportunities for me to unearth my leadership talent. The model of leadership he exhibited helped me learn the ways we need to be firm and kind at the same time. He showed time and again that a leader should accompany the people he leads more than he uses his authority to lord over them.

My special thanks to Dr Jebamalai Irudayaraj, SJ, provincial superior of Jesuit Chennai Province (CEN). His commitment to the poor and the marginalised defines the core of what a leader should be. My reflections on the last section on *backward* move are partly drawn on my observations of his decision-making style: ultimately, a leader must make a difference in the lives of people.

A debt is owed to Dr Francis P. Xavier, SJ, rector of Loyola College in Chennai city. His leadership approaches and strategies have showed me a new world of possibilities, and in fact, that helped to revise some parts of this book. His discipline and hard work inspire me, and the scientific temper he employs in his leading organisations is a skill I am yet to learn.

I want to thank Dr Gerard J. Hughes, SJ, the former master of Campion Hall, Oxford, for his contributions to the writing of the book. Campion Hall granted me the position of visiting scholar for four years during which I wrote most parts of the book. More importantly, I thank Father David Smolira, SJ, who suggested that I return to Oxford for annual research after my doctorate in Oxford, UK.

I am grateful for the fruitful discussions I had with Professor David Parkin, Professor Robert Barnes, and Professor Marcus Banks at the Department of Social and Cultural Anthropology, Oxford University. I benefited a lot in sharpening my ideas from Dr David Moss, professor at the School of Oriental and African Studies (SOAS), London.

I owe a lot to Dr Casimir Raj, SJ, former director of Xavier Labour Relations Institute (XLRI), Jamshedpur, India. When I wanted to combine anthropology, communication, and management, he showed great enthusiasm, supported my desire, and stood by me in my efforts. More importantly, he introduced me to business schools and gave me an opportunity to teach consumer behaviour to XLRI students in 2005. Later, I went on to teach in Singapore and in LIBA; *Loyola College*, Chennai; *Rajagiri Business School*, Cochin; *XIMR*, Mumbai; *Chennai Business School*, Chennai; and *Goa Institute of Management* (GIM), Goa.

My friend George Stroup inspired me with his business skills while I was writing this book. He has been a successful entrepreneur. He owns a chain of ice cream parlours called G&D. During my doctorate at Oxford and later during my annual visits to Oxford, he introduced me to the intricacies of entrepreneurship and to the 'underworld' of business.

Mrs Latha Pandiarajan, *Ma Foi Strategy*, remains a unique leader in my view in the corporate world. I treat her as my sister and call her *akka*, meaning 'sister' in Tamil. That fondness and affection was born out of the ways in which she related to me and the ways she introduced me to the world of human resources management. The road that she has taken to reach the position where she is now, as the director of one of the most successful management consultancy groups in India, shows the depth and quality of her leadership skills. I learnt from her about how important it is to keep the humane dimensions while leading people with certain firmness.

Late Mr Joseph Enok, CEO of *Venture Lightings Ltd*, showed me an example of a leader who had a fine blend of spirituality and business. With a tremendous ease, he demonstrated the art of living and the art of business. He inspired me. He is no more, but he continues to motivate me in intangible ways. I know that he blesses me from heaven.

Mr Marc Genuyt, director of *Icam Site de Bretagne*, Vannes, *IcamGroupe*, France, has exposed me to the French perspective of leadership. My work with him to start an engineering college in Loyola College campus in Chennai city, in collaboration with IcamGroupe, showed me a detailed picture of what the French felt, thought, and acted—the French culture—while they led a team. In that, my close friendship with Mr Jean-Baptiste, who remained as a link person for Icamgroupe, trained my hands on the dynamics of intercultural management.

I want to thank from the heart Dr Renu Isidore, research associate of Loyola Institute of Business Administration (LIBA), Chennai, who played a significant part in making this book happen by pointing out inconsistencies and effecting stylistic refinements. She was very patient with me and persevering in pushing me to return to her with drafts of chapters of this book.

I will always be grateful to Ms Rochelle Simon, who gave the support I needed at times of stressful work schedule for finalising the book and setting reminders to make me refocus on the deadline of completing chapters.

A large number of friends who are leaders of various organisations have directly and indirectly contributed to many ideas you will find in this book, and I could not list them all in any reasonable amount of space.

Finally, my gratitude to the editorial team in Partridge Publishing House that helped to create a much better manuscript.

C. Joe Arun
Chennai, India
2021

Part I

INTRODUCTION

Arunav Banerjee, president and chief researcher, School of Inspired Leadership Innovation Board at the Gurgaon-based SOIL Business school, says, 'The automotive industry requires a composite knowledge of sales and marketing, production and supply chain, engineering and design, human resource and finance. While expertise in other areas can be found within India, there is still a vacuum insofar as people who are able to understand the technical aspects and integrate them into a holistic approach are concerned. This competency is particularly critical in the start-up phase where key decisions on infrastructure, machinery and processes have to be taken.'[1]

We hear people say that our leaders have failed us. Some say we have reached the end of leadership. In fact, they argue that we are in a leaderless world. Recent research on leadership amplifies this idea (Kellerman 2012; Ross 2012; Kelly 2012). Tracing different trajectories of leadership in history, these authors feel that the people today who are governed have lost hope increasingly in today's leaders; they do not believe that the leaders are capable of showing any proper directions to successful and meaningful living. Ross (2012) puts forth passionately an argument that we no longer need any form of representative leadership.

To realise this, Ross invites us to look at the global economy and environment today. He argues a case for 'participative democracy' in which everyone comes together in person to discuss problems and find solutions through a well-informed debate.[2]

The top three in the list of the best-performing CEOs published by *Harvard Business Review* (February 2010)—Steve Jobs (*Apple*), Yun Jong-Yong (*Samsung Electronics*), and Alexey B. Miller (*Energy*)—did not hold any MBA degree, yet they stood above the rest in their performance as leaders. This demonstrates the fact that one does not learn leadership skills from a B-school, but she has to form her character by application of energy from within. It is the moves you make and the energies you utilise which makes you a leader. Today more than ever, we need leaders who understand the movements and energies. This book suggests a model of leadership based on energies and movements. A unique leadership style presented in this book consists of movements and energies.

It is intended to help evolve ways of leading a family and organisations. Special focus is given to leaders who plan, develop, and manage human resources in the corporate sector, although it applies to every individual who leads people in every realm of life. I believe that life is all about leadership—how you lead your life. That gives you either happiness or suffering. Influences, ideas, and experiences guide you to lead your life, your family, and the organisation in which you work. But you need competence and energy to make choices of your actions and words. So you need to build your personality in a competence (energy state) that suits your context and needs. Talent, knowledge, and skills are three fundamental principles that give energy to your personality, or what we call as competence. You uncover your talent, acquire knowledge, and develop skills to achieve what you desire in your life. This helps you perform activities leading to growth individually and collectively. Personal growth should not be seen in terms of narrow domains and specialised domains to succeed in life. We do not need specialists; instead, we need holistic persons who see life in an integrated way. Our education provides specialists with limited understanding of select knowledge. Realising this, the Chinese believe that better leaders are formed by liberal education that allows the person to see the whole person.[3]

The approach employed in this book is anthropological. The competence of a human person is the core of any anthropological discourse.[4] The new definition of the key purposes of management and leadership is 'to provide direction, gain commitment, facilitate change and achieve results through the efficient, creative and responsible deployment of people and other resources'. Fifty-one skill items are proposed and arranged into six clusters: providing direction, facilitating change, achieving results, working with people, using resources, and managing self. This is a state of energy of a person to grow physically, emotionally, intellectually, and socially and to live a life of happiness and to help others grow and live happily. Competence is not meant *only* to help you earn money, power, and fame. Competence is energy. When you have competence, you energise yourself and others. Energy cannot be destroyed. It only takes different forms. The real competence provides you a perspective to life, energy to act, and skill to face difficulties for making the family you live with and the organisation you work for a place where love and happiness rule supreme. Real happiness comes from energies that make you other-centred and do other-centric activities. This altruism gives you lasting happiness and a contended life.

The basis of the energy-movement-based competence, which this book suggests, comes from a triadic process of anthropology, communication, and management. An HR professional should be trained in this process and should learn strategies from it. She should understand the organic unity among anthropology, communication, and management. Managing human resources involve these three areas in which an HR professional should learn skills and build her competence. This serves as the foundation to the dynamo competence of movements and energies, which will be discussed in detail later in this book.

Leadership competence should be built on three pillars: *anthropology*, *communication*, and *management*. *Anthropology* talks about the study of human behaviour from its origins.[5] It studies people and their cultures. The central concern of anthropology is about how people behave and why they behave that way and not any other way. In other words, it explains about identities of different people. Before you manage people, you need to understand them and their culture, world views, and language. An HR professional should be a person who first knows how to study people and their behaviour. One of the skills the HR professional needs is the ability to build ethnography of any group of people. That is, the HR professional should learn the skills of an ethnographer who could stay with the employees in an industry and participate in their daily routine and observe their behaviour. This is what is called a 'participant observation'.[6] A participant observation is a research strategy which aims to gain a close and intimate familiarity with a given group of individuals (such as a religious, occupational, or subcultural group or a particular community—in our case, a group of employees of a company) and their practices through an intensive involvement with people in their natural environment, often, though not always, over an extended period of time. Although this is called a qualitative research in social sciences, anthropology gives emphasis to fieldwork by which the researcher participates in the normal activities of a company and observes at the same time. The strength of observation and participation over long periods of time is that the researchers will be able to discover the internal reality and power networks and will be able to unearth discrepancies between what participants say and believe, what should happen in the formal system of an institution, and what actually does happen, or between different aspects of the formal system. This is in contrast to what one gathers in a one-time survey of people's answers to a set of questions. What the method of anthropology can give us are conflicts among the different aspects of the social system or between conscious representations and behaviour. In a sense, anthropology provides the basis to the ways in which human resources are studied, trained, deployed, and awarded benefits and compensation.

More importantly, in HRM, we manage human beings who speak different languages, who come from different cultures, and who see things from different world views. As companies are becoming more and more globalised, employees are from different countries and cultures.[7]

An HR professional needs to have the capacity to manage across cultures in the process of achieving the goals. This means that she knows how to study the pattern of behaviour and patterns of culture of the personnel in a company and accordingly lead and direct others. Anthropology helps in this. Cultural anthropologists study human behaviour by means of first-hand observation and by interviewing within particular communities and companies and interpret that behaviour by comparing with the results of similar studies done in other communities and companies. They may focus on particular aspects of life or institutions such as how they view their jobs, their approach to life and relationships, or they may try to characterise a way of life as a whole. In studying behaviour, anthropology focuses on the internal logic of other societies. It helps us make sense of the behaviour that strikes us.

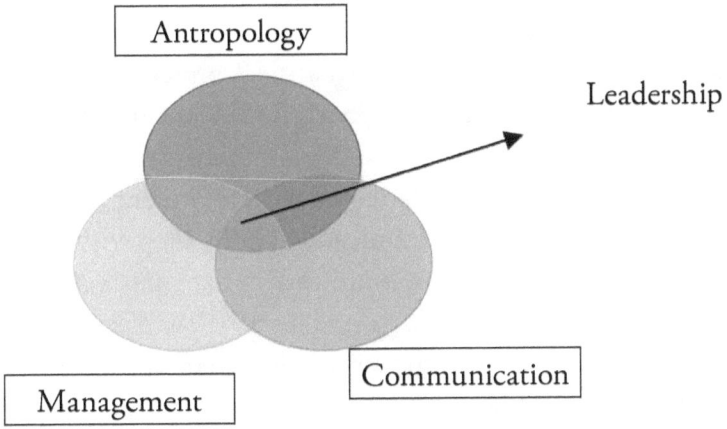

Cross-cultural management of human resources involves multiple ways of developing strategies.[8] In studying organisations, we try to unearth the existence of procedures for mobilising and coordinating the efforts of various, usually specialised, subgroups with different world views in the pursuit of joint objectives. Most of the time, social interactions and activities in the organisations/companies never correspond perfectly to what is officially prescribed. It is important that the employees in an organisation resocialise their behaviour to the prescriptions. For this, there must be a positive dialectic between the prescribed culture of a company and the culture the employees come with.[9]

The second pillar on which leadership competence stands is *communication*. An HR professional should learn to communicate the data gathered in anthropology, what is studied through the method of participant observation, to the employees who need corrections in order to make themselves able people to achieve the set objectives. An HR professional should have effective communication skills to transfer the data from the field study into simple observations and statements. These should effectively reach the people who need to know them. This is an important skill of a leader. An HR professional is a leader who should have the skills of an evangelist, who can talk through the hearts of people. Needless to say, good communication skills improve relationships and teamwork, enhance performance and productivity, foster an open and creative environment, and help solve problems effectively. More importantly, an HR professional should be able to decipher the data from the fieldwork for her understanding of the state of human resources and for the development and enhancement. When companies set high standards for its recruitment of new staff, they emphasise on effective communication skills along with analytical skills and good education.[10] Communication does not come simply because you have learnt a language and know how to speak it. You need to develop the capacity to conceive ideas, keeping the context and the people in mind. Further, you need to formulate them into simple language and then communicate them to the people who you think should listen to your ideas. What matters is how you articulate your ideas in managing human resources.

The third pillar of leadership competence is *management*. Management lies in the ability of one being able to persuade the other to listen to her own ideas and actualise them in the most effective ways. The act of persuasion involves appealing to the hearts, not so much to the head. Arguments by reason do not always work in making people work towards objectives. If you attempt to order the people who work under you by using your position of power, they would not listen to you. Even if they do, it would not be convincing to them. Once you have got a grip of the data available from your anthropological fieldwork and you are confident about your communication skills, what you need to do first is to empathise (*feel into*) with the persons and understand their emotional states. This understanding helps enormously to say what, when, how, why, and to whom. This is called appropriateness. An HR professional should be able to develop the skill to persuade the people with her appropriately.

This HRM process that produces this kind of HR professional will be able to affect success and create a culture of continuous learning and change in companies. Also, the targets in projects, however high and difficult, will be seen as positive and normal.[11] Such HR professionals will be able to develop their skills on their own and create jobs for themselves every day.[12]

Competence and Energy

Today we face two crises: one is energy crisis, and the second is economic crisis. The world in 2008 began to face that energy crunch. This centres on the ever-increasing demand for energy supply and natural resources, petro-dictatorship of oil-rich countries, irreversible climate change, and loss of biodiversity.[13] Later in 2009, we faced the credit crunch, economic crisis. This puts spotlight on the socially irresponsible behaviour of the financial markets, which have often seemed to behave in the smoke and mirrors manner of giant gambling casinos. The world market engaged in high-risk and short-term gains. We put moneymaking at the centre of our lives. That imbued our culture with acquisitiveness and greed.

These crises are not to be seen as natural disasters that we use easily to throw our hands up and blame it on nature. Instead, they are human-made. Greed is the epicentre of them. Luxury has been the aim of life. There were no strong regulations set by national leaders to apply restrain and moderation. It has become very difficult for nations to discern the signs of times, to decide and to design strategies and act upon them.

Lack of proper leadership with balance, maturity, and integrated energies has been a reason for the crises. And the engine of recovery for us lies in leaders with appropriate energies and appropriate decisions. We must stop our extreme ways. Leadership should emphasise on sustainable growth and ethical practise, not profit at any cost. And in this, we need balance and integration. We need appropriate energies and their proper use. For long, the world has been either left or right, communists or capitalists, conservatives or liberals. This extremity cost our growth, and we are in recession. We need leaders who are capable of using energies to help us lead an integrated life.

This book is about energy leadership that uncovers and uses appropriate energies with a deep sense of integration and organic unity. Put simply, this book is about how to become a leader who is integrated in person and uses energies to manage the resources effectively. Largely, it explains about the ways to build the competency that a leader needs to manage human resources in organisations. More sharply, this book discusses eight energies in eight moves which a leader should make in order to lead people efficiently and effectively. This is, in many ways, a source book for training people to become competent leaders in human resources.

This book is not only for people who want to be HR professionals but also for those who are already in the profession and need ongoing training to revive the spirit of leadership in them. In managing the talent pool to achieve the set objectives in an organisation, an HR professional needs to have directions and energies within that she would employ appropriately and effectively. This book suggests that she should be able to think, speak, and act guided by the eight moves and the eight energies. These energies are drawn from the resources of anthropology, communication, and management. A leader is the one who understands her and others (anthropology), communicates that understanding effectively and clearly (communication), and manages the people and activities (management) that produce results that contribute to human development at large in our society. A leader in the role of managing resources should learn to move in eight ways to gain the eight energies in order to become a resourceful HR professional and an effective and efficient leader. This applies to any leader in any organisation or even in a family who wants to effect change and development by allocating resources properly and organising activities efficiently that help achieve goals.

In the recent past, we have seen a rapid industrial and technological growth. This has given us many breakthroughs in many areas. But every step we take forward, we are pushed back by natural disasters, economic collapses, incurable diseases, war, terrorism, and weapons of mass destruction. More dangerously, now in 2008, we face serious crises of climate change, energy scarcity, and loss of biodiversity. Even great experts in finance have no clue about what is going on and how to fix it.

The elected governments in the world have failed to tackle these destructions, or they have been ineffective in handling the crises. The only hope for humanity is by forming individuals who are personally capable and empowered and socially motivated, who can effectively and efficiently conceive strategies to allocate resources and manage performance. In doing so, they should be able to change the way we live and the way we work. We do not need mangers today. We need leaders who effect social change through transformations in the corporate world—social entrepreneurship.[14] Many managers who manage human resources in organisations are left with frustration and conflict. The problem faced by them is typical of what Watson spoke about managing people:

> It's the people management thing. It's handling the people who work for me. They are a constant headache. I've tried to read the books and I've been on people management courses. I didn't miss one of the OB classes on my MBA course. But still despair at the difficulty I have with managing the in my function; sorting out who is going to do what, getting them to things I want, getting them to finish things on time, even getting them to be where to be where I want them. And that's before I get into all the recruiting, training, appraising and all that stuff.[15]

This frustration, I reckon, comes from lack of competence to deal with people. HR leadership competence is first and foremost the capacity to persuade others to listen to your ideas. The question here is, 'to what extent this individual gets people to perform tasks effectively without arousing hostility'.[16] This is the core area of human resource management. It lies in the ways in which we persuade people to listen to our ideas and act accordingly. Persuasion needs skills, talent, and knowledge. Acquired skills, uncovered talent, and informed knowledge give you the needed competence to persuade people to buy your products and ideas. This competence is the resourcefulness of a leader. She will be considered a competent leader. This resourcefulness cannot be measured by the grades you get in B-schools. Those grades come from your grasp of the subjects taught through many terms of the academic year. That does not demonstrate your resourcefulness. It is just a measure of your knowledge, cognitive capacity.

In HR competence, many books suggest three needs: cognitive learning, skills-based learning, and affective learning.[17] In most of the works on HRD, HRP, and HRM, needs (knowledge, skills, attitude (KSA)) are seen at:

1. the level of capacity, in the sense that one is able to think and process intelligently
2. the level of capability that gives practical abilities in work rules
3. the level of desired behaviour that facilitates interactive behaviour to effect best results.

In this, leadership in managing human resources is merely seen as a function of an individual. In other words, human resources are considered as machines that are capable of doing some activities. This is one-sided and a narrow approach to HRM leadership.

HRM leadership is based on energy. The leader draws energy from resources and energises her and others towards achieving the best results in organisations. This leadership is concerned mainly with how one is able to gain energies to energise others and the organisation. I believe that there are energies innate to us that are potential to make us competent individuals suited for any performance. We need to tap those energies at the right time and in an appropriate measure. We need to make moves to realise the energies. All we require is the passion to develop the competence we are in need of. Once we have the passion that guides us with ease to become competent, we can become powerful people who can persuade anybody to do anything. To train to become a competent leader who can persuade others effectively and efficiently, you need to understand the movements and know how to use the energies. I am not a management guru to propose definitive theory on management. I am an anthropologist who tries to apply anthropology to management, more specifically, to the ways in which we could develop human resources and manage them. I consider human beings as the source through which an organisation conducts a business. If that is to be successful, the right human resource has to be employed, trained, and redeployed in roles in that organisation. These HR skills do not come merely from a degree you get. It is a process of growth. You nurture it and become matured in it. This process is concerned with how you build the competence that enables to lead a group of people who would achieve their objectives with ease and style.

This book suggests the eight ways of moving with eight types of energies which help in the process of HR competence building. Consciously, one should move in the eight directions and realise the eight energies and apply them to oneself in the act of being a leader. This would make you a competent person who is intellectually sharp, emotionally mature, professionally skilful, socially adept, and morally sound. You will not be just a specialist in one area; instead, you will be capable of multitasking in a pluricultural environment and with people across cultures and societies. It is not just competence building that you could easily do by attending workshops and seminars. To develop this competence, one needs to enter into meditation in which you realise what you are, what you are capable of, and what you need in order to become a competent person. This competence I call *dynamo competence*. Before we explain about the dynamo competence that discloses the energies and moves, we need to look at the management scenario today.

Managing Persons Today

Managing institutions and people go through a rapid change. What was management in 1960s is not any more the type of management we have in 2008.[18] The way leaders and managers see the act of leading and managing is different in both content and style. The perspective has changed. Increasingly, it is not the material gain that is the focus but the means by which that material gain is achieved is the major concern of many organisations and companies. Being ethical, environment-friendliness, and corporate responsibility have become the parameters to measure the quality of companies. The ascending economic growth is often trapped in debate of how to bridge the gap between the superrich and the marginalised poor and how to make the poor enjoy the benefits of global capitalism. At the same time, organisations are struggling to keep pace with the change in commerce and culture. Deregulation has produced competitive anarchy across industries. The digitisation of everything possible has made the information available free of cost. Many industries struggle to adapt to this 'free world'. Internet has taken the power from producers to consumers. The availability of capital, power of outsourcing, and the Internet help greatly to start businesses quickly, and success and failure are equally quick.

We will see change in the ways we manage human resources and what type of leadership is needed for that change management. The context is set by a report by *the Charted Management Institute*.[19] This is the context against which we need to understand human resource management and leadership competencies. In 2018, human resource management will be different from now.[20] The report discusses the state of employment in 2018. It predicts significant changes in the ways by which companies would employ people. More people will be working from home than from offices. The concept of workplace will go through a sea change. There will be more virtual companies, which will organise the work of their employees by connecting to them using the computer. And these virtual companies will be mostly community-based enterprises. Companies will have to compete hard for employees since many would like to have flexible working hours and the freedom to choose their workplace. Employees will gain increasingly the power to dictate companies what they want. Many talented people will be multi-employed, working for many companies at the same time. They will get work and do them at home, and they will be available on the phone once they have done the work. Alternatively, they will be virtually present in meetings by the use of hologram technology. Work will be project-based, not conventional duty-based. Managers will have to be competent in managing people remotely, and their emotional intelligence and sensitivity to other people's values will be valued greatly, equal to their technical competence. Employers will hand over their power to employees; shareholders will lose power to all profits. Young people in the coming decade will choose jobs that are ethical and environment-friendly. They will refuse to enter into the rat race. The younger generation will demand a part in the power and in the structures of the organisation. This context will demand a different type of leaders and managers who have integrated competencies and comprehensive perspective.

The report suggests that we would need leaders/managers who will be knowledgeable, flexible, capable in managing flexibility, constantly aware of the evolving trends and changes, have humanness in their approach, highly motivated, and who will be in need of family support. The report considers these as action points for the future. The report also suggests what kind of organisations would evolve in 2018. Organisations should be able to be agile and alive and should have clarity in their purpose, flexibility in managing change, genuineness in their transactions, innovation in their produces, and openness to change. In this book, how we should develop human resources and how the HR should be managed gets special attention.

We would need leaders/managers who have the skills to mutitask and have integrated competence and personal character, because (i) they need to evolve HR policies that are based on trust, openness, equity, humanness, flexibility, innovation, and consensus; (ii) they are motivated to create conditions in which people are willing to work with zeal, initiative, motivation, and enthusiasm; (iii) they are competent to treat people, and prompt redress of grievances would pave the way for healthy workplace relations; (iv) they become agents of change in such a way that they are able to prepare the workers to accept the technological changes by clarifying doubts; and (v) they are devoted to quality and professionalism in all aspects of personnel administration that will ensure success. In other words, the HR manager should have the skill, the talent, and the knowledge to treat people as resources, reward them equitably, and integrate their aspirations with corporate goals through suitable HR policies.

HRM is understood as 'management function that helps managers recruit, select, train and develop members for an organisation'.[21] Properly trained and highly skilled human resource is perceived as the greatest asset of an organisation. Skilled personnel contribute to efficiency, growth, and increased productivity and market reputation of an organisation. Industrial, commercial, research establishments, and even governments have realised this. Invariably, a separate human resources development department exists in all these organisations to attend to the matters relating to recruitment, training, and deployment.

Technological advancements in various fields the world over are very rapid, and every other day, we see new products or machines or equipment with more and more advanced features, with which users have to be acquainted. In order to cope with the industry demand and technological advancements, we need to develop training strategy for our human capital to attain the required skill levels.

Many scholars define the study of HRM as efforts to train employees in learning, training, development, and education.[22] Learning and training changes an individual's knowledge and skill set. Much debate is on how we put learning into practice. But the HRD process—*observe, plan, act, and review*—is set to achieve some specified objectives by training and learning.[23] Training refers to methods to give a new entrant or an existing employee the skills, knowledge, talent, and attitude needed to perform the job. In this, there has not been one model to train the employees to develop their competencies and skills. Each company, keeping in mind its purpose, follows a model that need not be comprehensive and integrated. This is due to the complexity involved in understanding human resource development and management. This leads to performance management and talent management. Thanks to the increasing interest in HRD by learning societies, knowledge economies, flexible organisations and careers, and developers of new technologies, companies and institutions have realised the importance of the role of HRD and HRM in the success of their enterprise. And HR professionals have equally come forward to see their role as significant and challenging.

In the theoretical arena, HRD is fundamentally concerned with enhancing the competence of the personnel in an organisation. That competence leads individuals to be committed to the goals of the organisation, and the competence and commitment generate a culture that becomes unique to the organisation. Nurturing this culture is what ultimately makes the organisation stand above the rest. This has a huge impact on business growth and development. Many studies have looked at the performance of companies in which what kind of role the employees play was important to determine the success of the company (Pfeffer 1994; Yeung and Berman 1997; Macduffe and Krafcik 1992; Ostroff 1995). They have concluded that wherever the development of employees' competence through training and other practices was at the core of business practices, those companies have fared well in the long run, whereas the companies where profit and quick process of achieving the goals without a coherent design of competence building of employees have only failed them. The employees could not sustain their productivity, and they did not manage the companies efficiently.

The study by Wellbourne and Andrews (1996) of 136 companies (food service retailing, biotechnology, etc.) had two scales to measure the role and the function of HRD in those companies. The first scale was to see whether in the company's strategy and mission statement, employees' competence and training programme for them was mentioned and more competent HRD managers were not only in place but were constitutive in nature in the whole design of the companies. The second scale looked at the contentment of the employees in these companies. Optimum level of productivity and organisational culture were felt at every level in the companies in which the two scales were given sufficient emphasis. Even the companies that were awarded by the National HRD Network and the Confederation of Indian Industry (CII) from 1989 until 1996 have shown their success formula by having good HRD practices (Rao 1996; see also Rao 2006: 26, 27). In spite of changes and fluctuations in the market, they could continue their performance mostly by their robust HRD department that designed strategies and programmes that enhanced the competence and commitment of the employees and thus effecting a proactive culture in the companies.

Kaufman (2007), in his review of the development of HRM, traced its origin as a functional side of management and research teaching of HRM. Initially, there was no formal focus on management of human resources. There was no separate department that looked after the development of human resources and their allocation. The practice of HRD-M began to get a formal look only in the late nineteenth century. Hiring, training, discipline, and motivation of employees and termination were all done alternatively, and someone in the line of management looked after it. In the 1890s, many companies started to see the need of paying attention to human resources in terms of giving employees sufficient incentives and providing them with a proper environment for their work and family life (Spencer 1984). For this, the 'welfare secretary' was given the charge of managing human resources. Later, a kind of 'employment office' was introduced in many countries (Farnham 1921; Eilbirt 1959). In outside countries like United States, Germany, and Great Britain, it was only Japan that paid attention to HRD-M. The British colonial territories such as India and South Africa treated HRD-M as 'welfare work'. In the 1960s, application of psychology to industry and management of employees took shape, leading to the formation of the distinctive field of human resources management. For the first time, the term *human resource management* appeared in the mid 1960s (Strauss 2001).

At the strategic level of HRM, we must understand the main areas of HRM for which the personnel are deployed. There are three subfields of the theoretical areas of HRM. First is micro HRM, which deals with the policies and practices of HR (Mahoney and Deckop 1986). It includes local laws, customs and markets' condition, and recruitment of employees and their competency development. More clearly, cultural contexts play an important role in the area of micro level of HRM. The second area is strategic HRM. It discusses systematic questions and issues that connect the contexts and the organisational activities with the goals for which an organisation is founded. This focuses on measuring the impact of human resources on performance (Delery and Doty 1996). The strategic perspective should be considered not only by HR specialists but also by general managers. This, in general, altered the outlook of the human resource management as well as the development. In more than one sense, management is seen as resource-based and as strategic decision-making with regard to the development and the use of human resources. High performance is closely linked to the question of how the personnel in an organisation have been helped to develop and build their own competencies. The third major area of HRM is international HRM. More than theoretical concerns, here in international HRM, emphasis is on how companies operate across national boundaries—cross-cultural management (Evans et al. 2002). Strongly, this connects to the issues of how personnel are employed to measure up to international standards and requirements. One's competency is weighed more in terms of demands from the country he is employed than the competency understood in isolation of the context. The connection between one's competency and the country in which he is employed matters here. Therefore, one should enhance her skills according to the demands of the context.

In all these three areas of HRM, human resource has to be shaped according to the demands of the particular perspective that is taken for the type of HRM. These approaches would produce only employees and workers who will play their roles in industries and organisations, not leaders who are creative and innovative. They would lack attachment to the organisation they work for. In fact, most of them will be 'disengaged' in their work.[24] Mostly, the management process involves strategic planning, capital budgeting, project management, hiring and promotion, training and development, internal communication, knowledge management, periodic business reviews, and employee assessment and compensation. But there is hardly anything substantial about the development of leadership competence. Successful companies such as General Electric, DuPont, Procter & Gamble, Toyota, and Visa were consistently successful not because they followed the management process well. Their success is due to innovative leadership. General Electric was able to produce minor inventions within the structure of Thomas Edison's notable invention. DuPont invented a way of allocating capital rationally in the context of plenty of attractive projects. Procter & Gamble came up with how to build intangible assets—brands. Toyota became the most successful car-making company simply because it believed in the ability of the ordinary employees. They call it Thinking People System. In 2005, the company received more than five million improvement ideas from their employees.[25] In all these cases, the companies made efforts to develop leadership competence instead of skilled employees. The employees in these companies considered themselves as men and women leading their own companies and not working for them. To do this, we need men and women—human resource—who have multiple and integrated competence. They should be men and women who do not see profit and material benefits as their main objectives but as by-products of their role in contributing to the well-being of humanity. In other words, HR professionals should be social entrepreneurs who can create a competent workforce, a healthy work culture, and a conducive work climate.

Anthropos of Energy

All matter is energy at rest. Energy manifests itself in many ways, in numerous forms and conversions. Universal and planetary flows of energy have determined the course of history. All these are governed by the gravitational energy. Energy determines life. Innovation and growth in history revolve around energy and its effective use. What we have grown is driven by different strategies by which human beings have worked on manipulating energy. Conversion of heat by human labour (work) led to the Industrial Revolution.[26] From steam engines to search engines, it is energy that plays a central role in the ways by which leaders had gone through a fortuitous process that resulted in the life we live today.

Life on earth is determined by the 'photosynthetic conversion of solar energy into phytomass [plant biomass]. Humans depend on this transformation for their survival, and on many more energy follows for their civilised existence.'[27] The history of civilisations has followed a course of how energy is transformed and used for different works. This is why Nobel laureate Wilhelm Ostwald said, 'Vergeude keine Energie, verwerte sie.' Do not waste any energy, make it useful.[28] Initially, civilisation is founded on use of energy from coal; the entire metabolism of the Western world was dependent on coal miner since the manipulation of soil by human beings.[29] The structure and dynamics of any evolving societies have been centred on refinement of energy flux. For Leslie White, anthropologist, the first important law of cultural development: 'Other things being equal, the degree of cultural development varies directly as the amount of energy per capita per year harnessed and put to work.'[30]

In 1700, there were two kinds of energy: heat and work.[31] Human beings burned coal or wood to cook food and keep themselves warm. They used their muscle energy or the muscles of horses to move things. Later, Thomas Newcomen invented a device; Newcomen used steam to move things. The Newcomen steam engine remains the origins of all progress of the modern world. It introduced technology to make good use of work of human beings to be productive with ease and facility. In 1763, James Watt mended the Newcomen device to come out with an idea of 'converting the up-and-down motion of the piston into a circular motion capable of turning a shaft for use in mills and factories'.[32] With Thomas Edison's light bulb energy innovation moved to another level, he combined all the properties. He seemed to have tested more than six thousand things, to make a carbon filament to generate and distribute electricity. This changed the ways human beings lived their lives. Although incandescent bulb gave way to fluorescent bulb more than a century, it helped to transform societies. Nick Holonyak, a scientist in General Electric, and later Shuji Nakamura of Japan came up with LED lights using gallium nitride. Then came steam energy to give electricity to move navies and liners.[33] Charles Parsons saw energy and its effective use in turbine that spun on its axis. For a long time, steam was the main energy that determined the world's economy and expanded industries. In twentieth century, nuclear energy ruled supreme, with the development of civil nuclear power popularised by the Manhattan Project in the 1940s.[34] Later, natural gas came to occupy in the process of energy and its use, like coal and oil, particularly George Mitchell's Barnett Shale, the largest gas product of USA. Now the depleting natural resources directed the attention of countries to sustainable energy sources.

We realise that energy is a key source of economic growth because many production and consumption activities involve energy as a basic input.

Energy determines economic development; it is the oxygen of an economy and a driver of economic growth. The energy industry contributes to economic growth. Energy creates jobs and value by ways of extracting, transforming, and distributing energy goods and services throughout the economy. 'In 2009 the energy industry accounted for about 4% of GDP in the United States. In some countries that are heavily dependent on energy exports the share is even higher: 30% in Nigeria, 35% in Venezuela and 57% in Kuwait. The energy industry extends its reach into economies as an investor, employer and purchaser of goods and services.'[35]

Energy underpins the rest of the economy, and when the flow of energy is disrupted by price shocks and supply interruptions, it can destroy the economy. Heat, light, and power build or help function the factories and cities that provide goods, jobs, and homes and provide amenities, making life more comfortable and enjoyable. And job creation is such a high priority around the world.

Human beings unlocked both somatic and extrasomatic energies for various tasks. It starts from searching for food; any non-photosynthesising being needs food energy. Primate ancestors used their tool-using capabilities to gain energy for their existence, and tools have given mechanical capability to acquire food, shelter, and clothing.[36] Mastering of fire energy led to comfortable habitation, and in small ways, conversion of kinetic energies of wind and water gave some useful power. In fact, power explains the rate of energy. That finally helped to see every form of energy turned into energy.

Leadership should be seen from the perspective of structure and dynamics of realisation and use of energies within and without. Leadership must spring from the deep realisation of human nature and condition that explains how energies are used to make things happen. The success of leadership lies in the efficiency of energy conversion by both physical and intellectual moves. The best leadership is measured by the degree and the intensity of energy with which she understands herself, other human beings, networks of society, and the natural environment, not merely by her sharp intellect or versatile skills. You cannot acquire this competence from B-schools and research. A competent leader views the world, nature, and human life in a proper perspective. Her world view is important.

Lack of energy density and energy conversion are the reasons for failure in leadership. A leader must become aware of her energies that energise and vitalise the group she leads. The energy of a leader gives direction and meaning to others who follow her in a company or an organisation. Leaders, in fact, transform people by 'imbuing them with a new energy that did not exist before'.[37] Leadership is not just about tools and techniques, but it has much do with the level of energies. In the relentless drive to achieve a goal, a leader needs undivided energy to persevere in the presence of challenges.

I believe that anthropology provides a foundation of leadership that helps a leader understand first the vulnerability or fragility of human power, that human beings are limited, and that limitless energy is needed to achieve goals. If not, human beings conserve energy to perform tasks to achieve goals.

Fragility is the most fundamental core of human life. We are limited beings. Somewhere at one point in time in life, we reach that limit. There is an end to our power of reason and physique. Of course, our science and technology have enormous power, but even with the advancement, it has reached the limit. Every living being is born, grows old, and dies. Nothing is permanent. Everything is transient. If one learns effectively to make sense of the limitedness of humanity and the transience of life, she becomes a very efficient leader at the core level.

I want to dwell on this for a while. Imagine you are a ten-year-old standing by the side of an athletic track, holding your father's hand. You watch this magnificent athlete striding down the runway, with the pole gripped in her hand. With the effort of the run, her hair flies, and suddenly, she soars. You crane your neck, and it seems as if she were going up, up, up . . . forever, towards the skies, towards eternity. Suddenly, there is a break; it seems as if she were being snapped back to Mother Earth as she turns her body and comes down and falls on her back, spreadeagled on to the foam. You ask your daddy, 'Why did she not go higher and higher?' You father says, 'That is all she could do.'

From our birth until we die, we do so many things to rise above our human nature that is finite and limited, and at one point, we fall down. The acts of rising and falling are in the fabric of this human nature. We invent machines to make life convenient, invent medicines to prolong life, break atoms to understand nature, read our genetic code to overcome our nature. This makes us feel self-sufficient, and many times, we become arrogant and say that we do not need God and only the weak needs God, that we are strong and intelligent, that we can erase the limitations of this finite human nature. Ego gets inflated. Passionate individualism fills the air. However, at some point in this project, we come to realise that *we are fragile and limited*. That is the point where we begin to look for some meaning in this existence. We begin to feel that we need energy beyond the limited human energy.

Every human being has an urge within her to go beyond the limitation of the finite human nature. From the time we are born, we have a deep sense of restlessness that craves for something beyond what we are. There is that fire of energy that demands an expression. We want to reach the heights of this existence. Nevertheless, we reach a limit beyond which we are unable to go. Death, by nature or by accident, spells the end. We know we will have this end, yet we try to go beyond. We meet with failure. We did not choose where and when we were born, and we die when we do not expect to die. Our human nature *fails*. That failure drums into our mind that human life is fragile, finite, and limited. 'Then is there no meaning in this life?' we ask angrily. 'This life is simply an illusion!' we shout in frustration. Some reach the dead end in which death instincts eat them up. The end is suicide. Some others recognise in them the life instincts that urge them to search for some meaning in this limited life. They look for ways to have a sense in this senseless fragility. That impulse leads them to do something beyond their finiteness. I call it a spiritual impulse. Once they are in the grip of that impulse, life becomes meaningful, and such a life is transformed into a life of other-centredness.

Let me detail the process in anthropological terms. *First of all*, separateness is the first realisation of human beings, since human beings are the only creation who are *aware* of themselves by the power of reason. They are aware of them-*selves*, their capacities, their past, and the possibilities of their future.[38] They know that they are born without their will and will die without their will. They see and realise repeatedly that people who are younger than them and older than them die before them. They love something so dearly, but then they lose it. They love someone passionately, but then they lose them tragically. They experience this aloneness and separateness all the time. This capacity of self-awareness of aloneness in human beings begins from the time the umbilical cord is cut off when they are born from the womb of their mothers, where they had been enjoying a total communion. In the womb, there was no separation between the mother and the child; instead, there was an organic union between them. I call this union umbilical union. This union is not produced by human effort. Any force from outside does not will this. This is a natural, divine force that has produced the child from nothing and built this union. No one knew what shape, what colour, and what character the child will have. It simply emerges. I strongly believe that the divine force does this emerging. In this union, we experience the limitless power within us, which helps to grow and flourish into a beautiful creation. In the womb, every need is fulfilled without our asking. We breathe, eat, and rest with ease. From the time we are cut off from that umbilical union, we begin to feel not at ease with everything. The first thing we do is to cry. We cry for the reunion with the mother. We become restless. We start searching for such union in life and long for it constantly. From then on, every effort of human beings aims for that union. The deepest need of human beings is to overcome the separateness and the aloneness.

We need to situate leadership in this. Each individual human being longs to be-*long*, and longing to belong is a reservoir for activities of leadership. What I want to become energises us to focus on activities on the goal. To do things within the limit and beyond the limit, a leader requires energy, directed and focused energy. Choosing the right kind of energy makes a leader successful in a chosen field.

Dynamo of Energies

Building leadership competency revolves around a dynamo energy. The dynamo power comes from the use of rotating coils of wire and magnetic fields to convert mechanical rotation into a pulsing direct electric current through Faraday's law. A dynamo machine consists of a stationary structure, which provides a constant *magnetic field* and a set of rotating windings called the armature, which turns within that field. You need a field and a set of windings, and you need to rotate to produce energy that springs from the interaction between the field and the windings.[39]

Applying this dynamo theory, the magnetic fields are *energies*, and the armature is taken as the *moves* we make to realise the energies. A leader should move to one direction where she acquires one energy and then towards another direction and collects another kind of energy. Once the eight energies are personalised and internalised, she uses the energies in equal measure for her task of management. There is a constant movement from one direction to another. There is no stoppage or outage. As a dynamo provides electricity only when it is rotating, in this model, there should be constant movement to and fro in order to realise the eight energies. The magnetic field has to be constantly connected to all the fields of directions, and you need to move from one to the other while you are being connected organically to the other movements. Here, you move from one field and remove from one to the other. Moving constantly creates power and dynamism. Ultimately, this process makes you the person who is *dynamic*-ally competent. Here in this process, staying on with one direction will be against its very nature. It stagnates growth. Eight moves (windings) activate eight energies (fields). In this, *move*-ment is crucial to realise the energies.

In equal measure, there is organic unity between the different energies and moves. One does not have its energy isolated from the other. One move is useless without the other moves. They are interconnected and interrelated. This unity gives integral growth in a person. HR competence can be defined as movements that connect with core energies to realise the ends in an organisation. The HR professional is the one who moves backward, forward, rightward, leftward, inward, outward, upward, and downward and realises by activating energies of historical consciousness, futuristic vision, authority, emotional maturity, attitude, productiveness, transcendence, and pragmatism. The eight moves and the eight energies form the character of the HR professional. She becomes dynamic, energetic, and productive. Not one-sided but a multifaceted personality. Not a single-task professional but a multi-task leader. This dynamo competence can transform institutions and corporations. Largely speaking, she can transform the world.

Competence consists of the knowledge, skill, and experience of the application of the knowledge and the skill.[40] Knowledge explains about the intellectual grasp of your area of expertise, the information and the data about it. You know it. Skill is that you know the ways of acquiring the knowledge. And you know the language to communicate that knowledge appropriately and effectively. You become wise by the experience you gain from applying your knowledge into action by using your skills. Therefore, competence is the state of personality that is formed by the intersective process of movement between knowledge, skill, and experience of application. You gain competence by the experience of application rather than merely having knowledge and skill.

This dynamo competence of a person who manages human resources must develop a competence that consists of knowledge, skill, and the application of the eight moves and the eight energies. You develop the HR competence by having the knowledge of the eight moves and the energies (which we will soon discuss), developing skills needed to generate the energies, and having the experience of applying the knowledge into concrete actions that have been successful. In other words, when you are considered a competent HR professional, it means that you understand the eight energies and you have the skill to generate the eight energies.

The dynamo leadership refers to the organic capability by which a person realises energies within and without and actualises those energies to effect transformative changes in society. This leadership has distinctive features. *First*, a dynamo leader acts. Just does it, by functioning with powerful energies. Thinking and action are not two different acts, but they form as a single action—*think-act*. *Second*, this active nature springs from the realisation of energies deep within her person and from her social interactions. She is a person who lives consciously. Therefore, the *third* feature is that she is sensitive to the happenings around her. This makes the dynamo leader observant of what happens and what goes through the minds of people who work with her. By being observant of the reality around, it provides a better understanding of the situation for effective decisions. *Fourth*, since she is an active person, she is the agent of effects. She does something because she believes in it, not directed or influenced by someone. She is open to influences, but not overwhelmed by them. She owns her actions. In other words, human agency is with her in the sense that she takes personal responsibility for her actions. *Fifth*, she constantly reviews and evaluates her actions. This review refines her further actions in terms of making her actions productive and contributively useful. In this, there is honesty in accepting the truth. She does not hide deficiencies. Instead, she accepts them humbly in order to make the deficiencies into efficiencies. *Sixth*, the dynamo leader manufactures changes—change-maker. This is a way of creating an impact on the society, not merely in terms of creating a profit for the organisation she works for. And equally, she knows how to manage those changes. *Finally*, the most important feature of the dynamo leadership is that she knows how to handle the eight energies and use them appropriately in a mature way.

By these features, the dynamo leader stands and will stand above the rest in any place and time.

Agility of Energy

Energy makes a leader agile. She moves fast and manages all that stands in the process of making things happen in an organisation. Once a leader becomes aware of her core energy, she would move quickly and make faster decisions and search for the right type of collaboration from her team. Once full of energy, she finds the right sources and resources and continually learn and relearn in the process of growth. Agility gives the ability to create and respond to change and helps succeed in difficult and uncertain environment. An agile leader values individuals in the organisation and interactions with them to respond to change, finally achieving outcomes.

The agile methods in software product development are *Kanban*, 'which concentrates on reducing lead times and the amount of work in process' and *Scrum*, 'which emphasises creative and adaptive teamwork in solving complex problems'[41] are used. Many companies—such as *Amazon*, *Netflix*, and others—use agile methods. Most of the software developers use agile techniques. The case of Bosch Power Tools explains how it has gone through agile transformation in 2016.[42]

Every leader who realised energies within, particularly one who has become aware of her core energy by self-examination, becomes agile. It is an energy that drives her to do things and moves her every minute and at every level. The core energy could be seen in a child at an early stage, in what she likes and how she handles objects she sees. Later, she develops a style of doing things that is unique and different from others; it is a definition of her identity. The core energy makes her agile all the time. It maximises productivity. As seen in software development, an agile leader is full of energies and moves, continually learning from the moves she makes, and uses the energies not only in herself but also in others by moving away from a rigid and set plan of work. Interactions between moves and energies make the leader agile, who builds high-performing teams, putting emphasis on the performance of the teams over dominant individuals. Collaboration between energies of individuals in the team and communication of ideas get recognition in the process of performance. Energy that makes a leader agile results in transforming an organisation effectively and successfully.

The agile and dynamo leadership I will explain in the following sections lies in the cycle of eight moves with eight energies in achieving the goals of an organisation.

Part II
MOVES AND ENERGIES

Backward, *forward, rightward, leftward, inward, outward, upward,* and *downward* are the eight directions/movements. All the eight movements are guided or driven by eight energies. The *backward* movement has the energy of *historical consciousness.* It is one's own past—how she has lived, what has shaped her, and what has deshaped her. It directs us to the experiences in the past that have given life's convictions and world views. What I am is the product of what I was. Moving backward gives, in fact, your identity. If one wants to become a competent leader, she should know her past, her family background, and the ways in which she has shaped her life so far. She should be deeply conscious of the experiences that created wounds as well as the experiences that helped her grow. This consciousness of the past is the foundation on which a person's resourcefulness and competence are built.

Moves	Energies
Backward	Historical consciousness
Forward	Futuristic vision
Rightward	Use of authority

Leftward	Emotional maturity
Inward	Positive attitude
Outward	Productiveness
Upward	Transcendence
Downward	Earthliness

The *forward* move has the energy of futuristic *vision*. Moving forward denotes the future. It sets the vision for life. Against the backdrop of the lessons learnt from the backward movement, the forward movement helps us to evolve a design of life—the design that shows us what we want to be and what we should be. It maps our future. It points at the goals and the ideals that we need to achieve. A competent leader must have clear goals and a sharp vision to achieve. Understanding the past and the identity of the organisation, she should be able to evolve designs and plans for the future so as to develop the organisation. What we have done (backward) and what we will do (future) define the profile of a person and an organisation.

The *rightward* move denotes authority. Conventionally, the right hand refers to power. We have heard people say, 'He was like my right hand. I have lost him.' The use of the right hand points to strength. Here, a leader should be able to use her authority positively.

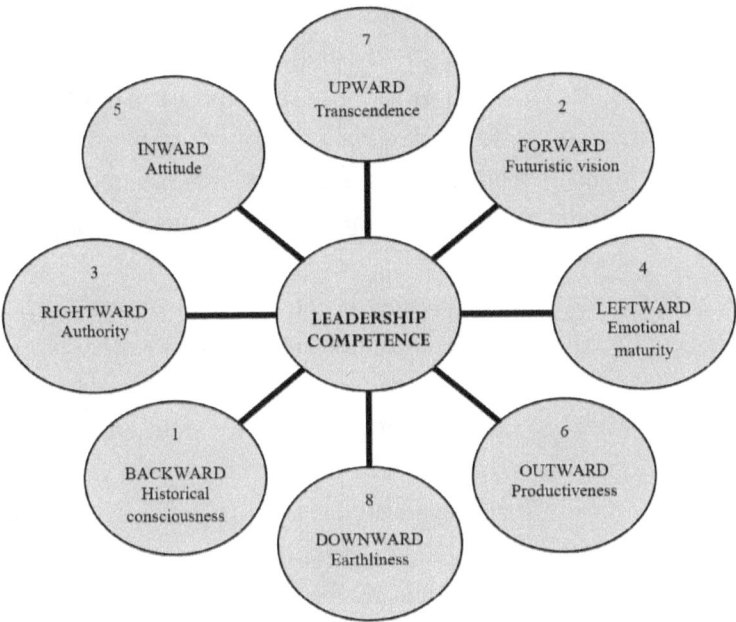

Figure 1. *Movements and Energies*

That is, she must be able to use her position of power, talents, knowledge, and skills for the growth that generates only life within an organisation and beyond. Authority is not to dominate the weak and to lord over the others. It is the responsibility that places one in a position of power to respond to a situation efficiently. The HR professional should activate responsible use of authority.

The *leftward* move refers to emotional maturity or emotional intelligence. A leader in an organisation should have the ability to understand her emotional states and movements and handle others' emotions and mental states. She should be able to inject intelligence into emotions in the ways she interacts with others and makes decisions.

The *inward* movement addresses one's attitude. It is the way by which one sees the world, her work, her life, and the people around her. All of us have a paradigm of life that guides the ways in which we behave and conduct our lives. This is crucial for a person in the process of setting her goals and her performance to achieve the goals. This applies to institutions as well.

Outward is what output or products one is capable of bringing forth. The first five movements talk about the inner capacity that places the foundation that gives the sixth movement the expression of one's worth. Historical consciousness, futuristic vision, proper use of authority, and emotional intelligence produce an attitude towards life and work. And these altogether make a person deliver in terms of achieving goals and objectives.

Upward refers to transcendence. It is not simply about God. It is a sense of going beyond the state in which one stands. If there is a failure in being productive, one should not get bogged down by it. In the same way, if there is success, one should not be overwhelmed by the glory of success. One should move on. Go beyond. This is a way of seeing both success and failure at the same level. This provides a balance in life. Once one reaches this level, she should move *downward*, which is being earthly. Being earthly refers to the earth that needs to be cared for—eco-friendly—being ethical about what one does, being practical about what one is involved in. Above all, this points to the importance of being people-centred.

At the end of the day, the HR professional is measured in terms of how she is sensitive to people. By all this, the HR professional is conscious of her past and the history of the institution she works with and for. She develops a design for the future—vision. And she makes proper use of her position of authority with a right blend of emotional maturity. This gives her an attitude that helps her deliver the products. She does not allow this achievement or failure to stagnate her dynamism. Instead, she goes beyond. She transcends the reality to see the larger picture of life. Finally, she grounds her life in terms of humanness by being and becoming people-centred. This is what gives meaning to one's life.

The following sections explain about the eight moves that produce the eight energies. In training yourself to become sharply intelligent, emotionally mature, skilfully capable, and visionarily far-sighted, you should know how to make moves to and from the eight directions and draw in the eight energies from them. In the following sections, we will describe the moves and the energies and the locus of learning about how to gain these energies. You do not need a training programme. You do not require money to attend a course on this. You can do it yourself. All you need is quality time and a conducive atmosphere. It is meditative and reflective. You need to make mental movements and observe internal movements in order to gain the power of energies. It is not a time-bound training. It is a lifelong exercise that trains you to become competent to manage human resources.

Backward—Historical Consciousness

> Man proceeds in a fog. But when he looks back to judge of the past, he sees no fog on their path. From his present, which was their far-away future, their path looks perfectly clear to him, good visibility all the way. Looking back, he sees the path, he sees the people proceeding, he sees their mistakes, but not the fog.
>
> Milan Kundera

History is derived from the Greek word *historia*, which means 'an enquiry designed to elicit truth' or 'information'.[43] *Conscious* is a Latin word meaning 'aware' or 'knowing'.

David McCullough, a two-time Pulitzer Prize winner and author of many books on leadership, in his interview, said that we needed leaders who have a sense of history in their roles as leaders.[44] For him, history teaches how to behave, what to do, and what not to do in different contexts. Being aware of what happened before and what impact that has on what is happening now is crucial for an HR professional.

History, culture, and language shape peoples' identity. The ways in which we lived our lives and the people who were part of our lives in the past contribute to the life we lead today and the type of people we are today. The past makes an impact on the present. We learn from the past. We shape our personality by the wisdom we learnt from the past. To gain the wisdom of the past, we need to move *backward*. Backward movement is to go back to the road we travelled, to the people who accompanied our journey, and to the experiences that we had. This *going back* purifies the present life and helps formulate the framework for the future.

Knowing your past provides your identity and a sense of the present and the future. It provides a guide map for the future and the wisdom to navigate that map. Managing yourself and organisations first involves understanding the history of yourself and the organisation you work for. The way you have lived your past and the experiences you have had provides a set of values, ideas of life, and guidelines to behave and conduct yourselves. If you are seen as an angry person, it is the result of your past life. There has been something that has made an impact in your personality to be and behave like that. The place you were born and brought up, the kind of parents and siblings you have, and the type of people you encountered in the past have all shaped you to become what you are today. These often do not get relived. It is just deposited in you. You are not conscious of them, but they remain within you and direct you to feel the way you feel and speak the way you speak. Therefore, you need to comprehend them in order to have a proper self-image.

Companies often recollect the history of their organisation only at anniversary parties and other important events.[45] They fail to be conscious of the history while focussing on the managers' day-to-day activities for the future targets. In this fast-changing world, no one has the time or the patience to recollect nostalgic moments or other less relevant details. The truth is that a sound understanding of the past will serve as a powerful tool to mould the future. The main duties of a leader would be to stimulate collective effort and develop strategies for the future. In both the tasks, history could be employed. When the leader communicates the organisation's history while making the employees work together productively, the employees would feel a sense of purpose and identity. History could serve as a case study, an explanatory tool and inspire people to face challenges better. History also offers valid generalisations, pragmatic insights, and significant perspectives. Hence, the leader needs to find the employable past in the history of the organisation. Knowledge of the history to which we belong is important in order to view ourselves and events as a part of a still unfolding story. It is important to remind people who we actually are. When leaders realise that it is history that shapes the culture, learning from the past would become essential. McKinsey's global managing director, Dominic Barton, said, 'We believe it is essential for every one of our partners and colleagues to understand our history and how our values were shaped over time. Although the context today is radically different from what it was 20, 40, or 80 years ago, we can still draw lessons from understanding how previous generations of partners confronted challenges and opportunities and responded to them.'[46] The organisation's history can also be successfully used to implement change. It is also useful during difficult times to fix rifts. History is not merely for adorning speeches, but it is the deep truth of the organisation. Leading with a sense of history does not mean to be slaves of the past, but it is to recognise its power.

Leaders need to strike an accurate balance between the present and the past and make decisions accordingly in order to be effective.[47] Too much of preoccupation in the current context prevents leaders from noticing the similarities with history. Appreciating both the present and the past needs to go hand in hand. The main drawback among leaders is, they tend to overestimate their abilities and hence fail to appreciate history. In this process, they tend to ignore their context. Leaders need to realise that they are not as unique as they judge them to be.

As an HR professional, you should always be in touch with your past, particularly the ways you were brought up. This historical consciousness makes a person more grounded. And you have to own up the past. When you do not own up the history, you will be inclined to hide it and you will attempt to put on a different persona. That is your unreal self, and you know it, but you have no other go because you have not made peace with your past. This kind of person is often an insecure person. You will not be able to lead a group properly. You might be successful, but at the end of the day, when you go to bed, you know you have not done it. There will be an emptiness crying for fulfilment. You need to learn from your past. You should be bold and open to say, 'These are my parents, this is the place where I grew up, and this is what I am.' For this, you need to go back to your past. And you have to relook at the major events and experiences you have had. Walk again with the people with whom you have travelled. It is an internal training process. It is a meditation, about which I will explain soon. This kind of person will behave naturally, and she will be at ease with herself. You need to have a positive idea about your past. If not, you need to develop one. Such a positive idea gives you an inner freedom and makes you a free person. In turn, this helps you understand the people who work with you. You can easily feel their persons.

Similarly, in working with and for an organisation, you need to know its past. It alters your ways and guides your actions. When it comes to analysing business scenarios, projecting organisations into their past might be as important as projecting them into their future. In this sense, historical knowledge might be seen as part of business knowledge. Past, present, and future would be seen as cycles of structuration, possibilities, and constraints.[48] You need to learn and understand first who started this company, why he or she started it, what their experiences are in the process of growth, and what the policies are that were given from their past experiences. You need to have a comprehensive idea about the organisation you work for. You need to make a trip to the historical milestones of the organisation and walk step by step on the road it has travelled so far. This makes you a member of that history—*remember*. You need to resocialise yourself into the organisation and imbibe the original charisma and vision for which the organisation was founded. By doing so, you will connect with the core structure of the organisation. You will root yourself in the soil of the organisation. There will be an emotional attachment to it. And automatically your work in the organisation will be authentic. People who work with you will feel your sense of loyalty to the organisation, and seeing this, they will contract this spirit. It is contagious. Then you do not have to tell them what to do. On their own, they would create jobs that would promote the growth of the organisation.

Pamela Marrone, the founder and CEO of *Marrone Organic Innovations*, says, 'I made a lot of mistakes on the hiring front in that I hired people who were technically competent and had the right industry background, but didn't actually have the same values that in the founding team did. This had devastating consequences for everyone because . . . they actually didn't believe in the mission and the vision of the company, and were working counter current to what we wanted."[49] It is a question of alignment that an HR manager or a leader should have with the organisation she works for. You may be technically competent, but if you do not know and understand the original vision of the organisation, you will one day, if not now, be seen as a liability. Therefore, you need to choose a company that suits your values and ideas of life and build your self-image by going back to your past and then emotionally enter the history of the organisation you work for and mould yourself into a leader who knows her past and has learnt from it and who has imbibed the history of the organisation.

Suddaby et al. (2010) proposed a framework for understanding history as a source of competitive advantage.[50] Research has proved that firms have enjoyed better access to resources owing to their past. History is considered as a malleable construct, a social and rhetorical construction, which can be used to motivate, persuade, and frame action both inside and outside the organisation. Hence, the capacity to manage history is a rare and inimitable resource. Suddaby et al. (2016)[51] also insist the understanding of history as a critical resource that can be deployed in order to manage membership with a wide range of organisational stakeholders. Mordhorst et al. (2015)[52] explains that the interpretation of the past is very important to forge organisational identities,[53] consolidate social memory,[54] set strategic direction,[55] understand entrepreneurial opportunities,[56] redefine market categories,[57] shape understandings of products,[58] and establish new industries.[59] Hence, the past can be used in many different ways in managing and organising organisations.

Historical consciousness is an energy that a leader needs to ground herself on what had gone before and what lessons it can teach her.

Historical consciousness is important as it transcends the exclusive preoccupation with what happened in the past, which has now become history, and this knowledge is used to shape the thoughts and actions that will determine the future.[60] It is not mere retrospective contemplation, but it draws conclusions from the past and applies them to future goals.

Hence, there is a crucial interdependence between the future action and historical consciousness. Therefore, any decision taken today will mark a turning point when viewed from the past or the future.

The historical consciousness concept was originally conceptualised by Jörn Rüsen.[61] He used it as a way of describing the role of history in education, how it shapes the orientation and helps to understand the world. Ahonen (2005) defined historical consciousness as an interaction between understanding the past and developing expectations for the future.[62] In the 1970s, Rüsen was one of the theoreticians who introduced historical consciousness as an important concept in history education in Germany. He later developed a theory of the personal development of historical consciousness. He presented his scheme of four phases of historical consciousness. 'The phases reach from [1] a recognition of a continuity of tradition, to [2] taking examples from history, to [3] critical deconstruction of the belief of continuity, and finally to [4] a temporalized, genetic view of the transformation of life.'[63] Arnold Gehlen defined historical consciousness as 'the ability to recognise the epochal quality of an event that is happening now; in other words, to see the event with the eyes of future generations'.[64] Glencross (2010) defined historical consciousness as 'the understanding of the temporality of historical experience, that is how past, present and future are thought to be connected for the sake of producing historical knowledge'.[65]

Lorenz et al. (2010) documented the core claim of historical consciousness: 'The confrontation with history has an immediate impact on our professional practice, but it cannot be constructive unless we introduce a critical distance vis-à-vis current issues and unless we guard against all linear notions of "historical development". The dialogue with history is a two-way process. We interrogate the past but are aware of our subjectivity. In a dialogue with history, we investigate the past and put the current "facticity" and the obviousness with which "new" challenges are presented in perspective. Only thus do we remain true to our social pedagogical mandate. Solidarity and social cohesion do not rest on a-historical facts but on a genuine, permanent quest for shared values, symbols and aspirations, in an ongoing dialogue with history.

Only the constant elaboration and re-elaboration of the ever-incomplete project called society can ensure social cohesion and at the same time respect for cultural diversity.'[66]

Kieser (1994)[67] identified four reasons as to why historical analyses should be revitalised within organisational research. Firstly, the behaviour and structure of the current organisations reflect culture-specific historical developments. Secondly, the finding of the real organisational problems and of their appropriate solutions is often not free of ideology. Thirdly, historical analyses make people interpret existing organisational structures as the outcome of past decisions, some of which were intentionally made and some more implicitly. Fourthly, by applying historical developments to theories of organisational change, the theories get subjected to a more radical test than otherwise.

The importance of historical consciousness for management scholars was documented by Suddaby (2016).[68] The paper explains how history both enables and constrains the ability to organise, to engage in productive economic activity, and to create institutions of social control and economic order. Hence, management scholars need to develop a more powerful literacy and facility with history, historiography, and historical theory. He recorded that historical consciousness in management will need specific attention to practices or techniques of history. The paper stresses the need to nurture a broad-based and a more inclusive historical consciousness in business history that widens our collective assumptions about the nature and function of historical knowledge. 'Knowledge stagnates when a single world view becomes so dominant that it excludes all other possible perspectives. If the historic turn in management is to fulfil its promise, it needs to turn toward a horizon full of theoretical opportunity inspired by a broad awareness of the range and possibility for new learning, insight, and understanding that can emerge from vibrant and interdisciplinary conversations about the role of history in contemporary society. Achieving this involves nurturing the nascent *historical consciousness* that first inspired the historical turn in management thought.'[69]

The study of how the *past* is used for managerial purposes draws together threads of organisational research from management scholars[70] and business historians,[71] who examine the powerful role history plays in broader processes of epistemological and ontological 'knowing' in organisations and organising. The approach, termed historical consciousness[72], takes history as constitutive[73] in shaping how we define our own sense of self and action in time and in emphasising how the interpretation of the past shapes the experience in the present, the expectations for the future, and the choices we make.[74] Lubinski (2018)[75] demonstrates how politically motivated struggles to define the historical context contribute to the construction of organisational reality.

Frímannsson (2017)[76] attempts to link moral and historical consciousness through the hindsight bias. Historical consciousness is an awareness of a series of events occurring one after another in a human community. It is oriented towards the past; hence, there is no direct knowledge of the events, and the view would possibly be biased by hindsight.

At General Mills, if the cultural values of the company were questioned by anyone in the organisation, most likely they would respond with the story of the 1878 explosion that demolished its biggest flour mill.[77] After the disaster, the founder invented a safer flour milling technique and then, instead of patenting the design, shared it with all his competitors. This story gets repeated among all the employees as it reflects the positive values the company holds.

The pharmaceutical company Mylan used the history of its founder in order to revive the spirits of the employees during the global financial crisis.[78] Mylan, which is now a Fortune 500 company, was initially started as a small West Virginia company that flirted with bankruptcy two times. When the company's stocks soared as low as $6 in October 2008 during the global meltdown, executives narrated stories of the company's initial struggles. The aim was to remind them that the company has come this far from very humble beginnings, and they could bounce back one more time. The CEO, Heather Bresch, still insists on reminding the employees about the company's history though they are now a growing global enterprise. She says, 'A track record speaks volumes. Here's what we've been doing for 50 years. We've persevered.'[79]

The smooth merger of Kraft Foods and Cadbury is a classic example of how history served as a powerful weapon to match the cultures of both the organisations and lift the fear of value deterioration post the merger.[80] Post the merger deal, Cadbury's management faced tremendous resistance to the deal, and most of its employees, nearly forty-five thousand, feared that both the product quality and the value might deplete. This clash of cultures was thought of as another failure of post-merger integration. But the senior executives stepped in to solve this culture clash by employing Kraft's archives, which were established in the past. Company archivists launched an intranet site immediately and named it Coming Together in order to honour the similar paths both the companies had taken. They investigated all the historical materials and found that a lot of values were shared between both companies. For example, the founders John Cadbury and James L. Kraft were both very religious individuals whose business transactions were deeply affected by their faith. Both the founders had showcased their dedication to producing quality products for their customers. Even at a period when workers were looked down as commodities, both founders valued their employees and also believed in giving back to the society.

Along with the stories of the founders, the intranet site also had iconic advertising images, brief documentary videos, interactive timelines, and dozens of detailed histories of brands such as Oreo cookies, Maxwell House coffee, Ritz crackers, and now Cadbury chocolate and Halls candies. It was all designed in order to portray how the Kraft and Cadbury brands had always been on grocers' shelves side by side. Ultimately, there was an illustration titled *Growing Together*, which showcased the previous merger deals of Kraft, along with the recent Cadbury deal. This was a well-thought-out road map which represented a continuous forward movement as a stronger, united company. This message was clearly sent out through CEO speeches, press releases, and training sessions of the employees and through every other type of communication. The integration of Kraft and Cadbury was the smoothest when compared to all the previous acquisitions of Cadbury.

One more example of historical consciousness is the formulation of governance structure at McKinsey.[81] When McKinsey expanded from being a self-governing partnership firm into a global network of several consultants, they had to reform their governance. A team of senior partners analysed different types of organisations. However, the partners knew that their issues in governance had risen in the context of their own unique ethical values and intellectual standards, and looking at other organisations alone would not help. Hence, they also closely monitored their own history and formulated a more formal structure of governance with wider distribution of authority and also with a firmer control over the culture of the firm.

An example of how history was helpful in changing the culture in organisations is UPS.[82] In the late 1990s, when the company realised the need for innovation in a large scale, the leaders had to instil confidence in their employees in order to move bravely. They mentioned about UPS's long history of developments, starting from bicycle delivery to trucks, then starting their very own cargo airline (which was the second largest in the world), and finally, starting their web-based package tracking. The main idea was to remind employees how innovative they had been, along with the routines of industrial engineering. CEO Jim Kelly loved to tell the employees, 'Yes, it's new and it's different and it's tough and it's a change. But that's OK. We've done that successfully for many years.'[83]

To become a person who has historical consciousness, there are three loci of learning:

Relive your past

Take off for a week to a quiet place of your choice. Spend two to four hours every day on reliving your past. Start from your childhood, from the time you remember clearly, until now and observe the kind of experiences you have had and the type of people you have met. They should have made an impact, both negative and positive. Relive them by going through them all over again. Realise deep within what is happening to you and become aware of your feelings and label them as anger, happiness, fear and so on. There are constructive experiences and destructive experiences. From them, you will learn a great deal about what you are today. Constructive or positive experiences formed what you have now as positive self-image, and the destructive or negative experiences have formed what you have now as negative self-image. In the negative self-image, you need healing and purification. For example, you had an experience where somebody has hurt you. Even today, if you think of it, there is a feeling of anger that swells up within you. You need reconciliation in that. Even if you are unable to heal the hurt, you need to be deeply conscious of it. Similarly, you need to identify your present feelings from the pattern developed from your past experiences. This would give you an image/profile of what you are, what you feel, what you think, and how you act/behave.

Recall the history of the institution

Similar to the personal review, you need to enter into the flesh and blood of the organisation you are working for. Go back to the roots of the organisation. Travel mentally to that day, that place, and that time when the whole idea of starting this company occurred. Feel the moisture of the skin of the struggle the founder(s) went through and the challenge she faced. Hold the hands of the founder and walk with her mentally. If there are films about the founding, watch them alone. Feel the heat under the skin of the moment of its conception. Talk to the people who were physically present during the moment of the foundation.

Recently, I met a person who works as a professor in an engineering college in Chennai (India). Everyone in that college told me that he was a committed and a competent man in the whole college. He managed the whole place with ease and efficiency. Personally, I saw people being highly respectful to him. I asked him, 'What is it that made you like this?' He said, 'I was with the founder when he bought this land at 11 pm. This place was mud and filled with thorny bushes. Along with others, we removed all the mud and bushes and started the foundation. In a sense, I was one of them who gave birth to this institution. I know

I am not paid well, yet I will work for this, because I never felt that this isn't my college.' He is the person who has become part of the history of that institution. When he asks someone in that college to do something, he or she will immediately listen to it and do it. You must talk to such individuals and listen to the stories they tell you about the institution. Feel the smell of the time, the people, and the place in which the foundation was laid for the institution.

You may sometimes feel that the ways in which the institution was started are not the ways in which you want to lead your work life as it does not suit your tastes. Then either you make an effort to personalise yourself with the institution or go for some other suitable institution. All you need to do is become a part of the institution.

Remember yourself

Becoming a part of the institution means that you have become a member of the institution's core ethos and values—*remembered*. There is a deep, organic unity between you and the institution, in the sense that any impact that the institution senses is felt by you in equal measure. Your position is unique. You are neither an employer nor an employee. An HR has this strategic position in an institution that you take orders from the employer and give orders to other personnel in the organisation. Your vantage point is a space between the employer and the employee. You need to be a member of both the worlds of the employer and of the employee. You are a part of the two worlds, and at the same time, more than anybody else in this context, you are responsible for achieving the set of goals which are set for the institution. You are invited to achieve the goals. This you could do only when you are a member of the institution, just like being a member/a part of the human body, organically united with the body in flesh and blood.

The sense of history and the way of becoming a part of the institution will make you own the institution. This makes your words more convincing and persuasive. When people who take your orders and the personnel you deploy in different sectors make a mistake, you will be there to make them become conscious of the past. You will feel that this is your institution. There is no difference between your home and the institution. You *live* your work and not *do* your work. You will effect an important change not only in the sense of growth of the institution but also in the sense of significant change in the place you work and in the lives of people you work with/for. Often, you are not at the optimum level of performance simply because you have not membered yourself to become passionate and committed.

Similarly, this has to be done at your personal level as well. By being in touch with your past and becoming conscious of your personal history, you construct your identity. This makes you sensitive to the past of people (human resources) in the institution—where they come from and what their past experiences are. You will empathise with others. This will add a magnetic nature to your personality. The people who work with you will be open to you. In brief, you become an agent of change.

If you want a real story of success by the energy of historical consciousness, listen to Howard Schultz, the CEO of *Starbucks* coffee.[84] He bought the chain from its three founders. He gave up his position as CEO in 2000 to be on the board but came back to it in 2008. The reason for his comeback was, he said, to revive the popularity of Starbucks. Recently, in 2007, its stocks slid about 40 per cent, losing more than 400 million US dollars. Why did the company lose its popularity? According to Schultz, after he left the management, the coffee house began to sell so many things—sandwiches, smoothies, and so on—that dominated what was the core product: coffee and beans. The people who took over him lost touch with the past of why Starbucks became famous. He felt that the best course to regain its past glory was to return to its roots. He said that keeping in touch with the past is the key to future success. Being connected to the past organically is like a tree's connection with its roots. The tree bears the fruits through that connection.

The process of becoming a competent leader starts with gaining historical consciousness. History provides lessons to build a future.

Without the consciousness, a leader can never give a proper leadership to an organisation.

Forward—Vision

> I guess—what may happen is what keeps us alive.
> We want to see tomorrow.
>
> John Steinbeck

Now after becoming conscious about the history of the organisation, through the backward move, the leader needs to move forward by visualising the future as being historically conscious alone is not sufficient. The past guides the leader to envision a future for her organisation. The lessons and experiences of the past help in many ways to avoid repeating mistakes and strengthen best practices. Forward move provides an energy of vision.

In 1996, George Stroupe, from North America, read anthropology at Oxford University.[85] One day, late at night, tired of writing essays for tutorial sessions to be held the next day, he looked for a shop that would sell ice cream or some drinks. He found none. This frustrated him. He told himself, 'When I complete studies, I would start one.' He did. It was a humble beginning. He named the ice cream shop George & Danver, or popularly called G&D. Students now flog to this shop. It was a very different experience for the Oxford students. They choose their flavours and make their own sandwiches. The ice cream sold here is popular for its home-made taste. Asked George what was it that made him achieve this, he would say, 'Vision.' His father used to tell him to envision the future and design your life accordingly now. He learnt from his past what he should do in the future. Knowing what he was, how he lived in New York, and what he learnt in the past helped him design his future.

Vision is what you want to be and what you want to do. It is a future state of *being* and *doing*. You are able to see in sight now what you want to be next month or next year—a mental map of the future life you will lead. You form this vision from the lessons you have learnt from the past. The past has given you the world view by which you see the world, your work, and your relationship with others. The life you have led, from early childhood to date, provides patterns of behaviour and attitudes. That forms the basis on which you draw the map of your future. The past gives you an identity (what you are), and the vision takes you to the future (what you want to be). Vision 'helps to legitimise grassroots innovation. It gives innovation a focal point. And it serves notice to those who would reflexively defend the status quo.'[86] More sharply, it is a design of the way you will live and the ways in which you will work. In other words, it is a way of being more insightful about the future.

Vision helps individuals to dream about an aspired state of being.[87] Visions are essential for both organisations and individuals in order to enable them to reappraise their existence continuously by examining the gap between reality and the desired vision. Visions will not become a reality without individual and organisational effort. In order to realise the vision, values need to be developed and operated. The values need appropriate behavioural responses in order to be realised, and if the behaviours do not abide with the desirable value, they could be easily identified and realigned.

Great leaders are aware that the experiences and insights of everyone who will be working towards the vision are important in developing the vision in order to establish a better connection.[88] For example, in 2003 in IBM, in the *idea jam* of Sam Palmisano, several stakeholders and employees were involved. The *Global Service Jam* process is another example. It has been employed by several city leaders over the years in order to involve their citizens in pointing out various opportunities for large-scale community development programs.

Another example of the visioning process was the process followed at the World Bank in 1995.[89] The president, James Wolfensohn, felt the urge to reinvent the organisation, different from its reconstruction role after the WWII. Right from the start, he wanted a more philanthropic direction, more to do with the reduction of poverty. In order to materialise his blurry intention, he summoned several meetings with the staff and junior executives all around the bank and also with government members and clients. Via this process of collaborating with all the stakeholders, the vision for the organisation was framed as 'pursuing a dream of a world free of poverty'.[90] At team levels, this vision was further broken down and translated into practical and tangible strategies for poverty reduction via brainstorming sessions within the teams. One such team led by Dennis Whittle came up with a vision that going forward, the new strategies for poverty reduction could come from all around the world and not just from the expert officials inside the bank. This translated to the series of 'development marketplaces' where people all over the world could display new innovative ideas for developing the economy and could also compete for funding.

An organisation's vision may sometimes escalate from lower-level leaders who use those visions in order to lead change and innovation in their own units.[91] This is the bottom-up visioning process. The broadcasting company PBS's launch of the exclusive kids' channel PBS Kids 24/7 is a classic example of bottom-up visioning. The CEO, Paula Kerger, made the decision only after Lesli Rotenberg, the SVP of children's media for the network, pitched the idea. He convinced her that this launch would be consistent with the educational vision of the company and can also be implemented cost-effectively in order to address the real needs of the audience, which was never being met. Another example of bottom-up visioning is the conversion of United Way in the early 2000s. Many local innovations helped to develop a new vision for the organisation, which converted the organisation from a corporate fundraising body, which was measured by the money raised, to a more community-based strategic network, which was measured by human welfare indicators. This vision which was more community-based was the assimilation of experiments which had more human service strategies and visions in various cities. Over the years, that was combined, refined, and institutionalised, and the process was appreciated for its bottom-up approach. In 2009, McKinsey's new MD, Dominic Barton, also realised that the vision for a new McKinsey could not be developed in the corporate office as a top management decision but had to be developed by assimilating the successful experiments of entrepreneurial innovators who were already changing how the firm served its customers.

More elaborately, the process of 'visioning' or leadership vision can be divided into three stages based on previous research.[92] The first step is the stage of envisioning or visualising the future state of the organisation, the next stage is the effective communication of the vision to the followers, and the last stage is empowering the followers using the communicated vision so that the vision could be enacted.

The elemental skill of a leader is to develop a unifying vision for the organisation.[93] A vision which is inspiring, strong, and yet simple can feel very mystical. It can bring people with different mindset and characteristics, throughout the company, together to work for one common goal. Strategies would be developed based on the formulated vision in order to achieve a better future. Developing the vision needs some element of looking into the future.

In the context of the organisation, from the employees' viewpoint, the emotional commitment of the employees to the organisation's vision is more important for the performance of the organisation compared to the vision merely guiding the employees in their daily activities.[94] Only the employees who are emotionally committed to the vision believe in the vision, work towards it, and make it a reality. Hence, in order to reap the benefits of a good vision, the employees need to be emotionally engaged to the vision.

Similarly, in the organisational context, from the leaders' point of view, the leaders who want to increase the effectiveness of their organisation should embrace a visionary leadership style.[95] Visionary leaders with strong leadership skills made possible the pronounced perceived effectiveness of the organisation. Visionary leaders contribute in triggering the organisation's vision, and they must be completely engaged in the organisation in order to realise and maintain excellence when leading the path to success. Visionary leaders are leaders who have a compelling vision for the organisation.[96] They have the ability to see beyond the challenges and ambiguity of the present and envision a compelling picture of the future. They infuse their team members and the entire organisation with the vision. They give their employees the liberty to choose their own paths in order to realise the vision. They hold the final picture in mind all the time with great discipline. Visionary leaders are inspirational, emotionally intelligent, open-minded, imaginative, resolute, persistent, collaborative, bold, magnetic, and optimistic.

A leader is believed to be visionary only if the vision provided by the leader is very clear, precise, attainable, motivating, and at the same time, appealing to the values of the employees within the organisation.[97] In describing the characteristics of visionary leaders, David Berlew (1974)[98] suggests that the first requirement is the presence of a shared vision for the organisation's future. A vision that is inconsistent with the values of the followers will not be received well. Hence, the vision must be developed from the values of the group being led. The leaders need to articulate the goals of diverse groups, and hence, only an outstanding leader can deliver the common vision acceptable to diverse groups. The outstanding leader needs to also act in compliance with the vision in a consistent manner.

The unique trait of a visionary leader is that via actions and words, the visionary leader makes the followers see his/her vision and makes them see a different way to think and act and thereby help the leader realise the vision.[99] The way the vision is communicated becomes as critical as what is communicated. Visionary leaders like Winston Churchill and Martin Luther King have skilfully used linguistic devices like metaphor, irony, alliteration, and imagery in order to make their audience visualise the vision as if it were real. The visionary leaders choose from a variety of mediums for communicating the vision. By matching the perception appropriately with the symbols, the visionary leader creates a vision and then this vision becomes the bridge between the leader and the followers. Visionary leadership involves sociological dynamics, psychological gifts, and the luck of timing. Strategic visionary leaders are the result of historical moments. Visionary leaders use emotions to drive the followers instead of employing the authoritarian approach.[100] The motivation is via words and action. The visionary leaders share a paternalistic relationship with their followers. Mahatma

Gandhi was a visionary leader whose vision of non-violence brought us freedom from the British rule.

In order to be a visionary business leader, a leader needs to be focussed and needs to inspire the team to achieve the goals of the organisation.[101] In order to achieve the goals, a business leader needs to have enough knowledge, strong willpower, and passion. The visionary business leader needs to know how to balance both action and vision simultaneously. Vision is the final destination to which the organisation seeks to reach, and the actions are the ways to get there. The leader needs to motivate his team after understanding them and providing what motivates them in order to work towards the vision. The work environment should be made conducive enough for maximum performance and for creativity, which translates to achieving the vision more effectively. Google, for example, has always maintained an environment conducive enough to encourage innovation. Google's vision of providing the world with information in one click was made alive by repeated innovations like AdWords, which revolutionised online sales, and other advanced search algorithms. This has put Google on the road to continuous success. Hence, vision can be made a reality only by proper actions. Visionary leaders need to also recruit the right talent and form a team whose skills complement each other and who work together to realise the vision. Visionary leaders need to assign specific responsibilities to each member of the team and strategise their path towards the vision. The value proposition of the brand needs to be communicated to the team so that they will work together knowing the competitive advantage over other competitors.

Visionary leaders need to have qualities like execution with confidence, self-made through their hard work, focussing more on the skills needed to achieve the vision instead of being liked by everyone, repeatedly innovating, delegation of decision-making to trustworthy individuals in order to increase team efficiency, creation of learning opportunities for themselves and for those around in order to grow together, recognition of employees' distinctive skills, focussing mainly on the future with stronger faith in actions than mere words, and a well-balanced mix of physical, mental, and emotional traits, along with strong integrity and core values in order to demonstrate the vision.[102]

Further, based on the individual's salient capacity, Westley and Mintzberg (1989)[103] divided the visionaries into different types of visionary leadership style. Edwin Land was categorised in the 'creator' visionary leadership style, Steve Jobs in the 'proselytizer' style, René Lévesque in the 'idealist' style, Lee Iacocca in the 'bricoleur' style, and Jan Carlzon in the 'diviner' style.

Edwin Land was the founder of Polaroid Corporation and also the inventor of the Polaroid camera.[104] He has been categorised as creator because of characteristics like originality of ideas or inventions and the quality of their realisation. He had foresight and was able to visualise his invention and understand the deep needs of people which they themselves did not know they had.

Steve Jobs, the founder of Apple computers, was a visionary leader categorised in the proselytizer style.[105] Jobs was outstanding in merging foresight and imagination. His visionary approach was the zeal to showcase the future potential of the product. He excelled in convincing people collectively to support a new product line. Unlike the creators, the proselytizers are very dependent as they depend on others to stimulate their vision.

René Lévesque was a minister of the government of Quebec and the founder of the Parti Québécois political party.[106] He was categorised in the idealist visionary leadership style. He had the characteristics of an idealist visionary leader, like speculating on the ideal, demanding perfection, and minimising the flaws of the real. Lévesque attempted to reduce the vision into practical realities of a rearranged political order. The challenge for Lévesque, unlike the other visionary leaders, was to sell an abstract idea whose results were just proposals on paper.

Lee Iacocca, an American automobile executive who held important positions in Ford and Chrysler, was categorised in the bricoleur visionary leadership category, owing to his capacity of myth-making and building ideologies, teams, designs, and organisations.[107] Iacocca never gave any original ideas, but he had the wisdom to build a team, the foresight to predict the market, and the insight to identify the winning design.

His distinctive style was creating a powerful outline around the core vision by combining operations, people, or parts with a lot of personal influence and hence creating a circumferential vision.

Jan Carlzon, a Swedish businessman and the president of the SAS group, was categorised in the diviner visionary leadership style because of his insight, which, in times of inspiration, came with great clarity.[108] But unlike the creator, the insight focused more on the process and the organisational structure and not on the product. His blueprint for the organisation was based on a number of small insights and distinct moments of inspiration. Carlzon had to convince his own employees to adapt to a new way of doing things.

Hence, like these visionaries, HR leaders should have a vision. They should move forward based on the knowledge of the past. Therefore, being historically conscious, the effective leaders should develop a futuristic vision and work towards it.

A leader should have a vision of what her organisation wants to be in the future and what she wants it to be known for. The success of an organisation depends mainly upon 'how well the organisation can anticipate or adapt to the unforeseen'.[109] You should be able to see the future in sight. This is the ability to see future in sight *now*. It is a capacity to predict what would happen by observing the present state of affairs. It is a *forward thinking*. You move forward by learning from the backward move. Normally, we always move forward to achieve anything. If we want to reach a place on foot or by a car, we journey forward, not backward. Of course, sometimes we need to use the reverse gear in order to correct or negotiate our forward journey. But moving forward always denotes making progress in our journey or in our work. We need to move on in life in order to realise changes or progress in the process of growth.

The energy of moving forward is the capacity to see the future in the present. If you want to be a successful person, you need to have a vision. Don't think that there is already a vision that is given by the organisation you work in. You need to have your own. Your vision is a combination of the vision of the institution and your life's vision. There must be some coherence between the two. This similarity only connects you with the organisation and you with the life and the work you are engaged in. As an HR professional, you have to keep the picture of what you want the organisation to be on your desk. You should make a map of it and keep it in your purse, and you should hang it on the rear mirror in your car. You should write it on a paper and paste it on the bathroom door, and you need to paste that on the ceiling in your house and above your bed so that it keeps you awake even in your sleep. The designs of that vision must fall in place in your mind constantly. It should run like a film with sound and images. At the end of every day, if you check, you will see how much you have progressed towards the goals of the vision.

Having a sharp vision keeps you strongly motivated. You have something tangible to live up to. This vision gives you the reason to get up from your bed every morning. You are seen as a fired-up person because you passionately love the vision of the work you are assigned to. You are alert mentally. You are conscious of your inner movements that direct you constantly. The vision would make you avoid events and activities that distract you from actualising the vision. Naturally, you become interested in making yourself physically fit so as to achieve your goals.

You need to make plans. You have to have a map of your daily plan, monthly plan, yearly plan, five-year plan, and life plan. The plan for your life manifests in all other plans. Daily, monthly, and yearly plans are just extensions of your life plan. The human resource management (HRM) process starts with human resource planning (HRP). Based on the organisation's objectives, the planning should be framed. How many people do we need? When do we need them? What skills and competencies should they have? Where do we find them? What would be the cost of employing them? How do we plan to allocate them in different positions? The HR professional aligning with the line managers must be able to answer these questions, and the type of answers will have the capacity to determine the success of an organisation.

When you are a visionary, you become a contagious person in your workplace. The people who come in touch with you feel the spark in you instantly. They see you as a single-minded person. They contract your visionary state. You will become a natural leader because you have something to contribute, and you are itching to realise the vision you have within.

How do you become a visionary? I suggest that it can be done by observation, discernment, and designing (ODD). You need to be an ODD person.

Observe reality

You form the vision by what you observe in reality. That reality consists of events, players in the events, and feelings and ideas you form from your experience in the events. What you taste, see, hear, and feel activate zones in your mind that help to form your own comprehension. In your organisation, what you see, feel, and experience give you an idea of the place, the institution, and the people in it. You make sense of how the institute functions and its dynamics in the framework of your previous knowledge. Before you initiate your own action in the organisation you start working for, you need to devote some quality for months for this observation. Stay with the people who work there with an open mind and listen to them. While you participate in the works done, you observe from a distance.

Discern a future

The observation shows you how the institution functions. Now you should evaluate to see how the activities and the people who do the activities will help achieve the goals that are set for the institution. This evaluation involves discernment. We often make decisions without making the initial discernment. Discernment refers to identifying between the positive spirit and the negative spirit. The positive spirit leads to lasting growth, and the negative spirit leads to quick growth but ends in disaster. You need to discern, as a responsible leader, the situation (people and activities in the organisation) by distinguishing between constructive agency and destructive agency. When the vision of the institution, the activities based on the vision, and the people who perform the activities contribute to the growth and the success of the institution, it is called a constructive agency, and if not, it is called a destructive agency. This helps you identify what and who will be and should be in your team and to whom you should allocate roles and formulate strategies in order to achieve the goals. This act of discrimination is crucial to formulate your vision of your work.

Design the tomorrow

The discernment will give you a clear picture and a state of mind about how you could proceed to evolve a design or a vision for your work. In this, you need to also keep your role as the leader of human resources. Managing human resources involves recruiting the right people, training and developing the competency of employees, allocation of the right people in the right places, managing performance, diversifying opportunities, creating healthy relations among different sectors, and providing appropriate rewards. In all this, you need to focus only on three core areas: designed action, competent actors, and conducive environment. You have processes and people that present you with human resource as strategic partner, human resource as change agent, human resource as administrative expert, and human resource as employee champion.[110] You need to decide which is your preferred emphasis only after the discernment of the state of your organisation. Alternatively, you could decide on an integrated perspective and evolve your design. The essential features of the design should be

- based on the main objectives of the organisation
- flexible to meet unseen demands and changes
- built in contingencies that would help use of personnel assigned for other purposes
- value-added in the sense that all the activities must have value in its productiveness
- reviewed periodically and replanned or deconstruct the plan to suit the new needs and the context

- concerned with the activities that directly and indirectly contribute to the overall strategic direction of the organisation and its business
- time-bound activities
- aware of the priorities that are more important than others
- clear about the identification of resources for the work.[111]

Observation, discernment, and design must demonstrate in every level your visionary energy that sees tomorrow now. Accordingly, the HR leader must keep the strategies in place in order to meet the needs of the future. This capacity of envisioning the future in an organisation, which helps to know well about the things that would happen tomorrow and how they would be faced, definitely provides security to organisations, and this gives them sustainable growth.

Rightward—Authority and Power

> Seven months ago, I could give a single command and 541,000 people would immediately obey it. Today, I can't get a plumber to come to my house.
> H. Norman Schwarzkopf III

Being conscious about the history of the organisation, through the backward move, and moving forward with a futuristic vision by formulating strategies are not sufficient. The leader needs to have the authority to influence others. The use of power and authority makes a leader effective in the process of achieving goals set for her organisation.

Authority is derived from the Latin word *auctoritas*, which means 'opinion, invention, influence, advice, or command' that is given by an *auctor*, which implies that 'authority originates from a leader, author, or master'.[112]

Oscar Pistorius was born in South Africa without major bones in his legs and feet; he had his lower legs amputated before he was a year old. Pistorius, at the age of twenty-one, runs on carbon-fibre blades popularly known as Cheetahs. A normal runner's stride needs tremendous energy, not efficiency. The ankles waste energy. But Pistorius's J-shaped blades take less energy and less oxygen. He can run just as fast using less oxygen than his competitors. He won gold in the 200 m at the Athens Paralympics in 2004, breaking 22 s.[113] Though later he became infamous for killing his girlfriend, for me, Pistorius is one of the powerful persons I have seen and heard about.

Authority comes from within. It is in the ways in which you have faced life and realised achievements. In fact, what we have seen in the last two moves and energies—historical consciousness and being a visionary—are the ones that give the power and authority to a leader in an organisation. What did you learn from your past? How did you infuse into you the history of the organisation you work for? What is your vision for your role in the organisation and for the overall realisation of the objectives of the organisation? These determine your power and authority in the role you have as an HR leader.

Rightward move denotes the energy of authority. We have heard people say 'He was like my right hand, I have lost him' or 'He is a right-hand man for that guy'. The right hand is used in many cultures to refer to power and authority. The right hand is used to rule or order and denotes authoritative power.[114] It refers to nobility. Moving rightward is to realise the energy of authority.

I use the word *authority* instead of *power*. Authority is the right given to act, as indicated in the structure of the organisational hierarchy. This authority helps one to influence the behaviour of others. Power is the potential force that others see you as a person to possess, and you are capable of influencing the actions of others. Power, then, is a psychological force that identifies the potential of a person as perceived by others. Power gives authority, and authority provides energy to influence others and their behaviour. At the same time, a person may be low in the hierarchy of authority, but she may have significant power due to personal talents, political connections, expertise in a subject, and so on. She may be able to wield influence more than the CEO of an organisation in order to achieve growth, 'increasing customer focus, enhancing employee involvement, instilling positive change into our culture and ultimately creating bottom- and top-line growth' as suggested by Six Sigma.[115]

Grimes (1978) points out that authority and power are the 'extremes on a control continuum. Power is conceptualised as influence and social control, the former reducing and latter reinforcing authority.'[116] Authority and power are conceptually opposites in terms of the kind of goals aimed at and the level of acceptance among the members of the organisation of the likeability of those goals and the means to achieve them. Exercise of authority is when common goals are arrived at in consensus with organisational members. Exercise of power is when the goals are more personal and the members comply. Identifying goals as common or personal can be difficult at times, and such fuzzy distinctions make the process of distinguishing between power and authority problematic. Gautschi (1997)[117] refers to authority as the 'right to command' and power as the 'capacity to command'. He insists that authority needs to be backed by power in order to gain dominance of one's goals. The factors which increase the real authority in the hierarchy include 'large span of control, lenient rules, urgency, reputation for moderate interventionism, performance measurement and multiple principals'.[118]

More sharply, in group nomenclature, authority refers to the power conferred in a role; however, the power is limited via coalition formation.[119] Authority is directed power which can be legitimately exercised only in channels defined by the group norms. The individual possessing the authority is obliged to govern. Thus, authority rises as the transformation of power in the operation called legitimation, which is mobilising collective assistance to challenge those who oppose power. This kind of supportive power is authority. In C. Wright Mills's words, 'Those in authority attempt to justify their rule over institutions by linking it, as if it were a necessary consequence, with widely believed in moral symbols, sacred emblems, legal formulae. These central conceptions may refer to god or gods, the "vote of the majority," "the will of the people," "the aristocracy of talent or wealth," to the "divine right of kings," or to the allegedly extraordinary endowments of the ruler himself. Social scientists, following Weber, call such conceptions "legitimations," or sometimes "symbols of justification.""[120]

Authority has five attributes, namely, decisiveness, accomplishment, persuasiveness, courage, and inspiration.[121] Efficient decision-making, especially the tough decisions, is an important trait of a leader. For example, the decision of launching a full-frontal assault by General Dwight D. Eisenhower on the Normandy coast on D-Day was very precise. The go-ahead decision was a result of several factors, like the weather conditions and the military build-up of material and personnel. Bad decisions can result in drastic failures. Hence, leaders need to cautiously take into account all the factors and make a calculative decision. Getting things done is another important attribute of authority. Leaders need to accomplish what they promise to deliver. Unrealistic promises about revenue and production could only yield unfortunate results. Leaders cannot achieve the desired results alone. They need the cooperation and support of their co-workers. The objectives need to be communicated clearly and in a way that is convincing. Leaders need to be courageous enough to stand up for what is right and ethical. They need to hold on to their beliefs only when they are ethical and in sync with the organisation's goals. Leaders need to inspire others by doing something beneficial, new, and different for their stakeholders. All these attributes reinforce the authority of the leaders in order to lead efficiently.

Leadership is infused with the concept of power. The main role of a leader is to influence changes, and power is an integral part of the influencing process. The power of a leader is defined by her position. The two perspectives of power—the power within or 'interiority' and the power without or 'exteriority'—were explored by San Juan (2005).[122] In the exteriority perspective, the power lies in the leader's external setting, which would be diverse and heterogeneous in nature. In the interiority perspective, the power lies within the leader, and the power mainly satisfies a desire, a need, and a motivation in leaders. The leader needs both the perspectives and has to understand them and confront the challenges they pose. These perspectives need to be integrated. The leaders need to make sense of the external power manifested in the environment and integrate that with their internal self. Filley and Grimes (1967)[123] identified twelve power bases, which include formal authority, function and responsibility, expertise, autonomy, manipulation, avoidance or default, collegial, control of resources, traditional rules, bureaucratic rules, equity, and friendship. The most frequently employed power bases include collegial, formal authority, responsibility, control of resources, and manipulation.

Further, the sources of power which leaders employ in order to influence peers were given by French and Raven (1959),[124] and it included coercive, legitimate, and reward categorised as organisational power and personal power, which included referent and expert.[125] The organisation's policies and procedures dictate the organisational power, whereas the personal power emerges from one's personality. Depending on the context, leaders employ all the power sources together in different combinations. Legitimate power refers to the power derived from one's position and is also known as formal authority. Leaders could exercise this power within the scope of their authority. This power could be enhanced by developing policies and procedures. Reward power refers to the ability to influence peers by giving away rewards, which could be financial or non-financial. Coercive power refers to the ability to punish peers in order to influence their behaviour. Expert power is the power to influence peers owing to one's own recognised expertise. Referent power is the influential ability evolved because of the admiration one receives from peers. The leader's behaviour plays a key role in the kind of power exercised.[126] Subordinates have implicit notions about their powerful managers. Managers who display high reward and coercive power are assumed to also possess high referent and legitimate power but lower expert power.

Moving further, let us discuss about the classes of power, which include objective power and perceived power.[127] Objective power exists objectively in the organisation and is very straightforward and direct. Mostly, people are unaware of this objective power. Perceived power is subjectively perceived to be present. Both these classes of power are essential. The leader's real behaviour has a significant influence on the perception of the exercised power, especially in the case of coercive power and reward power. The leader's reputation and behaviour does influence the perception of referent, expert, and legitimate powers. Hence, depending on the types of power a leader desires to exercise and desires others to perceive, she can alter her behaviour accordingly and also influence the information available about her reputation. The perception of an individual's power is significantly and independently related to behaviour and the position in the organisational structure, which is measured in terms of the level in the hierarchy.[128] The informal power positions depend more on the strategic use of behaviour in order to exercise power and influence peers. The model proposed by Farmer and Aguinis (2005)[129] suggests what combinations of perceived supervisor power and supervisor intentions to provide resources for subordinates' enactment are essential for quality leadership. Only when the perceived supervisor power is high and the intention is also high, the condition termed as confirmation, would the result be very high quality of the supervisor-subordinate relationship. Hence, a good leader needs to make sure that the perception of her power by her subordinates is high and should also exercise lenient control over the resources needed for the subordinates.

Successful business leaders have used their authority and power to demonstrate their significance in their respective countries and have also had international presence.[130] Lucy Turnbull was one such powerful leader who made her own mark without being under the shadow of her husband, Malcolm, who was the prime minister of Australia. She was the first woman to take up the position of Lord Mayor of Sydney in 2003. The newspaper *Australian Financial Review* titled her as the individual with the most covert power in Australia in the year 2017. Another powerful leader was Alisher Usmanov of Russia, who, through his wide networking skills, rose to become one of Russia's most powerful leaders. He gained power via profitable investments in Metalloinvest, which was a metallurgy and mining firm; in British soccer club Arsenal; and in the cell phone operator Mego Fon. In 2017, his personal net worth was around $16 billion.

South Korea's most powerful leader was Suh Kyung-Bae.[131] With a personal wealth of about $7.1 billion as of 2017, he is also one of the richest businessmen in the country. Suh's business of Amore Pacific, which was born out of his grandmother's store, soared to a great high with a market capitalisation of $14.1 billion as of May 2017 in a period of twenty years. There is a strong demand for his products in China.

David McKay is another powerful leader, in fact, one of the most powerful leaders in Canada in the finance world who leads Royal Bank of Canada that earned a total income of more than $10 billion in 2016.[132] He joined Royal Bank of Canada in 1988 and, through his knowledge and power, rose up in hierarchy and, in 2014, became the CEO, president, and director of the board of Royal Bank of Canada. In 2012, Retail Banker International titled him as Retail Banker of the Year.

Another powerful business leader was Richard Branson, whose philosophy was, 'If it's not fun, it's not worth doing.'[133] This entrepreneur started off very young. At sixteen, Branson founded a magazine whose advertising space was sold at $8,000 in its first issue itself. In 1972, he founded the first company under the Virgin brand, Virgin Records. His power story starts off then and has now earned a fortune of $5 billion with companies like Virgin Mobile, Virgin Atlantic, Virgin Trains, and Virgin Money, which are just a few to name among the 400 international companies owned either fully or partly by the Virgin Group.

In the process of HR leadership, there is always a conflict between line authority and staff authority. The line authority is in charge of productions proper, while the staff authority advises and provides consultancy to line units. HR leadership normally has staff authority. Line authority has more power and influence than staff authority in the production of goods and services. An HR leader could have greater influence purely by her competence of authority to create a greater amount of understanding across the organisation, of the values and goals of HRD programs and processes. Here, the HR leader is a specialist. She facilitates and functions as a change agent; she controls the process. In this context, an HR leader needs a sense of authority that comes from one's own personality rather than legitimate power given to her.

Therefore, the energy of authority we deal here in our dynamo competence for HR leadership is the ability to persuade others and influence in others' behaviour in an organisation. For example, you have an idea for progress of the organisation, and you want everyone, including your line manager, to listen to it and act accordingly to achieve the end. What you need here is persuasive skills. This does not come merely from the position of power you have in the organisation that your workforce will perceive as a threat. Power would not yield lasting growth for your organisation. Power can come from three ways: wealth, violence, and knowledge. The power based on force ('condign') will only produce workforce that work under fear. On the other hand, you provide incentives as a compensation for the work. When the incentives are not available, the workforce will lose the fire to work. These two are called the fear or fodder way of organising work. But if you are capable of persuading the workforce to work with a deep sense of emotional attachment to the organisation, the productiveness will be greater and long-lasting. Your authority should come from your capacity to persuade others to listen to your ideas.

Authority as the capacity to persuade comes from your knowledge of who you are and what the organisation intends to do. Going beneath your positional power, you need to touch the zones of coherence in others by the way you make your statements. This comes, I gather, from your identity that you have gained from your past (*backward* move), from your understanding of the history of the organisation you work for, and from the vision you have formed for yourself in the organisation (*forward* move). That gives you the framework of what you are and what you mean. This gives the persuasive power. It is powerfully influential.

A persuasive person should also draw energy from her physical fitness. Many think conventionally that if you want to be an HR leader who has the ability to persuade, you do not need to be fit physically. That is wrong. If you want to be physically fit, you need to be disciplined with your habits—eating and sleeping. When you want to go for a walk, there will always be a tendency to think, *Tomorrow I can go for walk*, and tomorrow will never come. We will always have excuses for not doing the workouts in the gym or going for a walk. This is because we do not have the fighting discipline. When you are determined to keep your body fit, your mind will also be sharp and focused. If you want to shed two kilos of your weight, you will do it against all odds. This disciplined life also gives you the persuasive power. In exercising, you constantly persuade yourself to train hard and to avoid excess eating and sleeping. You will make efforts to understand your body and its nature. You will have an insight into your body. And in the same way, you will relate to people who are disciplined like you. Physical power (physical quotient (PQ)) is a constituent part of your authority as a leader.

'Persuasive leaders conquer three hurdles—communication, power and authority.'[134] Persuasive communication is one of the important skills of a leader in order to differentiate oneself from a manager and establish leadership.[135] Leaders need to be persuasive enough to sell their ideas to the followers. The prerequisites of persuasion include rapport, emotion, and logic. The leader needs to build a good rapport with the group by placing the best interests of the group ahead of individual interests. Only a credible leader would be able to build a good rapport, and then using both logic and emotion, they persuade the group to achieve the targets. In order to embrace the group's emotions, leaders empathise with them and then use statistical facts to present the ideas' logic. Thus, rapport, logic, and emotion enable an easy persuasion for the leader.

Of all the sources of authority, the kind of discourse a leader, particularly an HR, develops has greater authority and influence. The discourses you articulate determine the successful leadership. *Discourse* is defined as 'ways of constituting knowledge, together with the social practices, forms of subjectivity and power relations which in here in such knowledge and relations between them. Discourses are more than ways of thinking and producing meaning. They constitute the "nature" of the body, unconscious and conscious mind and emotional life of the subjects they seek to govern.'[136] It is a form of power that circulates in the social field and can attach to strategies of domination as well as those of resistance. By formulating statements about the work to be done or done already controls the people who do the activities. Individuals in an organisation are constituted and governed as agents by discourses; power is exercised within discourses in the ways in which they constitute and govern individual subjects.[137] Each organisation formulates discourses when it sets its vision and mission statements that are put forth to all who join the organisation who would in turn assimilate them. This assimilation directs their behaviour, determines their activities, and forms the processes of growth and success. True to its Latin origin (*discursus*), a discourse *runs from and to* people and society. In this flow, it constructs behaviour of people and influences their actions. For example, in the *Amazon.com* logo, a yellow arrow starts from *A* and ends in *Z*, meaning that they have everything from *A* to *Z*. Also, it denotes the smile brought on the consumer's face. Another example is the BMW car logo, BMW (Bayerische Motoren Werke). It was founded in 1916 in Munich, the capital of Bavaria. The symbol is remarkably simple—silver lettering on a circular black band that encases four segments of solid blue and white, the colours of Bavaria. The image has its origins in World War I, when the Bavarian *Luftwaffe* flew planes painted in Bayern blue and white, affording the pilot a view through his propeller of blue and white segments. This inspired the stylised design we now recognise on vehicle logos, such as the one displayed beneath and on other BMW products. It is designed to project an identity that is smart, clean-cut, sporty, and image-conscious. In its website, it says about the company's strategy:

> Identifying potential and encouraging growth. Knowing what we represent. Recognising where our strengths lie and making the best use of every opportunity. Following a clear strategy. Goals we have attained are in essence the point of departure for new challenges. This is the philosophy that inspires every individual at the BMW Group. It influences the company's structure and it plays a vital role in the decision-making process. Our corporate ethos finds its expression in the uncompromising pursuit of the superlative. The result? Outstanding brands with an unmistakable profile. Automobiles and motorcycles which fascinate people all over the world and which win legions of new admirers every day. And a degree of

success which sees the BMW Group go from strength to strength.[138]

This discourse of BMW, in Foucault's view, constitutes and controls the ways in which the company functions and the ways in which the workforce takes up its different roles towards realising the overall plan. This is the case in every organisation and any institution. Every institution has a vision, and it is formulated as discourses unique to the company. That discourse is what the HR leader teaches to everyone in the organisation and persuades them to translate the discourse into concrete actions. As the HR leader, you should develop evocative and appealing discourses that persuade people who work with you. This is the authority that helps you influence the workforce to be productive and committed.

The discourses that the leader constructs should (a) *be vision-centric*, (b) *use positive discourse*, (c) *be empathetic*, (d) *be persuasive*, (e) *be courageous*, and (f) *be grateful*.

Be vision-centric

First, when you speak to your workforce, you must use words and phrases that help recall the original vision of the organisation. When the people in your organisation do their work, they are deeply conscious of the roots of the organisation. They also feel that you are aligned with it, and you expect them to do so. This is essential for employees to feel their personal stake in the whole enterprise's growth and success. Your statements make the people around you feel that you are the owner of the organisation. You infuse by your ways of talking—discourse—a spirit that makes people own the company. The owner's discourse will never have this: 'I do not know. This is what we have been asked to do.' That is the discourse of the non-owner. The owner will always make every effort to focus on business results, not on the job descriptions or roles really. You should have ownership discourse, not employee discourse.[139] This ownership discourse should disclose the vision, goals, and strategies set for the whole organisation. The Starbucks coffee chain is a good example of dissemination of this kind of discourses. Starbucks, from the beginning, sold not only coffee but also beans. This was the vision of Howard Shultz, CEO, who first suggested this idea to the original owners who summarily rejected it. But when he took over, he is the largest purchaser of fair trade–labelled coffee in the world, buying 4 per cent of global supply.

Use positive discourse

Always use phrases that can generate positive and optimistic feelings in others. Never use words that are construed as negative. Sentences such as 'I do not know how you are going to do this', 'I knew this already' 'You are a waste' will make you a weak person in front of your workforce. A negative person is a weak person in the sense that she does not have the strength to be creative with weak resources. Even with an incompetent workforce, you could produce results simply by infusing positive energy with positive discourse. There are millions of positive words to use. Ideally, if we are interested in promoting growth, we should use positive words. Negative words are meant to cause destructions. When you find a staff who has failed to do an assigned job and you know that she genuinely tried her best, for her, when you utter sentences like 'You have that skill', 'Try to do it in some other way', 'You will do it', she will see herself in a different state of being and doing. In places like Central America, the Maya are known to use words to influence the weather, cure illness, and get favours from the gods. The shamans of Africa are adept in the use of songs, chants, and words of power to heal illnesses. The explorers in Congo have seen people heal the sick, bring on rainstorms, ease the pain of childbirth, and even calm the fury of raging animals all with the utterance of positive words.[140]

Positive discourse is your strength that helps you to persuade your workforce to listen to your ways of doing.

Be empathetic

When you empathise with your workforce, you can yield enormous influence and power in your use of authority. One of the powerful ways of motivating the workforce to achieve results is to feel *into* them (empathise). Not only do you know them and understand them, but in great measure, you also feel into their total person. This is an umbilical connection you develop with your staff as a mother does with the child in her womb. This you can do only by participating in their lives. I know a manager who spends most of his time in attending family functions of his workforce. Once they know you care for them, they will consider their jobs as their personal duty.

When Jacinda Ardern, prime minister of New Zealand, was asked, 'If you were to summarise the qualities that have underpinned your path to this leadership role, what do you think has been most important for you?' she said, 'Kindness, and not being afraid to be kind, or to focus on, or be really driven by empathy. I think one of the sad things that I've seen in political leadership is—because we've placed over time so much emphasis on notions of assertiveness and strength—that we probably have assumed that it means you can't have those other qualities of kindness and empathy. And yet, when you think about all the big challenges that we face in the world, that's probably the quality we need the most. We need our leaders to be able to empathise with the circumstances of others; to empathise the next generation that we're making decisions on behalf of. And if we focus only on being seen to be the strongest, most powerful person in the room, then I think we lose what we're meant to be here for. So I'm proudly focused on empathy, because you can be both empathetic and strong.'[141]

Be persuasive

A leader must be persuasive. She should persuade her audience/employees at three levels: *logos*, *ethos*, and *pathos*. This is called the rhetorical triangle of Aristotle.[142] Logos appeals to the reasoning mind and her arguments. Pathos appeals to the emotions and, more importantly, to imagination. Ethos appeals to character and actual behaviour. Authority must appeal to the mind (thought), heart (emotions), and behaviour (actions).

The strength of leadership is in collective thinking. Often, we tend to be individualistic in our ideas: 'Listen to what I think and say.' This does not lead to autocratic leadership, and many do not own up plans/strategies in an organisation that persuade actions. There will be no sense of belonging. The term *logos* means that you reason before you enter into actions.[143] It is the antithesis of action. Before any action, we conceive an idea that gives a guide map to our actions and behaviour.

This you should reason out collectively in order to frame your ideas as the HR professional not only with the people in the boardroom but also with everyone in your organisation, from top to bottom. Listen to what they think about your strategies. Consult experts on the issue at hand. Spend some quality time in discerning how you need to formulate your strategies. Then come out with a sharp plan for managing people and guiding them to produce results.

This creates an atmosphere of family in which each feels that bond with the organisation. This provides you connection with everyone in your work. When you need people to actualise your ideas, most of the workforce understands your thinking. This makes your authority.

Once the collective thinking is achieved, you need to make them feel one with every movement of your organisation. It is like being conscious of the internal states of one's body. Your leadership should transform everyone in the organisation into being a part of the whole. In an organism, there is a certain basic unity between the whole and the parts—organic unity. Your empathy with the organisation should also be a similar case with others. They should feel as you feel. The term *pathos* means 'emotions', and if used properly, they could alter one's judgement. In your authority of leadership, the people who work with you are not only connected to you in the sense of abstraction/ideas but also connected to you in the sense of feelings. There is an abiding commitment of the heart to the work you allocate for the workforce. The leader and the ones being led are united in hearts and minds.

The term *ethos* refers to the habitual behaviour of a person/community. This forms fundamentally the character of a person and the culture of a community. As an HR leader, once you have connected with the people you work with in terms of ideas and feelings, they begin naturally to act in the ways you intend them to do so. Habitual behaviour, ethos, is the result of the combined function of practical skills (*pronesis*), virtue (*arete*), and goodwill (*eunoia*). Although you could simply make people work if they are talented with skills and still produce results, you will not be able to train people to become part of the whole organisation. That you can achieve by making them develop a virtue of commitment and goodwill towards the organisation and its vision.

If persuasion gives authority to/of leadership, logos, pathos, and ethos are three modes of persuasion. By using your authority, you convince people with your ideas, appeal to their hearts, and direct them to form their character by developing productive work habits. Then your authority is not based on commands, order, and control but by persuasion.

Be courageous

Courage is a moral strength to persevere with a constructive idea or a project to withstand any opposition. It means to do the right thing despite threats. Without courage, no vision could be realised. Aristotle views courage as the first virtue that follows all other virtues.[144] A leader should be courageous to stand by the principles and vision of her organisation when activities to realise the vision suffer setbacks and failures. A leader should see the setbacks as an opportunity for learning to grow. Being courageous does not mean that you dominate others. Instead, it is to be bold enough to be transparent to your stakeholders. Even at times of making mistakes, you are courageous enough to apologise for things you have done.

Accepting your limitations is part of your leadership capabilities. That should not be seen as a weakness, but it is a moral strength that will be considered by others as a positive quality of a leader. Fragility is a source of strength that makes you connect with the weak in your organisation. There are times in which your organisation makes mistakes or is involved in a crisis, affecting the reputation of the entire organisation. As a leader, you should not hide yourself, but you should show up to the media and explain the reality and accept your mistakes. This is to show your honesty to the stakeholders who have trusted your organisation. Often, when something goes wrong, many leaders shift blames on others and find scapegoats. It does not demonstrate real leadership.

Be grateful

Many leaders become arrogant as soon as they are given positions of authority. That creates a negative ecosystem in an organisation in which fear engulfs everything, leading to pretending employees and loss of confidence in leadership. A leader should always remain grateful to the people whom she manages. There may be very small things or trivial acts done by the employees, but when you tell them that you are thankful to them, it makes a difference. It gains respect from employees. Take time to observe acts of employees and those who are under your leadership and find an appropriate time to thank them. When you are grateful to your employees, you will see goodness around you. Saying thank you stimulates prosocial behaviour that leads the person who is thanked to be thankful to others. It is a cyclical influence. When an employee hears a word of thanks from her leader, she feels that she is valued. It has enormous positive effect in her, and this impact will be seen in her performance. The power of thanks is what makes a leader stand above the rest. Researchers who have looked at the effect of being grateful argue that it increases self-efficacy, becoming capable of achieving goals and seeing concrete outcomes.[145]

The *rightward* move makes a leader authoritative in the sense of being a person who accompanies an employee in the process of achieving outcomes for an organisation.

Leftward—Affective Maturity

> At twenty years of age, the will reigns; at thirty, the wit; and at forty, the judgement.
>
> Benjamin Franklin

A leader who has gained historical consciousness by the backward move, has moved forward with a futuristic vision, and has authority in order to influence others is not complete.

Emotional maturity is the key to an effective and efficient leader. If a leader has hurt feelings, she will be unable to address organisational problems. A leader needs to have the capacity to channel emotions and be emotionally intelligent in order to handle her own emotions and that of her peers. She needs to be flexible, understanding, compassionate, intuitive, and free from hurt feelings. Decision-making skill comes from emotional intelligence. Hence, a leader must have affective maturity in her dealings with people. She must be self-aware of her internal movements, her intentions, and her emotions. This awareness would help her respond and not react to situations. An emotionally mature leader would have high self-esteem, composure, and stature.

Mature is derived from the Latin word *maturus*, which means 'ripe or timely'. Now the rationale behind having the leftward move for affective maturity or emotional intelligence is because the hand can express several sentiments, like acceptance or rejection, doubt, love, hate, judgement, hospitality, and questioning. In India, the right hand and left hand are related to various social activities. The right hand fulfils tasks which are considered to be 'clean', whereas the left hand fulfils activities considered to be 'unclean'. In all important life events, like marriage, death, birth, etc., this distinction between the right side and left side is maintained. In French, the word for *left* is *gauche*, which means 'awkward'. In general, left represents 'evil' and 'weak'.[146] Hence, the left denotes emotions, and so affective maturity is the energy for the leftward move.

Blaise Pascal, a philosopher, says, 'The heart has its reasons which reason knows nothing of... We know the truth not only by the reason, but by the heart.' The rationale of the leftward move is that the left denotes the heart and not the left hand. The heart of the matter lies in how the heartfelt emotions are handled as most of the decisions taken are the outcome of emotions.

Randy Pausch was diagnosed with terminal pancreatic cancer in September 2006, and he had only a few months left to live. This devastated his three children and his lovely wife. In 2008, he accepted to give his 'last lecture' in which he told the Americans 'how to live' at Carnegie Mellon University in Pittsburgh, USA. Sadly, that day was the birthday of his wife, Jai. As he was nearing the end of the lecture, he wanted to express his love for his wife. The prearranged large birthday cake with a single candle was wheeled on to the stage. He told the audience, 'Dear friends, I have never given Jai a proper birthday party, and thought it might be nice if I could get 400 people to sing to her.' The audience applauded and sang 'Happy Birthday'. His wife, Jai, came towards him on the stage and embraced and kissed him. The crowd gave a standing ovation. Suddenly, there was dead silence. As they held each other, Jai whispered something into his ear, 'Please don't die.' He hugged her more tightly. Randy Pausch, a forty-seven-year-old computer science professor, still lives on.[147] In his website, he updates the state of his health and his activities. He demonstrates enormous sense of maturity in adversity.

The earth is the only home we have ever known. Though the earth is a very small part of the vast cosmic arena, it is the only world known so far to harbour life. There is nowhere else, at least in the near future, to which our species could migrate. Like it or not, for the moment, the earth is where we make our stand. From a distance, the earth might not seem significant, but when you look again, that's home, that's us. On the earth, everyone you love, everyone you know, everyone you care for, everyone you have ever heard of, every emotion you have ever felt for, every human being who ever was has lived out their lives. The distant image of our tiny world is a good demonstration of the folly of human conceits. It emphasises our responsibility to deal kindlier with one another and to preserve and cherish the earth—the only home we've ever known. It is very important to understand the emotions of others who live in this home and be affectionate and loving towards them.

From a distance, though the earth is a small dot, the emotion attached to it is what makes the earth more special.

In our dynamo competence, the *leftward* move brings in the energy of affective maturity. As a leader, she should be aware of her emotions and internal mental states, and she should know or learn to handle them. In the same way, she learns about others' emotions and handles them effectively and appropriately.

Elaborating on the treatment and constitution of emotions, 'emotions are treated as material things; they are constituted biologically as facial muscle movements, raised blood pressure, hormonal and neurochemical processes, and as "hard-wired" instincts making up a generic human psyche'.[148] Emotions are viewed as organised responses to either external or internal event that has had a negative or positive influence on oneself.[149]

A mature person maintains a state of mind that faces crisis with composure and a sense of balance of the mind and heart. We call this emotional intelligence. As Goleman suggests, you inject intelligence into your emotions. You understand your emotions and know how to handle them.[150] And equally you understand others' emotions and handle your relationship with them. This relationship demands a change in your approach and behaviour. You learn gradually how, when, why, where, with whom, at what level to speak and do. This is called appropriateness of your speech and action. Changes, especially at work, can be frustrating, fearful, and emotionally draining and can cause helplessness and anxiety.[151] Emotional intelligence strategies can be adopted for adapting to change instead of resisting it. Strategies like identifying the source of resistance, questioning the bias of emotional response, owning a part in the situation, and turning up a positive outlook would help to manage the emotions and be more mature to handle change. By being self-aware, the source of resistance could be identified. The emotional reactions which are exhibited owing to change could be very superficial and unreal. By questioning the bias of the emotion, the reality check can be done. Only a self-aware individual can know how one's attitude can influence the experience of the change. A positive outlook can also welcome changes with wider arms.

By gaining this affective energy, you will demonstrate competence that helps to

- *perceive emotions* that enable you to recognise and decipher emotions in faces, pictures, voices, and gesticulations
- *use emotions* that help gain energy to do cognitive activities, i.e. thinking on things and solving problems (an emotionally intelligent person can capitalise fully upon his or her changing moods in order to best fit the task at hand)
- *understand emotions* in order that you not only comprehend the language of emotions but you also become sensitive to the fluctuations of the emotional states
- *manage emotions* so as to handle and regulate emotions in yourself and in others. When people see you as emotionally intelligent, it means that you have the capacity to use and handle your emotional states, both negative and positive, and achieve objectives.[152]

Maturity consists of being and doing with a deep sense of appropriateness. There is a space between too little and too much, scarce and excess, strict and kindness. That is a mature space. Leaders should occupy that space. This competence of maturity, affective energy, leads to the formation of your character in such a way that you learn to consider criticism as a moment of grace in order to grow. When others give you corrections, you sincerely see that as an opportunity to develop your competence. It is the immature character that cannot stand criticism and corrections. The persons who have affective energy will look positively for people who can give constructive criticism. Even when people give destructive criticism, they will be able to see through it and take from them what they mean for their growth.

Leadership is an emotional process.[153] Implicitly, emotions are the centre of management practice especially with respect to leader-member relationships. The employee's productivity and behaviour is dependent on the leader's emotion. Organisational members need to be high on emotional intelligence so that illegitimate leadership could be identified and resisted. Emotions and moods play a major role in the process of leadership.[154] Emotions are more short-lived compared to moods, owing to their high intensity. Emotions usually flow into moods. Hence, when the emotion's intensity reduces after dealing with the source behaviourally or cognitively, the emotion translates into a mood, which is a less intense feeling. Emotions and moods have the propensity to influence information recollected from memory, deductive and inductive reasoning, judgements, creativity, and acknowledgement of success and failure. Hence, they are intricately connected to the ways individuals behave, think, and make decisions.

Emotional intelligence has been defined by various researchers in different ways. Salovey and Mayer (1990) define emotional intelligence as a branch of social intelligence that 'involves the ability to monitor one's own and others' feelings and emotions, to discriminate among them and to use this information to guide one's thinking and actions'.[155] Whereas according to McClellan et al. (2017), 'Emotional intelligence relates to the use of the components of mind associated with emotion as opposed to purely rational thought in the application of intelligence.'[156] The process of emotional intelligence includes six steps. The first step includes being aware of the emotion which starts to emerge via a significantly emotional event, the next is the emotional response which happens subconsciously, followed by being aware of the emotional response, then detachment and control of the emotion, then choosing the appropriate behaviour, and finally, goal-driven regulation of behaviour and emotion.

Emotional intelligence is the capability to comprehend and handle the emotions and moods in oneself and peers.[157] And emotional intelligence is instrumental to effective leadership. The main aspects of emotional intelligence include understanding the emotions, employing emotions to improve the quality of decision-making and cognitive processes, assessing and expressing emotions, and managing the emotions. Individuals vary with respect to their level of awareness of the emotions experienced and the level of expression of the emotions, either verbally or non-verbally. Perfect expression of emotions is key for effective communication so that the needs are met and the objectives are achieved. It is important to be knowledgeable about both the causes and the effects of emotions and also how they evolve and vary over time.

Emotional intelligence consists of four main domains, namely, self-management, relationship management, social awareness, and self-awareness.[158] Within each are twelve emotional intelligence competencies which are either already learnt or learnable capabilities that enable the leader to fare par excel. Self-management domain includes competencies like positive outlook, adaptability, emotional self-control, and achievement orientation. Relationship management includes teamwork, influence, conflict management, inspirational leadership, coach, and mentor. Social awareness includes organisational awareness and empathy. Self-awareness includes emotional self-awareness. Leaders need to have a balance of soundness across the various competencies in order to perform exceedingly well. Leaders need to work on the areas of emotional intelligence deficit.

A leader achieves maturity by blending reason with feeling. Reason alone will make a leader dry and arrogant; there would be rigidity in her approach. A leader must reconcile reason with feeling that would bring in harmony in the calculation of things. Giving a due place for feeling, leftward energy, in daily tasks, helps to create sublime success.[159]

Affective energy of the *leftward move* of the dynamo competence makes you a person for others—other-centredness. Others in your work life and family life become more important than your-self. You reach affective and moral maturity by genuflecting before others, not by adoring yourself. If you do the latter, people around you will easily see the deficiency in your leadership, and you will sooner or later begin to self-destruct.

A leader has to be less of herself. Without this, we hugely inflate and behave silly, even to ourselves. In the process of human growth, we realise a congenital push towards making ourselves centre around something or someone higher than ourselves. When we put ourselves in the centre of the world in an organisation, we will soon end up in depression. We will only feel right when we give ourselves away more and more. Leadership competence is built for altruism. A selfish leader is an unhappy person. Deep in the recess of her heart, she is a sick person.

To live out leadership fully is to let one's ego go. In an organisation, the leader is not the focus. It is the work and what the work effects change in that organisation and in the society at large. The leaders who have kept their picture at the centre of the organisation have always ended up earning more enemies. After they step down from their position of power, they are hated. Through being selfless and putting the interests of others and of the organisation ahead, you build your leadership competence. This type of leader knows well that our lives are not about ourselves. It is about others. If a leader thinks that life and work is about herself, she will end up too full of herself or too empty of everything else. The result is depression and isolation.

Mature leadership is to 'promote not herself, but the goals of the organisation and careers of the people she leads. It is all about alignment of what's inside your heart and what the world needs. It's about finding what you love and doing that to serve others.'[160] This is what gives meaning to leadership. This other-cantered approach creates passion in you for your work and life. You become passionate by experiencing the lasting impact you make on individuals and the organisation. Mother Teresa had this passion. When she saw more and more people who were abandoned in streets, they were later taken care of in her homes, and she became more passionate in doing that again and again against all odds. The smile of the marginalised people infused an incredible energy into her blood. She spoke about only the poor and lived for them alone. This is passionate leadership. This is what is called self-giving love (*agape*), when a leader gives herself totally for the organisation's growth and for a meaningful life of the people who work with her.

Emotional intelligence contributes to effective leadership by mainly concentrating on five important elements of leader effectiveness:

1. *Develop goals and achieve them.*[161] Leaders with high emotional intelligence would have higher information processing capability, would employ their positive emotions to visualise better organisational functioning, would cautiously revisit prior decisions, would employ their emotional knowledge to sense the

followers' emotions, and thereby influence their emotions so that they are receptive of the organisation's vision.

2. *Inculcate in others the appreciation and knowledge of the significance of work activities.* Emotionally intelligent leaders would be able to effect the followers' emotions so that they are aware of the organisational problems, keen to solve the same, and also feel positive about their contribution.
3. *Develop and continue the optimism, cooperation, enthusiasm, excitement, trust, and confidence in an organisation.* Leaders who are high on emotional intelligence can instil these feelings to the followers by having quality interpersonal relations with them by identifying, responding, and influencing their genuine emotions. Leaders need to also be able to predict how the followers would respond to various changes, events, and situations and manage them accordingly.
4. *Motivate flexibility in decision-making.* Emotionally intelligent leaders would have the capacity to prioritise demands without biases and thus take effective decisions both by using emotions and also by managing the emotions which intervene.
5. *Develop and maintain a relevant identity for the organisation.* The leaders with high emotional intelligence have the ability to deliver the emotion-driven values, beliefs, and norms which make up the organisation's culture, which translate to the organisation's identity, in an appealing way to the followers. Hence, emotional intelligence is essential for effective leadership.

Leaders need to be self-conscious about their own emotions and comprehend their weaknesses and strengths.[162] Emotionally charged decisions and behaviours could be prevented with this kind of understanding. Leaders can employ emotions in order to create eagerness towards a task, to motivate the team to achieve targets, to resolve problems, and to support critical decisions.[163] There is a significant relationship between the competence of the leader's emotional intelligence and the emotional competence of the team being led. Hence, leaders need to be emotionally competent. The traits of an emotionally intelligent leader include being able to notice the nuances of a given situation, being intuitive about others' needs, being seamlessly responsive enough to generate positive outcomes, and making the right decisions about what is most needed for the group and for individuals in several scenarios.[164]

Research has documented that there is a positive relationship between the emotional intelligence of the supervisor and the organisational commitment of the subordinates.[165] The emotionally intelligent organisations and individuals are more productive, and they also encourage productivity in peers. Effective managers with high performance ratings are found to be high on emotional intelligence. Hence, emotional intelligence contributes positively to job performance. Emotional intelligence enables leaders to deliver better ideas in the process of developing goals for the organisation.[166] With the understanding of peers' emotions, the emotionally intelligent employees build good social relationships and hence build organisational commitment. Emotionally intelligent leaders who are able to assess their own emotions and that of their followers have better exchange relations with their followers and are also more effective when compared to the leaders who have lower emotional intelligence.[167] Emotionally intelligent leaders have higher probability of leading an effective team, working towards success, and being more content working with others.[168] The leaders need to employ their positive emotions to promote organisational performance. They also need to differentiate between the emotions expressed and the emotions actually felt by the followers. They need to handle both the negative and the positive emotions both in themselves and in their followers via emotion management. Organisational effectiveness could be achieved only when both the highs and lows are managed. Controlling emotions at work is key to effective leadership. Feelings like satisfaction, security, and trust can be imbibed in the followers only if the leader holds a positive outward appearance.

The most prosperous CEOs are emotionally intelligent enough to handle their power and use their emotional intelligence to bring out the best in others.[169] Elon Musk, the CEO of SpaceX and Tesla is one such leader. When there was a claim of a higher rate of injury at the

Fremont factory in Tesla, Elon Musk wrote an email to the workers, urging them to give an account of all the injuries, and also mentioned that he would come and personally visit the factory and do all the tasks of the injured workers. When a CEO who works for nearly eighty to ninety hours weekly shows genuine care by offering to work along with the factory workers, it shows how the emotional intelligence of the leader has enabled him to act empathetically. Actions speak louder than words. This act of Elon Musk was motivating for the employees, and his attempt to better understand their perspective was appreciated.

The CEO of PepsiCo, Indra Nooyi, was another emotionally intelligent leader who realised that the best way to earn the employees' loyalty was to hook them emotionally to the job via the business model of the company.[170] During her visit to India, she realised that the many people who visited her actually spoke less to her but more to her mother. They told her mother how well she had raised her daughter. That is when Nooyi realised that her parents were worthy of the praise as they were accountable for her success. On the same note, she decided to write letters to the parents of her employees, thanking them for the gift of their child to her company. The parents replied, saying how honoured they felt. The employees also mentioned that that was the best thing that ever occurred to their parents. Nooyi connected personally well with her team in order to develop loyalty via her distinctive display of thankfulness.

Richard Branson, the chairman and founder of Virgin Group, was an emotionally intelligent leader who was able to direct his emotions of being dyslexic in the right direction.[171] He is a very renowned business icon, adventurer, entrepreneur, and activist who has initiated many billion-dollar businesses and other companies. He extends help to other young people suffering from dyslexia via the charity organisation Made by Dyslexia. In his recent letter, which he published, addressing his younger dyslexic self, he brings about all the components of emotional intelligence. He agrees that dyslexia is both a strength and a weakness. His condition of dyslexia was a reason for his success. He is empathetic towards other young people with dyslexia.

Satya Nadella, the CEO of Microsoft, was another emotionally intelligent leader who handled the emotions of the drastic failure of a Twitter bot called Tay very maturely.[172] In 2014, he took over as CEO and proved himself by boosting the annual revenue to more than $85 million and also invested in quantum computing, artificial intelligence, and augmented reality. Under his leadership, Tay was designed with the goal of improving artificial intelligence communication. In less than sixteen hours, this experiment failed as profane and racist comments were being tweeted, and Microsoft had to call off the project. Nadella sent a very consoling email to the engineers who worked on Tay. He mentioned that it was human to err and that they always had his back. He said that this should be treated as a learning experience. His motivation, instead of scolding them for the public failure, encouraged the team to create a new AI chatbot, Zo, which has been working well so far.

To become a passionate leader who is mature in being and doing, you need to follow the process of realising your personality, reforming what needs to be reformed, and transforming your life and others' lives.

Realise yourself

You need to realise what you are, your staple emotional states, and your affective energy. There are hurts, anger, and bottled-up feelings. Label them in the sense of where they came from and what impact they make in your personality. You recognise their nature and dynamics, and you are aware of the sources of disruptive emotional states and constructive emotional states. By this, you gain accurate self-assessment that you know your strengths and weaknesses. There is nothing to feel bad about what you are. In fact, it helps you build your self-esteem. When you have the profile of your personality, you gradually become self-confident. To map your personality, you should first ask your mother what you were from the time you were born. She would give you a good view of your root personality. Then ask your classmates and close friends; they would give you your social personality. Ask yourself honestly. We always have an area that is only known to us. That hidden area often controls our behaviour and thoughts. This personality mapping should give a picture of yourself.

Handle your vulnerability

Mapping yourself will show a picture of you as deficient in many ways, weak in many areas, and limited in capabilities. Real leadership is born out of one's own realisation of vulnerability. In vulnerability, one finds strength and courage to move forward. As a human being, you are fragile, limited, and weak. Physically and intellectually, you are limited. There is a point at which you see yourself powerless, but all the time, you try to go beyond the limits, push yourself so hard beyond the limits, and refuse to recognise the limitedness. Most of the time, what happens is that you end up in depression. Instead, you need to accept what you are, your limitations and weaknesses. Surrendering to the unlimited reality makes you stay humble and composed. That in a way makes you see unlimited possibilities and draw a huge unlimited strength and energy. Accepting that you are fragile is in fact a sign of strength, not a weakness. In front of employees in your company, when you say that you have done something wrong, you will become strong in their perception. It is a moral strength that outsmarts the deficiencies you have.

Reform yourself

Once you realised your inner states, then you should regulate your feelings and moods. You should make an effort to see growth in the areas in which you need positive change. Correct the wrongs and strengthen the rights. Form again yourself—*reformation of self.* You need to develop skills to keep your destructive emotions in check. Often, this reformative initiative should involve interior modification in that negative emotional states have to be cured and positive emotional states have to be built qualitatively. If a leader in an organisation is called to be pleasant in interaction, have high self-esteem, and manage people in the work efficiently, she needs to be an emotionally healthy person free of inordinate attachments.[173] To reform is to free oneself from inordinate attachments[174]—attachments that are obsessive and compulsive—which make people immature in their behaviour. If a person is full of herself, egoistic, she is attached to self-glory. This is an inordinate emotional attachment. This can cause only aversion in others, not attraction from others to her.

Inordinate attachments in a leader can lead to self-destruction, and she will be an unsuccessful leader. There are ordinate attachments that can effect healthy changes. It will be ordinate when a leader is emotionally attached to the people she manages in her workplace, and that attachment produces a cohesive team to achieve the goals of the organisation. Because the function of a leader is to lead people to be productive in terms of contributing to positive change, if something in your personality distracts you from this function, it is inordinate, and if something strengthens your resolve in the function, it is ordinate. As said earlier, ordinate attachments should help a person to speak and behave appropriately in situations. This type of reforming self is a way of healing oneself to be fit for being and doing in a particular life situation.

Transform your life

Realisation and reformation should reach transformation in the process of growing mature as a leader. It is like a genetic alteration of self. You realise what you are, and you reform yourself to be fit for the work you do and life you lead. Then you generate energy around you that transforms the atmosphere of the place where you work and of the family you live with. Every interaction you have with people produces energy that transforms people and places. Although the people you lead will do the same work or roles in an organisation, they will do it in a very different mental state. A mature leader, in fact, transforms people every time she interacts with them in her efforts to lead in order to achieve the goals. A transformative leader in an organisation regularly shifts her focus from situational coaching and training, which is aimed at helping people who work to make incremental performance improvements, to leading and coaching them to grow in their search for meaning and authentic living.[175] The leader who has transformed herself into a mature person not only wants the people around her to change but she also remains to change. As Mahatma Gandhi said, a leader is the change that she wants to happen in her organisation and in the people she works with.

Be authentic

Gaining affective maturity makes you an authentic person who believes truly that you are at the core of yourself. You need to recognise who you truly are before what you aspire to become. Any attempt to get away from your true self is a neurotic disorder.[176] To be really authentic, you need to become conscious of your state of incompleteness. This is to realise that you are limited. You need to pull out of the game, playing or pretending and become happy and comfortable with who you are, with strengths and weaknesses. Once you have pulled out of the game, you should engage yourself in activities that express truly who you are.[177] These expressions will be either accepted or rejected by the people around you. A kind of social embodiment of your personality happens. That acceptance or rejection defines your identity. By this, you realise that being authentic is not merely a personal act or behaviour but a social act that completes the process of being authentic.[178] Authentic leaders always develop social conversations to identify with their personal conversations within. Often in this process, the personal interests go away, and a synergy between what they think they are and want to be and what the society really requires emerge automatically.[179] Being authentic is therefore directly related to what you do to the society you live in, or what we call authenticity in context.

To get a picture of where we are so far, an energy of affective maturity of the *leftward* move in the dynamo competence makes a leader mature, and that maturity is manifested in every move she makes in her managing and leading human resources. Authority (*rightward* move) and affective energy are the sources of power that function as an engine of leadership. The authority of persuasion, which is drawn from the historical consciousness (*backward* move) and the vision (*forward* move), needs the maturity of affective energy in the performance of leadership.

Inward—Inner Attitude

> The greatest discovery of my generation that man can alter his life simply by altering his attitude of mind.
> James Truslow Adams

A leader who has historical consciousness, who can move forward with a futuristic vision, who has authority as an influence, and who has the affective maturity by moving leftward is not complete. She needs to have the right attitude.

'Attitude is used to refer to a person's overall evaluation of persons [including oneself], objects, and issues. Thus, one's attitude refers to how favourably or unfavourably or how positively or negatively in general one views some object of judgement such as "the defendant," "capital punishment," or "ice-cream." These global evaluations can vary in a large number of ways in addition to their extremity such as whether they are based on emotions, beliefs, or past experiences and behaviours and whether they are internally consistent or ambivalent.'[180] *Attitude* is a French term coined from the Italian word *attitudine* and the Late Latin *aptitūdō* and *aptitūdin*. Synonyms of *attitude* are approach, mindset, position, way of behaving, orientation, manner, feelings, outlook, way of thinking, stance, and thoughts.

Attitude is defined by three main characteristics. It is (1) a mental state, either unconscious or conscious; (2) a feeling, belief, or value; and (3) a predisposition to action or behaviour.[181] The predecessors to attitude are the opinions one experiences, concepts, objects, and situations. The possible results of an attitude are very diverse and multiple in number.

The important attributes of an attitude are that it is bipolar; it consists of affective, behavioural, and cognitive components; and it is a reaction to a stimulus. An attitude may not be acknowledged consciously by an individual as she may or may not reveal it. The attitude towards an object affects the entire range of responses to that object; however, that may not forecast any action.[182] Intentions, which are functions of one's attitude, determine one's behaviour. When there is a high correlation between behaviour and intention, actions can be predicted based on the attitude towards them. Hence, if an individual holds a favourable attitude towards some object, her behaviour would also be favourable. Similarly, unfavourable behaviour if the attitude is unfavourable. 'A person's attitude represents his evaluation of the entity in question.'[183]

A leader's attitude and behaviour play a vital role in influencing the employees' performance capacity and drive.[184] It is the attitude of the leader which would evoke the desired behaviour from the employees. The right attitude is an important trait of a good leader.[185] A person's upbringing, the influence of peers, and life experiences play an important role in the formation of one's attitude. Though childhood experiences form the initial attitude, the people who we meet later and the events which occur could change the initial attitude formed if we are open to listen and learn. The workplace influences the attitude mainly via mistakes and the learning from them. The behaviour of a person is an important indicator of her attitude. The main factors influencing attitude are beliefs, education, upbringing, socio-economic status, influential people, peers, and media. Attitude is being influenced continuously and is evolving each day. Attitude change is the alteration of one's evaluation from one value to another.[186] The change is often calculated relative to the initial attitude of the individual.

Attitude is key to both professional and personal success.[187] It is the factor of success over which we have control. It shades our vision of how we view other individuals and the world as a whole. Attitude influences one's beliefs and behaviour. It influences the ability to handle changes, motivation, customer relations, and teamwork. It is attitude that changes a dreadful work environment into a more pleasing workspace. Successful people tend to adjust their attitude consciously when theirs is below par, owing to a bad attitude experience. They also tend to stay away from those who have a pessimistic attitude. It is very difficult to change a person's attitude. Individuals with a good attitude will be those who do not play the blame game, those who are optimistic and are able to see the brighter side of the problem, and those who are committed to continuous learning, open to feedback, and are good listeners.

Maya Angelou is the first bestselling Afro-American author, popular poet, and award-winning actress and university lecturer. She mentored Oprah Winfrey. She was the first Afro-American woman admitted to the Directors Guild of America. But her personal history is traumatic. She was sexually abused by her mother's boyfriend. After that incident, she refused to speak to anyone. To subsist in the world, she had to dance in nightclubs and work as a cook in a cafe and even as a madam in a San Diego brothel. But today she is a stalwart in her own right whom the world adores. She read a poem at the inaugural ceremony of Bill Clinton, as president in 1993. When asked about the secret of her success, she said, 'If I see something I don't like, I try to change it, and if I can't change it, I change my position of looking at it, and then seeing it from a different angle, I might be able to change it; or I might find some good in it that I can use, which might make it change itself.'[188]

Ben Rumble, who is well-known for his telecommunication business, reaped huge success because of having the right attitude.[189] He employed the McDonald's retailing method in telecommunication retailing. He believed that attitude comes in the forefront before everything, and life's attitude towards oneself is determined by one's attitude towards life. He ensured that his staff were well-trained with manuals which were supported by his own twelve rules of attitude to business and life.

This is the attitude that one achieves by moving *inward* in building up the dynamo competence. Moving inward in the process of building the competence provides the ways in which you see this world, people around you, and your life. This is your view of the world. This is your attitude. This makes you who you are and what you can become. Attitude to life is what gives meaning to one's life. Maya was able to overcome the horrendous suffering she faced in her life, and this transformation into the person that she is today has been possible simply because of the attitude she developed towards life.

Attitude is composed of various forms of judgements. It develops from affect, behavioural change, and cognition. The *affective* response is a physiological response that expresses an individual's preference for an entity. The *behavioural intention* is a verbal indication of the intention of an individual. The *cognitive* response is a cognitive evaluation of the entity to form an attitude. Most attitudes in individuals are a result of *observational learning* from their environment.[190] What you went through in your experience from your childhood to date forms your ways of looking at this world.

In your experience of life from your childhood, you develop a mindset that helps you to perceive everything, and that perception guides you to respond to a situation. As an HR leader, you need to know about your attitude to life:

- ✓ What is your attitude to food and eating?
- ✓ What is your attitude to your physical body?
- ✓ What is your attitude to gender differences and discriminations?
- ✓ What is your attitude to human relationships?
- ✓ What is your attitude to God/religion/spirituality?

Your answers to these questions will demonstrate clearly your ways of seeing the world. They form your attitude that would determine your performance as an HR leader.[191] People around you would see this attitude of yours in the ways you think, feel, and act. You can easily identify the attitude of people by learning their attitude to food and eating. Food and eating might look trivial, but it can open doors to one's world and ways of life. Consider this example. I know a friend. Let us call him Valentine. From his childhood until his college days, his mother scolded him always before serving food and hated him for eating heavily. He hated his mother for this. He loved eating. And after eating good food, he would sleep for hours. He was passionate about it. Later, he went abroad for work where he enjoyed the freedom of buying his food or cooking his food. Sometimes he would buy two kilograms of lamb and cook it in ghee and eat it himself. He related with people who like good food. He used to drive many hours, ten hours sometimes, to go to a place or a restaurant to eat. On weekends, he would go hiking and eat a variety of food and go to sleep for twenty-four hours. He hated people who disliked eating. He would get angry if anyone commented on his liking for food. His attitude in life centres on food and eating. Deep down in him, he thinks that good life means eating good food. Good life is a life in which you earn good money and eat good food. He wants his future wife to love food. What would be his performance as a leader? He is an efficient leader in an IT company. But his attitude to food controls and dominates his work ethic in the company. He looks for any excuse to organise a dinner. This has enormous impact on his performance. He ignores or isolates himself from the people who have no liking for food. From this stems his approach on life that it is meant to satisfy desires and fulfil just physical pleasures. Values such as justice and equality would be relegated to the background. Enjoyment would be his prime aim. And he would consume everything, even human beings, to satisfy his cravings. This person's leadership role would be poisonous in the body of society or in an institution.

A leader must have a proper attitude. Attitude is composed of different forms of judgement. Attitude is developed from childhood. A competent leader would have the attitude of authenticity. Being authentic implies that the person has a good attitude. To be authentic, one should be driven by the values of beauty, goodness, and truth, which are the three fundamental values/principles. This is the foundational philosophy of life. Hence, a person with good attitude should appreciate the world's beauty, defend the truth, and be responsive to goodness. When you are true to yourself, attitude is formed. Being true to yourself and being authentic mean being responsive to goodness, being appreciative of beauty, and being able to defend the truth.

One can study from the experiences of others, but it is not possible to be successful when you try to act like them.[192] Trust is built only when you are authentic, when you are yourself. Kevin Sharer, the president and CEO of Amgen, had earned a lot of experience when he worked as Jack Welch's assistant in the 1980s. He mentioned that everyone attempted to be like Jack Welch. But leadership is all about being your true self and not trying to emulate anybody.

As competent leaders need the attitude of authenticity, leader authenticity becomes an important dimension.[193] *Leader authenticity* is defined as 'the extent to which followers perceived their leader to be maximising the acceptance of organisational and personal responsibility for actions, outcomes, and mistakes; the non-manipulation of followers; and the salience of self over role'.[194] Authentic leaders need to be true to themselves, to be accountable, and to accept the mistakes committed. The followers would view the authentic leaders as real and genuine, one who takes responsibility for the organisation's actions and that of her own, one who is cautious not to repeat mistakes, and one who does not manipulate peers. Authentic leaders have an agreement between their expressions and actions. Authentic leaders would help to build organisations where ethical behaviour, job satisfaction, interpersonal respect and trust, and positive morale dominate. Organisations would also be high on effective employee supervision, accountability, leader effectiveness, employee self-efficacy, and productivity. Authentic leaders have a lot of trust in their employees, and hence, they delegate more responsibilities and thereby empower them.[195] Via effective communication, authentic leaders have in-depth knowledge of all the staff in their workspace. Authentic leaders need to self-change via continuous learning, have emotional strength to deal with uncertainties and fear, are motivated to learn from their errors, and have self-trust and self-discipline.

When leaders, who are the main driving force in an organisation, become authentic, they would stimulate employees to perform better.[196] Authentic leaders act as role models for the organisation's values and earn the trust of peers. They instil optimism, hope, resilience, and confidence among the employees in order to improve their performance and hence the organisational performance. Authentic leaders also help to inculcate in employees a positive attitude and behaviour, which in turn enhances the performance of the organisation. Authentic leaders consistently practice their values, showcase desire for their purpose, and lead with both their heads and their hearts.[197] They get their desired output with self-discipline, and they develop meaningful long-term relations. They are well aware of who they are. For the authentic leaders, leadership arises from their own life stories. They reframe their own stories in order to comprehend who they really are deep within instead of just passively observing their story. They repeatedly test themselves via actual life experiences in order to create self-awareness. In the process, they identify the purpose of their leadership. Authentic leaders are driven by their inner core values. Authenticity is the only way to be effective. Authentic leaders build excellent support systems to help them stay grounded and to remind them of who they really are. These leaders have a very confident and stable presence. Professional and personal lives are not a zero-sum game for the authentic leaders. With a lot of discipline, they have integrated their lives. They need to sustain their authenticity. Authentic leaders generate continuous superior results over the long term. Only short-term results can be generated without being authentic.

Beddoes-Jones and Swailes (2015)[198] advanced the three pillars of authentic leadership as ethics, self-awareness, and self-regulation. Majority of the leadership fails are because of the absence of one or more of these pillars. By being self-aware, the leader is well aware of her own motives, feelings, and beliefs and how they influence her and the others around. Self-regulated leaders possess high self-discipline, keep their ego and mood swings under control, and remain accessible even during difficult times. Ethical leaders have their core values held very strong and do not compromise as they believe that they are ethically accountable of others.

In order to be an effective leader, one has to be authentic.[199] Authentic leaders are true to themselves and don't have the pressure of acting in order to achieve results. When leaders are not genuine to themselves, they would not mean what they say or do. Moreover, those who work with/for them would see through this eventually, resulting in uncomfortable relations. More importantly, leaders will not be able to act for long away from their true self. Soon, the actions, behaviour, decisions, words, and body language will begin to reveal their true self, which creates mistrust in the long run. Authenticity is both an ethical virtue as well as a practical virtue. Authenticity is a social ability. Being authentic, that is, being exactly what you claim to be, is an important quality of interactive behaviour. An authentic person would express what she believes in, in her conduct towards others. Authenticity is the message given out about the true self.

Authentic leaders lead with empathy, which is enabled by their strong core values and self-awareness.[200] They identify, share, and assist in achieving their followers' goals. Barack Obama and his messages are a reflection of an authentic leadership. He was one of those leaders who resembled the common man and understood the struggles. In spite of all the surface dissimilarities, there were deep commonalities beneath. Most authentic leaders have a tragic past, which translates into a strong character moulded by core values.

Howard Schultz, the CEO of Starbucks, is one such authentic leader. His father endured an injury when Schultz was young, which led to the loss of his job and healthcare benefits. With this background, when Schultz led a company, he in turn offered very lavish benefits to even the part-time workers.

Daniel Vasella, the CEO and chairman of Novartis, also struggled hard in his childhood days and has now reached the pinnacle of success.[201] His journey to authentic leadership was filled with difficult trials. He was born to humble parents in 1953 in Fribourg, Switzerland. His desire to become a physician stemmed from the medical problems he faced as a child. At the tender age of four, he was hospitalised for food poisoning. And then at the age of five, he fell sick with asthma and was sent to spend two summers alone with a caretaker to Eastern Switzerland. This separation from his parents was terrible for him as his caretaker was an alcoholic and did not attend to his needs. At the age of eight, he suffered from tuberculosis and then meningitis and was left at the sanatorium for a year. His parents visited him very rarely. He suffered from loneliness and homesickness. His sister succumbed to cancer when he was just ten years old. His father also passed away in a surgery three years later. His mother began to work in a faraway town in order to support the family. She visited him only once in three weeks. He was in bad company then until he met his first girlfriend, who changed his life with her affection. At twenty, he joined the medical school and graduated with honours. He chose psychotherapy as a result of his history and to refrain from feeling like a victim. His reframing of his past enabled him to realise that he wanted to reach out to a larger crowd than he could if he practised as an individual practitioner. Vasella wanted to increase his influence on medicine with his abilities. He joined Sandoz's US affiliate as a sales representative and then went on to be a product manager. He rapidly went up the hierarchy of the marketing division. In 1996, during the merger of Sandoz with Ciba-Geigy, Vasella was made the CEO of both the companies, which eventually was named as Novartis. When he bagged the role, he was very young with very limited experience. He took it upon himself to revolutionise the pharmaceutical industry using his powerful role. He bloomed as a leader. He built a completely new culture for Novartis, which revolved around compassion, competence, and competition. He wanted to reach out to people via new life-saving drugs by building a global healthcare company. He is one such authentic leader who has found strength from his life experiences, which has enabled him to understand the purpose of his leadership.

Authentic leaders have a great sense of self-awareness.[202] One such authentic leader who exhibits great self-awareness is David Pottruck, the former CEO of Charles Schwab. He was a football player in high school. At the University of Pennsylvania, he was the MVP of his college team. Upon completion of his MBA at Wharton and after a small tenure with Citigroup, he became the marketing head at Charles Schwab. He was very hardworking and vigorously put in long hours of work in order to push for results, which annoyed most people at work. His boss made him realise that his colleagues do not trust him. He was in denial, and that was the biggest obstacle to becoming self-aware. He had to overcome his blind spots in order to succeed. Authentic leaders understand that they need to be receptive to feedback, especially the ones they never like to hear. Pottruck realised his large blind spots only after his second divorce. It was a counsellor who told him some hard truths, after which he was determined to change himself for the better. Now he is able to accept healthy criticisms from his wife. Though he falls back at times to his old ways during stressful situations, he has found ways to battle stress.

The foundation of an authentic leadership is the core values which result from one's convictions and beliefs.[203] The real values will come to light only during stressful situations. The principles of leadership are these values which convert to action. Jon Huntsman, the chairman and founder of Huntsman Corporation, is one such authentic leader. His core moral values were questioned during his tenure during the Nixon administration in 1972 when he worked under H. R. Haldeman, Nixon's powerful head. Huntsman was made to work in an amoral environment as Haldeman's orders were questionable, and Huntsman wasn't willing to take orders which were unethical or against his values. He did not think twice before refusing to carry out the orders which were against his moral values though he was working under the second most powerful man in the country. Huntsman later quit.

In spite of vivid differences, authentic leaders relate deeply with others and encourage them to take up daring challenges.[204] Anne Mulcahy, the former CEO of Xerox, was an authentic leader who worked meticulously to encourage Xerox's dispirited employees to work together and lead the company to great heights.

As a competent leader, you need to have an attitude of authenticity. To be authentic is to be driven by the values of beauty, goodness, and truthfulness. These three values are the foundational philosophy of life. The attitude of a leader should stem from these three values. And she should approach her life and work with this attitude. This would define her character. Character is more than personality traits. Personality traits such as ways of acting, habits, maturity, preferences, skills, talents, and abilities are superficial dimensions in a person.[205] Character refers to your moral worth that is formed by beauty, goodness, and truthfulness. One's character does not wholly come from the money she earns or the position she holds or the background she comes from. Rather, it comes from the responsiveness to the objective values of beauty, truth, and goodness. If one denies these values or uses them for selfish ends, she will lose first of all the meaning of life.[206] She will not be a leader who attracts people and persuade them to action. These three virtues provide the ground on which a personality stands. A good character formed by the virtues becomes responsive to good reasons that reveal good values. People with good character will feel and behave 'at the right times, about the right things, towards the right people, and in the right way'.[207] Therefore, the attitude of a leader in an organisation should come from her character that is formed by the virtues of beauty, goodness, and truth. In brief, the character of a dynamo leadership must be able to sense and be receptive to the beauty of this cosmos, should be eager for truth, and find fulfilment in mutual help and love.[208] This is necessary in today's modern (or postmodern) life that is devoid of beauty and meaning, only frantic rush and craving for pleasure and money. This has made our lives bleak and nothing but transient moments of consumption. The dynamo leadership should have the competence that helps to see the beauty of the world and be responsive to goodness and truth. Let me elaborate the virtues that form the proper attitude of leadership.

Appreciate the world's beauty

A leader should have an attitude that appreciates the world around her and sees the human life as beautiful irrespective of its flaws. She should perceive intensely the immeasurable beauty of the life around her. As William Blake persuades us, you should see 'a World in a Grain of Sand and Heaven in a Wild Flower'.[209] Human beings will not be able to live happily without being responsive to beauty of the natural world and, by extension, to the beauty of human beings. Deep inside, you should develop an approach to the world that everything and everyone is basically beautiful. Not merely in appearance but underneath every human being is the beauty that reflects the structure of the universe. This approach distances from the conventional approach that sees skin colour, structure of the body, and make-up as beauty. The dynamo leadership we propose here perceives that every living organism is beautiful. You must appreciate the fact that everyone who is human is beautiful. This is an attitude that perceives beyond external reality.

In reality, more often we see a person spontaneously with her negative qualities. Rarely are we able to appreciate her beauty as a human being. This is why we turn negative, and that makes us less productive and creative. We waste our energy and time in handling negativity. If you look at individuals who work with you as basically beautiful, you will be positive, and you will be able to spend your time and energy for productive purposes. You will be more concerned about 'He is good at it' than 'He is not good at that'. You become positive and see only the positive and always set aside the negative.

This approach helps you as a leader. You become a person who gives a good interpretation to any event. For example, someone in line commits a mistake. You will automatically think that there must be some good reason or situation that made her commit that mistake. You first give a good interpretation of the event. This is very important in leading an organisation.

Awe and wonder at things seen and unseen make a leader creative, and this also helps her see 'what is distinctive, efficient, and excellent in certain parts of the world'.[210] The leader who is able to appreciate beauty in others and their cultures will be able to work in a team, and she would connect with others quickly, which enables any work to reach its completion with a certain ease. The workplace is likely to be filled with joy and happiness. When you appreciate beauty, you become less fixated with your views, and you begin to be open to new ideas and possibilities of doing a thing in different ways.

Start your day with appreciation of the morning brightness, feel the water, and smell the soap. Look at the beauty of size and smell of the food you eat. See the lovely curls of the hair of the person you see first. This will make your day beautiful. Realise that the world is charged with the grandeur of God, as poet Gerard Hopkins said. This is the inner attitude that makes the life and work of a leader meaningful.

Be responsive to goodness

If you are able to see the beauty in people and in life, you will naturally respond to goodness. By goodness here, I mean natural disposition that generates life and fights against death. Responding to goodness means that you take the side of life generation. Whatever you think, feel, and act is oriented towards generating life, resulting in happiness. Your being and action are beneficial, helpful, and useful to others. Others appreciate your presence and your actions because they produce life, not death, not suffering but happiness. This is one of the important qualities of leadership.

Every decision you make as a leader of an organisation ultimately produces life in others and in the organisation. Often in the rat race of corporate life, people go all out to hurt people and destroy lives in their search for money and power.

Think that everything and everybody around you is good and full of goodness. Metaphysically, all are made to be good. Your employees are basically good; only circumstances make them not good. Try your best to see the goodness in them. This attitude will bring out their strength. Often, you see what is not good in others, only looking at their weaknesses. By doing so, you as a leader would not be able to achieve anything. Responding to goodness in others means to work on the strengths of others who work for you. This increases your moral strength that would automatically attract respect from others. As soon as others with you realise that you see mostly what is good in them, they would try to see what is good in you. There is a mutual recognition that leads to an atmosphere of fraternity. This is what makes an organisation better than others.

Defend the truth

I define *truth* as 'realisation of the gap between what we are and what we want/aspire to be; and believing that no technology can fill that gap, only inner change can change our way of looking at our life'.[211]

As said in the introduction of this book, we human beings are born into the world as diseased persons, not satisfied with what we are. We want to become something else and are not contented with who we are. The reality is transient, and in that transient world, we human beings are finite, limited, and fragile. We are born, grow old, and die. But all the time, we make efforts to overcome this finite nature. We create machines and invent medicines to prolong life and youth. But what we should do is to accept it and modify our inner attitude in order that we see our finite world, which could be lived only by having a spiritual impulse. That impulse educates us. Despite this transience, there is meaning in life. That meaning comes from our efforts to hold the hands of other human beings and walk our journey of life. As a dynamo leader, you should defend it and promote this idea in the place you live and work.

Accepting and defending the idea of fragility and finitude of humanity helps you as a leader to become humble in the first place. You will understand who you are before (being) and what you aspire to be (becoming). That humility and self-acceptance puts you at ease with yourself first. This provides you with a certain ease in your leadership. This ease comes when you love who you are and accept it.[212] A leader who is at ease with herself will have an attitude to life that is responsive to beauty, goodness, and truth. You will gain a way of behaving that respects others, does the right action, and finally, gives you a unique meaning to your leadership, in fact, to your life.

Outward—Expressions and Productivity

> I believe that you should gravitate to people who are doing productive and positive things with their lives.
> Nadia Comaneci

A leader who has gained insights about the past by being historically conscious, has a futuristic vision, has influenced others via her authority, has emotional intelligence via the affective maturity, and also has the right attitude towards life is not competent enough. She needs to be productive and hence move outward by translating creative ideas into innovations—all that you have and what you need to be expressed as concrete actions and as visible effects. An effective leader would know how to produce and does not merely speak about it. Just do what you believe within. The learnings from the past (*backward*), designing of the future (*forward*), and formation of inner attitude (*inward*) must show concretely in actions.

So far, what we discussed were moves within. Now they must be seen visibly.

The energies of historical consciousness, futuristic vision, authority, affective maturity, and attitude should be seen tangibly by means of action, behaviour, body language, and verbal and non-verbal expressions. What you express should be born out of these energies. The expressions must be creative and innovative. These expressions create a positive impact on the life of others, which ultimately leads to optimum performance.

Productive is derived from the French word *product if* and also directly from the Latin word *productivus*, which means 'fit for production'.

The following analogy explains the inward move perfectly. Now if you are holding a cup of coffee when someone comes along and bumps into you or shakes your arm, making you spill your coffee everywhere, what would you say when asked why you spilled the coffee? 'Because someone bumped into me!' Now that is the wrong answer. You spilled the coffee because there was coffee in your cup. Had there been tea in the cup, you would have spilled tea. Whatever is inside the cup is what will spill out. Therefore, when life comes along and shakes you, whatever is inside you will come out. It's easy to fake it, until you get rattled. So we have to ask ourselves, 'What's in my cup?' When life gets tough, what spills over? Joy, gratefulness, peace, and humility? Anger, bitterness, harsh words, and reactions? Life provides the cup, and you choose how to fill it. Hence, what is inside you comes out as your expression, behaviour, and action.

Expressions

Outward move is about how a leader expresses herself. Expressions are an important medium through which the five energies of historical consciousness, futuristic vision, authority, affective maturity, and attitude of the leader are expressed.

Expressions play an important role in influencing the quality of the bond between the leader and the followers.[213] Leader's expressions have the power to influence the attitude, behaviour, feelings, cognitions, and the performance of the followers. The leader's expressions could also trigger the followers to unconsciously adopt the leaders' expressive behaviours. The emotional expressions of the leader are a source of information about the leader, which would be used to form judgements and beliefs about her. The followers keenly observe the expressions of the leader, her non-verbal behaviour, and her vocal cues, both positive and negative, which in turn impacts the likeability of the leader. Hence, leaders have to be cautious of their expressions if they have to maintain good relations with their followers. There are four processes via which the emotional expressions of a leader impact the affective state of the followers. They include '[1] an unconscious, reflexive response, [2] a conditioned, schematic response, [3] conceptual-level processing and [4] emotional contagion'.[214] It can be concluded reasonably that the leader's expressions provoke affective responses among the followers, whichever the processes at work are at any point in time.

Leaders need to be knowledgeable about their emotional expressions.[215] A leader's expressions perceived by the followers are strongly related to the followers' trust in the leaders. A leader's expressions of emotions like pride are connected with lesser perceived kindness of the leader. On the other hand, expressions of gratitude are related to higher perceived kindness of the leader. Hence, the expressions of the leader influence her trustworthiness, which includes integrity, benevolence, and ability. A leader's expressions of gratitude lead to greater job satisfaction and lesser turnover intentions among the followers, whereas a leader's expressions of pride result in lower job satisfaction and higher turnover intentions.[216] A leader's expressions of emotions are signs of outcome attributions.

Hence, expressions could be used to build good relationships between the leader and the followers. Leaders who express positive emotions are more effective when compared to the leaders who express negative emotions.[217]

Another aspect of expressions is the facial expression.[218] The facial expressions of the leader play a key role in emotionally influencing the followers. Even microexpressions, which last for less than a second and used mostly during speeches, do influence the emotional response of the followers. Though microexpressions are short-lived, sparse, and ambiguous independently, they significantly influence the followers' response, though the followers are unaware of their presence. Thus, expressions are crucial in delivering emotional content. Effective leaders are those who have the ability to express a wide range of emotions as they could gain empathy and support from their followers via communication. Therefore, communication of the leader—either through the television, social media, or face to face—is important for encouraging the followers.

Outward mindset

Outward is a mindset that sees others' needs and interests more than one's own agenda. In any organisation, people with outward mindset will make every effort to contribute to the growth of organisations they work for; they would give very little consideration to their own benefits. You could find some employees who do not bother about their salary or what they would get from their work; instead, they would focus always on what benefits the organisations. It is an innate push that they have to express their worth. Moving from narrow self-interest to seeing the larger reality is what outward move does to a leader. She thinks less about what she needs; all the time the needs of others who work under/with her matter most. Many companies have solved major crises when leaders in them displayed outward mindset.[219] They make their companies larger than themselves in which they see their roles as parts of the whole. This is a perspective that drives a leader to be a selfless servant to the vision of her organisation. The impact of their actions is given more emphasis by the leader with outward mindset, not like CEOs who gulp down a huge per cent of incentives while their companies are straining to give returns to their shareholders. The case of Alan Mulally, former CEO of Boeing, illustrates this mindset. He turned around Ford by making the people inside the company develop outward mindset. He said 'people first', not profit. With a compelling vision and inclusive approach, he guided the entire company to focus on the needs of customers.

Behaviour

Outward move is about how the leader behaves.[220] A leader's behaviour is the result of experiencing all the five energies of historical consciousness, futuristic vision, authority, affective maturity, and attitude. A leader's behaviour is whatever the leader does in order to fulfil her position or execute her role. A leader's behaviour plays an important role in influencing the confidence perception, collective and self-efficacy perception, and the perception of leader effectiveness in the work environment, which in turn impacts the organisational performance via the behaviour of participative management and performance feedback.[221] The leader who constantly interacts with her subordinates is capable of affecting their performance, feelings, and day-to-day perceptions, thereby affecting the creativity of their job via her behaviour.[222] Hence, the creativity of the work environment is influenced by the leader's everyday behaviours, like supporting the subordinates and their job by observing their growth fairly and efficiently, discussing important decisions with them, giving them emotionally support, and appreciating them for their good work. Leadership behaviours have a direct influence on the organisational outcome.[223] Leaders choose from a variety of behaviours and even behave in complex, paradoxical ways so that the desired outcomes could be achieved.

A leader's behaviour could be categorised into three independent dimensions, namely, task behaviour, change behaviour, and relations behaviour.[224] The main objectives of task behaviour are high dependability on services, operations, and products and high efficiency in utilising personnel and resources. The main objectives of change behaviour are adjustment to external changes and innovative enhancements in services, processes, or products. The main objectives of relations behaviour are enhanced mutual collaboration and trust and strong dedication to the organisation and its mission. The task behaviour of a leader includes monitoring performance and operations, clarifying the expectations of the role and objectives of the task, and planning activities for the short term. The change behaviour of a leader includes motivating innovative thinking, proposing innovative strategies, observing the external environment, and taking appropriate risks in order to bring about changes. The relations behaviour of a leader are supporting, developing skills and confidence, empowering the followers, consulting during decision-making, and recognising achievements. All the behaviours are equally important for effective leadership, and depending on the situation, each behaviour becomes relevant.

Leading in deeds

Going by the famous saying 'Actions speak louder than words', a leader's actions are one of the important dimensions of the outward move.[225] Actions showcase the inner energies of historical consciousness, futuristic vision, authority, affective maturity, and attitude. The way the leader acts is very crucial as what great leaders do is recorded in history. The leaders' actions need to be creative and innovative. 'Innovative leadership means introducing something new like an idea, method, technique, process, product, service or discovery to solve current problems and satisfy people's needs at the present and in the future. Innovative leaders can solve current problems with a focus on the future. Innovative leaders have several qualities in common, such as leadership knowledge, skills, values, and talents to recognise the danger of the current problems and anticipate their negative impacts on the future. They are visionary and committed to increasing peoples' economic, political, and social well-being and protect the environment and the planet, for creating a just society.'[226]

A leader's action is defined as 'the translation of self-knowledge into specific activities that can help enhance leadership capabilities'.[227] Action plans are important for leaders in order to achieve goals. Action plans could be implemented in three different ways, namely, vision focus, goal focus, and process focus. In vision focus, the action plan is not very extensive and is just the initial steps which eventually evolve the vision. In goal focus, the action plan is very specific in order to achieve the desired goal. Process focus involves an action plan which is ongoing. Jassawalla and Sashittal (2000)[228] formulated theories of action depending on the objective. When the objective is to ensure commitment, the leader's action should be to ensure that the employees equally commit to the inputs and, at the same time, share the responsibility for the results equally, thereby generating the notion of interdependence. If the objective is to build information-intensive environments, the leader's action would be to encourage the exchange of high levels of information in order to develop integrative thinking. When the objective is to play facilitator, then the leader should only coach and empower the employees. If the objective is to focus on human interaction, then the leader's action should be to ensure that the employees are equipped with not only technical expertise but also skilled at human interaction. When the objective is to focus on learning, then the leader's action is to maintain a work environment conducive of learning, which is important for developing flexibility and creativity.

Actions as small as microactions, which last for less than merely five seconds, play an important role in developing new leadership skills as they serve as a break in habitual routines.[229] Microactions, once practised, get merged with the leader's work style, team, project, history, culture, personality, and relationship. Examples of microactions are smiling in order to be a more optimistic leader, asking questions instead of merely stating so that communication could be improved, greeting peers to be a more inclusive leader, and waiting before answering for improved listening.

Nadia, the famous gymnast, was known for her creative and innovative skills in gymnastics. On the uneven bars, she created a move, which was a hip-to-front salto. This move was later named after her. And on the balance beam, she was the first gymnast who performed an aerial walkover and a double-twist dismount.[230]

We experience real happiness when we are creative. All of us are creative in the ways we can. I believe that God has created us in his own image. If he is the creator, then we should be co-creators. Creativity is not just a mental process of generating new concepts. The Latin root of the word is *creatus*, which literally means 'to have grown'. Creativity is, in that sense, a growth that is not normally achieved by people in the conventional way.[231] In the Greek world view, the expression *poiein* ('to make poetry') refers to bringing to life a new world. Later, in the age of Enlightenment, creativity means imagination. In the Eastern world view, creativity is viewing life from a totally different perspective. The East refuses to believe that you can create out of nothing. The cosmos in itself moves in creative dynamism. We need to approach changes from a perspective that is sensitive to the nature.

Closely associated with this concept is innovation. In fact, innovation encompasses creativity.[232] Innovation refers to change in thinking first, in things produced by that thinking, and in the processes of this change. In method, content, and process, innovation brings new change that increases the efficiency of an organisation. Innovation begins with a creative idea. In real sense, creativity and innovation are interchangeably used. The former mostly is in art and literature, and the latter in business sectors. The dynamo move of *outward* mainly refers to how a leader is productive—her ability to realise ideas into actions and plans into reality. Walking the talk. This productivity must be innovative in terms of resolving conflicts in the process of leading a group to growth, and she would be seen as an innovative leader who could clear all the obstacles in the way of growth. In this process, she should be able to chart a new path, new trend, and new atmosphere of work and life. This improves efficiency, productivity, quality, and competitive positioning in the market.

In the knowledge economy, innovation is a very important element.[233] The PWC 2015 study on global innovation shows that nearly $145 billion dollars is spent on research and development by the companies in the United States every year. 'Human capital' and 'innovation' were ranked as the top two challenges in the long term to business growth by around 943 CEOs in the Conference Board's 2015 CEO Challenge study. Thus, innovation is very important in order to compete, and leaders need to imbibe innovative thinking. Innovative leaders manage risk better than the other leaders as they are braver to take up experiments. They attempt to minimise risk and also take action when the outcome of the risk is negative. Innovative leaders showcase curiosity and always attempt to learn more. Keeping the organisational goals in mind, they venture out to learn new information. Their consistently learning attitude serves as a competitive advantage against others and helps to lead efficiently, thereby passing on this stimulus to the other employees. Innovative leaders lead bravely with authority and confidence. They welcome difficult situations with wide arms and use them as an opportunity to showcase their decision-making skills and also take responsibility for their decisions. They never avoid conflicts and are always upfront in meetings and discussions. Innovative leaders are very flexible and adapt paths quickly when new opportunities come up. They are very proactive and are always ready to take up responsibilities. They are capable of working independently without expecting peer support. Innovative leaders maintain a strategic business perspective. They have a holistic understanding of the industry, its effect on the business, the customers, and the marketplace. They use every opportunity to understand the external environment via active participation. They articulate convincing strategies for the future of their business.

The leadership of *Google* has demonstrated this idea of innovative strategies. In 1996, two Stanford University doctoral students in computer science, Sergey Brin and Larry Page, infused innovation into the Internet world. In May 2007, *Google* had 65.2 per cent of all US Internet searches. It is innovative in the sense that web-based links and 'click-through' ads bring in for a searcher/surfer all-in-one page.

Every page is connected to other million pages. The key ingredients of Google innovation are 'a wafer-thin hierarchy, a dense network of lateral communication, a policy of giving outsized ideas, a team-focused approach to product development, and a corporate credo that challenges every employee to put the user first'.[234] Innovation is the behaviour in the world of Google. Innovation becomes an attitude in most of the successful companies and organisations. A leader leads by example this innovation. That produces results, which contributes to social growth and change. An innovative leader is a productive leader. This makes her stand above the rest. Not what she talks but what she does is what makes the kind of leader she is.

Innovative leaders have a clear picture of the future in the form of an appealing, strategic vision.[235] They are strongly focussed on the customers, and they identify what factors fascinate the customers by getting into their heads via networking and repeated questioning about their demands. Innovative leaders develop a trusted, collaborative workspace where the employees are never penalised for genuine mistakes as innovation demands some level of risk and the probability of errors is high. They never fear doing what is right for the customer and the organisation. They believe in a culture which encourages upward communication as most of the innovative ideas bloom from the bottom levels. They display energy, optimism, and receptiveness to new ideas. They master the art of persuasion, which helps make their employees embrace their innovative ideas willingly because of the effective presentation of the ideas, and the employees work effectively towards them. Innovative leaders are efficient at setting stretch goals which demand not just working harder but going beyond and finding new ways to accomplish a higher goal. These leaders are very quick in their working style, and instead of long, time-consuming studies by big committees, they prefer quick prototypes or experiments. Innovative leaders always give straight and honest feedback which their subordinates can rely on in order to progress further in the right direction. For innovation to work, these leaders inspire through their work in the form of actions, which is both purposeful and meaningful.

Leaders need to show that innovation is important, and it really matters via their everyday actions as it is the most powerful sign for their team and the organisation as a whole.[236] In most organisations, senior officials felt that they have only facilitated the process of innovation for others and have felt responsible for the facilitation. They did not feel personally accountable for coming up with innovations. However, in the most innovative companies of the world like Amazon, Salesforce, and Procter & Gamble, the senior executives Jeff Bezos, Marc Benioff, and A. G. Lafley took the process of innovation in their own hands and did not delegate the process.

Innovative leaders valued the skills of innovation like observing, questioning, experimenting, networking, and associational thinking in other individuals as well.[237] As a result, the other individuals in the organisation would feel that it is the personal innovation capability that is needed to reach top positions within the organisation. Steve Jobs of Apple is a clear illustration of this. Apple reached an innovation premium of 37 per cent during Steve Jobs's first tenure from 1980 to 1985, wherein Jobs himself was involved in the innovation process at Apple. Important ideas for the Macintosh computer were derived by Jobs during his visit to Xerox PARC. Jobs even took his entire programming team to visit PARC as he was taken aback by their graphical user interface. Upon returning to Apple, the team initiated work on a personal computer that integrated an improved version of the technology they had seen at Xerox PARC. Like an innovative leader, Jobs put together a team of talented engineers and provided them with the resources needed and immersed the team of Macintosh with the vision of what was possible. The team at PARC lacked the innovation skills and did not look beyond the technology they had in hand. During Jobs's break from Apple, from 1985 to 1998, the innovation premium of Apple crashed to an average of 30 per cent as Apple stopped innovating and the investors lost faith in the ability of Apple to innovate and grow. It was only during Steve Jobs's second tenure at Apple when he rejoined and redesigned the top management team that Apple's innovation premium hiked to 52 per cent during 2005 to 2009. Steve Jobs had reignited the innovation engine at Apple and made the team more discovery-driven.

Procter & Gamble is another leading innovation company with an innovation premium of 23 per cent average from 1985 to 2000.[238] After A. G. Lafley took over as CEO, he increased the innovation capability at P&G, and hence, during his period from 2001 to 2009, the innovation premium went up to 35 per cent. Bob McDonald, who took over after Lafley, carried forward the tradition of innovating at P&G. Hence, innovative leaders should first understand how innovation functions and then lead the innovation charge. They should build up on their own innovating skills and also promote the discovery of others. They should inhabit their organisation with innovators who are discovery-driven in order to enable innovation as a team which converts to long-lasting innovation premiums.

Innovative action is an outward move in the dynamo leadership—*innovation*. Innovation does not lie merely in ideas; it is seen in action, not simply being productive but being innovatively productive. This makes the leadership shift from leading people into moving people to be productive—*movement leadership*.

The outward move in dynamo leadership makes a leader actualise ideas into concrete actions. In other words, if a leader wants to achieve results, she should have actualities and factualities. The *Toyota Production System* (TPS), which is a byword for Toyota, was born out of passion for facts.[239] 'Good thinking should lead to good products,' said Eiji Toyoda. Productivity, in TPS, consists of 'actual object, the actual site and the actual facts'. If you want to perform and produce results, you should show it in actuality. What use do ideas have if they are not translated into actions? In Toyota, they developed a system in which workers in the car plant must conceive an idea for a component and make that component on that day itself. In the TPS, every day a definite number of units are planned, and workers produce them on that day itself before they go home; if they have not done so, they are not allowed to go home.[240] It applies to leadership in any organisation. Real leadership lies in the application of ideas to produce results. Concrete actions, not merely abstract ideas, form the core of leadership.

A productive leader needs to do more than merely getting things done.[241] She needs to recognise a goal which is measurable and achievable and is crucial to the success of the organisation's mission. She then needs to form a core team of colleagues, subject matter experts, and mentors whom she can turn to for any help at any time. She needs to establish milestones and ensure that she is making progress towards achieving them, especially the list of most important things. A productive leader earns success by recognising and qualifying what the result will seem like, identifying those involved in achieving the result and the positive influence that would have on the organisation.

In the dynamo leadership, the energies and moves of the historical consciousness (*backward*), vision (*forward*), power (*rightward*), affective maturity (*leftward*), and inner attitude (*inward*) must be expressed in concrete output (*outward*). Thinking, feeling, and skills that a dynamo leader gains from five moves and five energies lead to the production of results.

The following characteristics make a leader innovatively productive:

Read the signs of time

Being productive must be based on relevant actions for a particular time. Your productive approach should be born out of a careful reading of the signs of time. Observing what goes on around guides your ways to a productive and positive life. That observation gives you what you should think and act. There is no action relevant for all times. Every moment in time and history demands a particular action apt for that time. Therefore, you need to read the signs of time that would give you an idea of what you should do. Put it differently, you need to understand trends and patterns of life and human behaviour and accordingly design your leadership. And you need to be sensitive to grasp what the world needs today and would need tomorrow. Accordingly, you need to evolve your style of leadership. When India was in need of subaltern leadership, Ambedkar stepped in to provide a brand of leadership that echoed the yearnings of the marginalised. In the time of war and killings, Mahatma Gandhi provided a non-violent leadership that focused on the importance of inner resolve against evils and domination. But for our times, that kind of leadership would be rendered irrelevant, although some ideas of that leadership might be helpful. Every time and historical junction require a type of leadership style that insists on being productive specific to that time and reality. You need to read it in the pages of reality. That would inspire you to be innovatively productive.

Experiment constantly

Based on your reading of the signs of time, you need to develop different ways of making the group for which you are responsible for productive, and not just only one way of being productive. That design must be experimented in your activities of leadership. When you put the style of leadership into use, you will surely come to know the impact of it. When you insist on being productive and putting words into action all the time, you should also constantly check with people about their impressions about it. Experimentation should begin with a small group that would give you an objective feedback. You should be able to give the group different ways of being productive and realise carefully what impact it makes on individuals and the organisation. Then choose those ways of being productive that are sharp in their content, style, and dynamics. As always, experimentation purifies the ways of doing things in life and helps us choose the best possible way of doing it.

Organise performers

Performance needs direction and focus to achieve goals. Often, high performers tend to become self-centred and egoistic. In the same way, they need appropriate and timely recognition. This would accelerate innovation and production. In your group, you will see performers who do more than they speak. Performers tend to lose sight of boundaries, and they fail to be moderate and appropriate. They need gentle reminders to help them not to cross the limits. Leadership lies in this sense in guiding performers not to lose sight of the fundamentals of the vision and mission of the organisation while they are productive and creative.

And the performance should be regulated performance. This regulation lies in organising the performers in a way that they inspire others who are underperforming. Usually, high achievers and performers tend to disregard others as 'useless'. They become an elite tribe isolated from the rest. Instead, the dynamo leadership should be able to stand in between the performers and non-performers to initiate the performers to infuse their productive energy into the non-performers. A leader, in many organisations, has a tendency to align with performers to achieve goals. What greatness is there in making the performers perform? Instead, a leader should organise the non-performers or underperformers to become performers by placing them in the school of performers. This needs persuasive skills with performers and enormous patience with underperformers.

Learn to do better from mistakes

Being innovatively productive often is stalled by lack of humility to learn from mistakes. High performers accept their limitations and mistakes by which they refine their performance. Humility is a fine quality by which one realises the real worth of herself and removes pretentions. This helps us shift our focus from one's ego to the purpose that is set before us. By being humble, one becomes open to possibilities. Mahatma Gandhi puts this in a nuanced way. Truth liberates, but truth without humility enslaves. Truth here is energy, but if that energy is not accompanied by the energy called humility, that energy (truth) will not be useful. In the process of being and becoming productive, we tend to lose sight of the mistakes we make. This oversight costs us dearly. Seisei Kato summed up the leadership model by saying, 'Never fail to reward merit, but never let a fault go unremarked.'[242]

This is to find strength in weakness. Productivity is conventionally seen as something which results from strength. Not entirely true. It lies more in the ways by which we learn from mistakes we make in the productive process. You see this in the lives of high achievers. The origin of their greatness is in their realisation of *low*-ness (*humilis*). In this sense, a leader should often direct her attention to her mistakes and deficiencies in order to achieve goals in concrete terms.

Persuade to perform

A productive and innovative leader is skilled both in word and action. Communication skills are crucial to persuade others to perform. Communication is not simply speaking some words. Instead, it is a transfer of energy. In any good communication, only 7 per cent is in the words we speak; 55 per cent is in body language, gestures, and eye contact; and 38 per cent in the tone/voice.[243] Leadership cannot achieve results unless she has the ability to communicate. A leader should communicate a sense of confidence and control to the people she works with. She should let her people know her own feelings about the change. The people around her learn the degree to which she trusts their abilities to get through the change. More importantly, she must communicate a sense of purpose and commitment. Communication, the leader has, connects with the people. This connectivity produces results. Effective communication decreases resistance and encourages moving through the change effectively and positively. If there is any miscommunication, it will not only decrease productivity but will also lead to conflicts. A leader sends, through words, actions, body language, and tonality of voice the messages about her and the changes she intends in her organisation. In addition, she should verify that the message she intends to send is actually received and interpreted the way she intended. To do this, she must listen to the people she communicates with. This type of communication builds bonds between the leader and the people she leads. This is what is finally realised in concrete productions.[244] And the dynamo leader is a person who achieves goals to make significant progress in an organisation.

Speak in actions

Often, leaders speak but don't act. As an effective and efficient leader, you should show your leadership in action. When you ask someone to do something, first you need to realise whether you would be able to do it. What you think must be a thing that could be translated into action. It is being realistic. Even in your commissioning report or in a business plan, avoid writing something that you know well you cannot actualise. If you can't do it, don't write it. If you write what is not realisable, you will be seen as a leader who speaks but does not mean what she speaks. This is why many plans remain as mere plans, only leading to environmental degradation. If you value anything, show it in action. If you love something, it must be seen in deeds. This requires courage because you need to say what you think. That should be in the best interests of the organisation you lead.[245]

Actions are expressions of your identity as a leader. But they should be congruent with the values the organisation promotes. Your actions must speak the values that you hold as important. When there is a difference between what you really believe and what you show that you believe and see in actions, it will lead to loss of trust. You will soon exhibit your insincerity. There must be a cohesive link between your actions and what you really believe. That way, your actions are expressions of what you are and what you are capable of doing.

Outward expressions and actions lead to conflicts and challenges from others. Not all actions are seen by others as good and beneficial. A leader will have to handle criticism and accusations. If you don't do anything as a leader, many will not find fault with you. Some even would say that you are a good leader. But when you start doing something different from what has been so far, you will immediately face resistance and opposition.

As a leader, you should go beyond and see the common good of the institution—*upward* move that gives you an energy of transcendence.

Upward—Transcending Limitations

> Literature, at its best, and despite the recent attempts of critics, can never be murdered and dissected, as it's an immortal yet organic thing, drawing on the richness and complexity of Experience yet somehow managing to transcend its mundane origins like an alchemist transmuting base metals.
> Sol Luckman

> He who has a why to live can bear almost any how.
> Friedrich Nietzsche

A leader is conscious about the history of the organisation through the backward move, moves forward with a futuristic vision, has the authority to influence through the rightward move and the affective maturity to handle emotions through the leftward move, has the right attitude by moving inward, and becomes productive by moving outward with the right expressions, behaviour, and creative action. When one is productive and involved in the actualisation of her vision, she will face conflicts and challenges. They should not stand in the way of achieving goals. She should be able to transcend the limitations. Moving on and going beyond the challenges is a key to be a successful leader. Transcending limitations is what makes a leader a great leader.

Transcendence originates from the Latin prefix *trans-*, which means 'beyond', and *scandare*, which means 'to climb'.[246]

According to the *Cambridge Dictionary*, *transcend* means 'to go further, rise above or be more important or better than something, especially a limit'.[247] A leader faces different kinds of limitations, which lead to irrational behaviour and prevent her from choosing optimal solutions. A leader faces political, cultural, ethical, knowledge, emotional, motivational, and informational limitations. Political limitations are those involving power play and company politics. Ethical limitations prevent the leader from behaving ethically. Cultural limitations are the challenges related to the organisational culture. Emotional limitations are those involving the leader's emotions which intervene in sound decision-making. Motivational limitations are limitations which interfere in the leader's motivation to perform. Informational limitations are the constraints related to the process of information collection in the work environment. Knowledge limitations are the challenges associated with leadership knowledge and competencies which could be understood by self-analysis.

Transcendence is a freedom to stand up beyond internal limitations and external inhibitions.[248] It is also a freedom of choice and a freedom to live authentically. The ability to transcend is built in our spiritual nature. Transcendent leadership is defined as 'a leadership of wholeness, consciousness, simple wisdom, service above self, and global healing'.[249] Being of service to others and trust are the foundations of transcendent leadership.

Deep within each human being, there is a yearning for transcendence. John Cottingham (2020) believes that the whole idea of transcendence is 'linked to the human longing for meaning, the yearning for completion'.[250] It is seen as neurotic nature of desire as it springs from innate archetype located in the deep collective unconsciousness.[251] This is what actually helps a human being reach maturity towards fullness and wholeness. At the time of suffering, this yearning for transcendence provides a certain sense of going beyond the reality to see a possibility of overcoming the suffering. If there is no such yearning, I believe one would reach the dead end of her life. Mostly, this is a moment in which one resorts to suicide. Of course, there are people who take refuge in substances that would give a temporary relief, but yearning for transcendence has the capacity to provide a comfort of peace within. When he says that the world is charged with the 'grandeur of God', Hopkins sees this yearning as energy that tones and energises one's being.[252] Even Nietzsche, who proclaimed the death of God, recognises the reality of life in the absence of God that is grim and lifeless; human beings will have nobody to lean against.[253]

Yearning for transcendence does not mean that it takes us directly to God. But it is fundamental to human existence to long for the unlimited as she is limited in power and actions. Carl Jung sees the desire for transcendence as an innate archetype that remains in 'collective consciousness of the human psyche, an ultimately benign presence that offers the key to healing and wholeness'.[254]

We can see this sense of transcendence in many leaders. The president of Egypt, Anwar Sadat, was a transcendent leader who modelled integrity and courage.[255] Sadat became a very well-known president dedicated to the Arab cause as he swore that even one inch of Arab soil would not be given to Israel. He realised in solitary confinement that if one does not change one's thought process, one will never be able to grow, as reality can never be altered. He therefore changed his thought process as a transcendent leader and went to Knesset in Jerusalem to commence the peace process. He transformed human history by modelling the integrity and courage of transcendent leadership, and then like most transcendent leaders, he gave his life for doing the right thing just to his conscience.

Other transcendent leaders who also modelled courage and integrity of transcendent leadership are Bill Gates, Melinda Gates, and Warren Buffet. They used their wealth to take on the cause of healthcare of the world's poor. Billionaires who practise what they preach have formed the world's biggest non-profit foundation by pooling in their wealth to take care of global health. Bill Gates, as a person of integrity and conviction, would be resigning in his post as the head of Microsoft in order to organise the foundation. Warren Buffet sets an example for the upcoming transcendent billionaires by donating his wealth to another foundation for healing the poor. He also modelled courage and integrity. Melinda Gates helped collect and distribute the acquired resources in an efficient and effective manner in order to leverage donating to new standards and thus modelled the compassion of transcendent leadership.

Steve Jobs, CEO of Apple and of Pixar Animation Studios, shows a type of leadership that transcends limits. Transcending limits is one of the core dimensions of leadership. Steve Jobs does not hold any academic degree. He was born to an unwed mother and was given up for adoption. He did not have a dorm to sleep in. He slept on the floor of his friends' room. He returned Coke bottles for the 5¢ deposits to buy food, and he would walk the seven miles across town every Sunday night to get one good meal a week at the Hare Krishna temple. He found the company named *Apple* at the age of twenty. Later, when he was thirty years old, he was sacked from the company he started. He said in his address at Stanford, 'So at 30 I was out. And very publicly out. What had been the focus of my entire adult life was gone, and it was devastating.'[256] But he did not give up. He started another company named NeXt and later another company named Pixar. He created the world's first computer-animated feature film, *Toy Story*, and is now the most successful animation studio in the world. The company Apple, from where he was fired, bought NeXt, and he returned to Apple. The technology he developed at NeXT became the heart of Apple's renaissance. The reason for his success is that he never saw any limitation or failure as an obstacle. Instead, he saw everything that stood in his way as something that would give him a new way of realising his dreams. He moved on; he was never happy with settled foundations. This is the spiritual energy that helped him tide over the obstacles in his life.

Transcendent leadership introduces a third dimension of planet to the existing bottom lines of people and profits, thereby offering a wholesome frame.[257] Hence, the focus shifts from interdependence to wholeness. A transcendent leader leads from a consciousness of wholeness, which is key to global sustainability. Transcendent leaders believe in the natural, inborn goodness of people and their unlimited prospective to do good deeds. They have faith in the strength of people working together for noble causes. They release confidence and hope in their organisations in order to achieve greater good. Transcendent leaders are an embodiment of humility as they forego their egos and put their corporate goals ahead. They are persistent enough to travel the distance needed to actualise their vision. They are courageous enough to stand by the truth with conviction. Courage, humility, and persistence are their core values. Relationship, purpose, and renewal are important criteria in transcendent leadership. Relationship is all about service to our fellow beings. The attitude to serve should surpass the self. Transcendent leaders are empowered by a strong sense of community. Purpose helps in the alignment of the mission of the organisation with the core values. The personal passions and talents are amalgamated with the broader goals of the organisation. It is the purpose which pulls people towards a desirable future. Renewal is about transcendence. Renewal is fastening to the surrounding wholeness via renewal activities like community building, prayer, reflection, intuition, meditation, and nature, which personally increases satisfaction.

There are several transcendent corporate leaders of today who use their fame, their name, and their visibility to important non-profit causes.[258] They remind us that self-transcendence and human goodness found in Mother Teresa and Mahatma Gandhi are also found in today's leaders. They bring out the humanness which lies within each of us. One of the transcendent leaders who inspire us today is Bono/Paul David Hewson, the co-founder of the non-profit organisations EDUN, Product Red, DATA, and ONE Campaign. He is the lead vocalist and lyricist of U-2, an Irish rock band. Via his non-profit organisations, he was involved in global activism in support of the poor of Africa, for which he was knighted by Queen Elizabeth II, and also for his global campaigns, the benefit concerts, and the personal diplomacy he started with the world leaders in support of the third-world debt relief.

Another transcendent leader of today is Dikembe Mutombo, the NBA defensive star of Houston Rockets.[259] He donated $15 million towards the development of a 300-bed hospital in Kinshasa, Congo, worth $29 million. Paul Newman, the superstar actor, was the co-founder of Newman's Own. It was a food company whose profits were all donated to charity. The amount donated so far as of November 2008 is over $250 million. These leaders showcase transcendence of self.

Bill Drayton, another transcendent leader of today, was the assistant administrator for the US Environmental Protection Agency (EPA).[260] He then resigned, and at just thirty-five years of age, he started Ashoka, a global non-profit organisation whose role was to recognise, support, and celebrate the leading social entrepreneurs across the world. Functioning in over fifty countries, Ashoka today provides over 1,500 social entrepreneurs with direct funds of over $40 million. They attempt to share the patterns of creating major social change with the rest of the world. Their team of 120 members have attempted to recognise people creating positive social changes and have converted them as global social change models. Ashoka is now funded by a huge grant from the Omidyar Foundation.

Jane Goodall has initiated the Jane Goodall Institute for developing the environment for all living beings and Roots and Shoots for interconnecting the youth of all age groups all over the world in order to develop a more sustainable world.[261] The hopefulness of Jane Goodall about the youth lies at the heart of transcendent leadership.

James P. Grant, the head of UNICEF, saved nearly 25 million children by leading a child survival revolution which provided affordable healthcare to children worldwide. He showcases how one powerful transcendent leader could revolutionise the world. In 1990, he also conducted the first world summit for children, which formulated objectives and goals for the health of children by bringing together over seventy heads of state. International law was formulated in 1990 based on the United Nations Convention on the rights of the child which was started by Grant. This transcendent leader saved the lives of more children than any other person in the world. He was instrumental in developing the Global Alliance for Vaccines and Immunization (GAVI) in order to strengthen immunisation programs for children. He worked towards the betterment of healthcare of the children in the developing world. He worked in coordination with global leaders for modelling cheaper solutions for complex health issues.

Ryuzaburo Kaku emerged as a transcendent leader who worked towards creating a better world post the bombing at Nagasaki.[262] He became the chairman of Canon Inc. As a citizen of the increasingly interdependent world, he laid out the roles the corporations should play. He advanced the principle of 'kyosei', which implies harmoniously living together and interdependence. He inspired the fourth-stage companies' vision of serving people via words and actions. Kaku is another transcendent leader dedicated to global sustainability. He still inspires via his public speeches and publications.

Wendy Kopp, the founder of Teach for America, is another transcendent leader who has made a difference for those passionate about teaching. Her belief is that many would choose to make a difference over earning more money and teaching over other money-generating professions led to the establishment of this prominent teacher corps. Functioning in more than thirty regions in the United States today, Teach for America is a promising teacher corps envisioned by Wendy Kopp. It consists of around 3,700 members and over $75 million of operating budget. It also assists similar ventures all over the world.

Jean Monnet modelled leadership way past the nation's boundaries. He developed international governmental forms.[263] He was a transcendent leader who employed his methods as the message. He modelled the potential of a transcendent idea and the power of determined effort. He worked towards Europe becoming one society using the power of a constructive idea which many could not accomplish by force. He was awarded the Freedom Prize by John F. Kennedy. Monnet always wanted to be remembered as the one who took the initial steps towards a more unified world and not as the creator of a unified Europe.

Pierre Morad Omidyar, another transcendent leader and the founder of eBay, along with his wife, Pam, started the Omidyar Foundation in order to help non-profit organisations as they had the willpower to make a difference in the world. In order to enhance their work of making a difference to even profit organisations and other public policy groups, they formed the Omidyar Network. By deploying the power of markets in order to develop opportunities for the betterment of the lives of people, they gave back to the communities.

James D. Sinegal, the founder of Costco Wholesale, modelled transcendent leadership.[264] Costco Wholesale had revolutionised the corporate model of short-term profits and shareholders and has brought focus to the community and long-term growth. The success story of Costco proves that cutting of wages and others' benefits need not necessarily convert to low prices for the consumers. Sinegal's low CEO salary and a rich package for his store workers, which included an average hourly wage of $17 and only a payment of 9 per cent of the health insurance's cost, symbolised fair compensation in this penny-pinching retail industry. Costco Foundation assists children's hospitals all over the country.

Jerry Zucker also modelled transcendent leadership as the CEO of InterTech Group and Hudson's Bay Company and as the first American governor. Jerry turned Hudson's Bay Company, which was initially a fur-trading initiative, into the largest retailer in Canada. He also made the InterTech Group one of the largest privately held companies in America. Jerry secretly aided many international missions financially which supplied medical reserves to people worldwide. He believed that evil came only because the good people did not do anything. Even during his last days of brain cancer, he worked towards fighting darkness in the world. Even after his death, his wife, Anita, worked towards living up to the founder's legacy by using a transcendent theme of *Tikkun Olam*, which means 'the repair of the world'.

A leader should not be stuck with failures. She should move beyond obstacles, boundaries, and limitations. Failures should be viewed as a time to learn and as an invitation to grow. Failure is a grace given by God as it's God's call to grow. Godliness is in how you overcome failures. Successful leaders are those who have not avoided hardships but those who have taken the cross and resurrected. They have experienced failures and moved beyond imperfections by using the imperfections to reach perfection. They see goodness in failure. The dynamism of reaching perfection knowing that you are imperfect is transcendence. Leaders who transcend are godly, and they have a grand strategy. They are more worried about the world than about oneself as they look at the bigger picture.

A leader must transcend boundaries and limitations. Some trivial matters or deficiencies in the organisation she leads should not bog her down. She must move on and stand above all that is destructive. Crisis or conflict should not limit a true leader from acting effectively. Rather, she must learn from it and go beyond. This is a spiritual energy. Carnality shows limits. It is weak and fragile. Spirituality is limitless and strong. It helps a person to be hopeful in hopelessness. When you feel that everything is lost, the spiritual energy guides you to gain energy in order to regain yourself. The word *spirit* in Latin means 'breath'. Breath refers to life. Any spiritual person must breathe life into others and into the world around her. She should never experience breathlessness. In any situation of death/darkness, a leader with this spiritual energy generates life and takes efforts to give life to lifelessness.

This is why we should not understand the idea of transcendence narrowly, referring to God or in the religious sense only. The word *transcendence* has three meanings: it is (a) an act of surpassing usual limits, (b) a state of going beyond the normal perception, and (c) a state of being free from the constraints of the material world. For a leader, limits and boundaries should not be seen as restrictive forces. Instead, in an integrated leader, limits must open up new ways of being creative. Every time she faces a limit or a restriction or a deficiency, she must be energised to look for innovative ways to flourish.

The movement of transcendence is all about going beyond. For the leader to transcend, she should extend boundaries and look for infinite possibilities. 'Transcendence is a way of framing the host of challenges that leaders face at the levels of self, relationships, and context.'[265] With respect to the level of self, leaders are challenged to transcend the propensities of narcissism, power, and self-centredness. With respect to the relationships between the leader and the follower, leaders are called to transcend the propensities of projection and transference that disturb the relations. With respect to context, leaders are challenged to transcend the unpredictable dimensions of reality and see it from system-oriented, intuitive, and adaptive viewpoints.

Breakthrough leaders seek transcendence.[266] They transcend above the travails and trials of life. The pursuit for transcendence may take any form like philosophy, science, spirituality, space exploration, religion, devotion to career, etc. Victims of hazardous accidents and other disasters transcend their sorrow by seeking meaning in those experiences and using that to enrich their life and that of others. When leaders have a better purpose in life, they can rise above all odds. Breakthrough leaders use every moment to examine new opportunities for themselves and for the organisation, live with a purpose, have beliefs, and have a sense of belonging, which improves the well-being and the health of the body and the mind. They are obliged to contribute, to receive, and also to repay. Breakthrough leadership is important for revealing the need for belonging, believing, transcending, and contributing especially during difficult times. Leaders of self-transcendence generate innovative ideas, motivate their subordinates, and build a moral workspace with high standards.[267] Self-transcendence surpasses boundaries and focuses on values and meanings. Self-transcendent leaders have higher understanding, tolerance level, democracy, attentiveness, morality, and equality. They strive to reduce dishonesty and corruption, increase the flow of information, and ensure effective execution of decisions. They are encouraged from within and strive to meet the needs of customers.

Leaders can transcend limitations and organisational paradoxes by gaining the trust of both superiors and subordinates, by earning and giving respect, by communicating and listening across all levels of management, by being self-confident and taking risks, by being occupied in daily activities in order to know the subordinates well, and by being passionate about their work.[268] Leaders need to incorporate transcendence into the mission and vision statements as they are the core of the organisation, and strategies evolve based on them.[269] By this, the leader adds limitlessness to the existence of the firm, and hence, the firm becomes powerful beyond means. The firm will become more robust with motivated employees and a more accepting client base. The firm will earn a competitive advantage against competitors. Firm transcendence will also encourage employees to go beyond limitations and hence develop high-quality outputs. Transcendence encourages limitless learning.

Transcendent leader makes connections with 'the larger universe and help individuals experience meaning in their lives, including in the workplace'.[270] The energy of transcendence takes a leader to see a higher purpose in all that she does. This is more like seeing goodness in the world beyond all its imperfections. Immediately one feels a sense of gratitude for the beauty of the world and the people around. One begins to feel that there is more to life than merely making money. This has positive impact on the organisational performance as well as on the well-being of employees. Employees are guided by the leader who is driven by the eight energies to realise a sense of altruism.

In Davos, at the 2007 World Economic Forum, transcendent leadership was introduced as a global imperative.[271] Over the last decade, two threads have defined the meaning of a transcendent leader. One (doing) was connected to planet, profits, and people given by John Jacob

Zucker Gardiner, the professor at Seattle University. The other (being) is the transcendence which happens internally, from lower self to higher self. *Merriam-Webster* defined *transcend* as 'to succeed over restrictive or negative aspects and to go beyond or rise above limits'. Transcendent leaders rise above the thresholds of self. These leaders showcase multidimensional awareness. As they are aware at many different levels, they impact the environment more. Transcendent leaders observe both their stakeholders and their own experiences, both outer and inner, that has translated from knowledge cycles, data, and information. Wisdom moments result from insights of these experiences, which in turn become the next set of data which produce radically different knowledge and results. The qualities of transcendent leaders include acceptance, reverence, presence, courage, gratitude, and highest good. Transcendent leaders do not judge people as wrong or right but instead accept the value differences of individuals. They choose values which guide their organisation. Transcendent leaders are responsible for embodying and teaching reverence, which is a state of awe for one another, inside the organisation. Transcendent leaders are present in order to listen keenly to the other stakeholders despite other pressing distractions. These leaders are courageous enough to view growth opportunities by facilitating between the various stakeholders. They are appreciative of the self and the stakeholders. They employ self-compassion and compassion for others in order to gain wisdom. Transcendent leaders need to function from a conscious of the highest good of all concerned. All concerned could be owners, employees, suppliers, communities, and all those responsible for the profits.

Transcendent leaders need to transcend the levels of self, the organisation, and others by going beyond and above as well as between and within the levels.[272] Transcendent leaders are in a better position to lead when the environment gets turbulent and difficult. Transcendent leaders understand that they are just a part of the organisation, and hence, instead of strategising specific plans which are controlled, they formulate performance aspirations within which experimentation is possible. Striking the right balance between innovation and stability is an art. The status quo of the organisation needs to be distributed creatively. In order to match today's dynamic environment, the transcendent leader should design flexible career paths for the members of the organisation and also motivate ownerships. Transcendent leaders enable learning via collaboration, experience, experiments, and opinion diversity. They aim to strike the right balance between exploration and exploitation by ensuring that the firm's strategy and structure are in alignment to assist the flow of learning to the teams and the individuals from the organisation and also the flow of ideas to the team and the organisation from the individuals. This kind of learning orientation was embodied by the president and CEO of the metropolitan hospital who has built the strategic map of the organisation on growth motivators and learning. After identifying the key strengths needed in culture, structure, and skills in order to succeed at the desired financial and customer results, it is then manifested in the organisation in the form of formal programs like NineSigma review of operating procedures and Kaizen analysis of workflow bottlenecks. This leader not only adopts the best practices from within the healthcare industry but also from other 'high consequence' industries. He has a clear vision to support the ever-changing environment and to ensure that all the internal processes are in place at the hospital. Hence, in order to ensure transcendent leadership, a deep awareness of oneself and alignment of the strategies with internal beliefs is required.

In order to cope with today's uncertain environment which is complex yet transparent, leaders need to transcend the organisational level and master leadership at the societal level also.[273] Focusing only on the society and disregarding the organisation is the worst form of corporate theft and the best form of self-serving. Transcendent leaders must understand the networking of leadership across the various levels and should also be capable to do so. If leadership is restricted to just one level, it will not be sufficient to promise high performance of the firm in the long run. Leaders with singular focus would only succeed in the short term, but not in the long term, guaranteeing sustained performance. If leadership of the self is absent, employees would be assigned to the wrong projects, and if leadership of the organisation is absent, there would be a huge possibility of organisational failure.

Hence, only the transcendent leader who has high leadership levels of the organisation, self, and others, capable to lead among and within these levels, would be in a position to deliver higher firm performance in a sustained manner in today's ever-changing environment and in this heightened ethical and moral climate.

If you read the biographies of leaders, you will learn that at every moment of deficiency, a successful leader has seen the deficiency/failure as an opportunity to grow, and she has transcended it to reach the goal set before her. A sense of transcendence gives us a feeling of movement. If we know how to transcend what tries to restrict us, we will move further and never be stuck in deficiencies. Like a river, we will run, tiding over obstacles, and every obstacle teaches us something to reach the end.

Energy of transcendence in a leader will give an attitude of temperance. Temperance refers to 'control over excess, including any form of auspicious self-constraint or self-control'.[274] The more a leader is able to keep her personal passions under constant check, the more she is able to see the greater good of society and the organisation she is in charge. This is to guard against excess and maintain self-control in dealing with issues and at the time of making important decisions. The leader who demonstrates temperance becomes automatically modest and humble. She will not seek for personal glory; instead, she will project her organisation and promote the interests of it.[275] Intemperance leads a leader to arrogance and narcissism. It will undermine all that a company or organisation has built over the years. It will also weaken the trust people have in the leader.

In order to successfully transcend boundaries, leaders need to have the following characteristics:

Detach from inordinate attachments[276]

Leaders with the energy of transcendence detach themselves from limiting, inordinate attachments. Detachment is a key to a mature leadership. Detachment from power, money, and possessions gives a leader enormous mental facility to be calm and take discerned decisions. Attachment to them makes a leader insecure, and to protect them, she will use her position. 'Detachment is essentially the process of removing one's inordinate attachments [affections and related emotions] to temporal and sensory experiences that hinder a person's ability to love and unite one's will with God above all else.'[277]

Do I suggest that leaders should not have possessions and attachments? No. There are two kinds of attachments: one is ordinate attachment, and the other is inordinate attachment. The former is healthy and purpose-driven, and the latter is unhealthy, as it distracts one from the goal that she has set for herself. A mature leader transcends inordinate attachments; she does not allow them to distract herself from the purpose of life and work. If you delve into the history of failed leaders, you will find that their inordinate attachments made them go away from the goals of the companies. Attachment to power, money, and wealth creates negative energies that give insecure mental states.

Transcend pettiness and triviality

Leaders need to transcend trivial and petty issues and look at the larger picture. By looking at petty issues, leaders' resources—like time, money, and manpower—will get restrained around unimportant issues, thereby leaving the more important issues unattended. This small-mindedness must change, and a leader needs to transcend their petty attitude. By focusing on micro issues and minor problems, you will lose the big picture of your leadership. Often, small and minor mistakes happen, and it is normal. It will always be the case as long as human beings are limited and fragile. You must ignore them. But when the minor mistakes develop into a pattern, it will be a serious concern. For this, leaders need to be more conscious about their self in terms of their expressions, actions, and behaviour. A self-conscious leader would always think before acting, and her moves would always be very cautious and calculated. This mindfulness helps to become what is important and what is not. The more the leader is self-conscious, the better her actions.

Go beyond personal likes and dislikes

Successful leaders should never be biased in their judgements. They should transcend beyond their personal feelings of likes and detests. Fair decisions would become skewed if personal preferences come in the way. Only a neutral leader with no personal attachments can make a difference in society. Personal appetites make a leader selfish, which influences the decisions she makes, and the greater social and common good is relegated to the background. There must be a constant check while you make decisions and implement the decisions whether what you do is driven by the common good of the organisation or driven by your personal whims and fancies. When you put your organisation and its reputation at the centre of your leadership, your personal likes and dislikes have no place. As soon as you start looking for personal gain, you will start compromising on everything, leading to dilution of values, and in fact, it will lower the level of overall performance.

Gain holy indifference

Holy indifference is the Ignatian principle of indifference. It speaks of a capability to let go of what does not help to love others and a larger purpose. It is a virtue of freedom to participate in the development and transformation of the organisation by which the society at large advances in all aspects of life. This indifference means being freed from things, people, and experiences that take a leader away from the common purpose. What is the most important here is the love and loyalty the leader has for the organisation that makes her distance from her personal gains and glory. In another way, you could see this as your love for the organisation and its purpose. If you love someone really, you will definitely want that person to be good and happy; your personal comfort becomes secondary. In the same way, the holy indifference takes you beyond yourself to see what is good for the society. A leader wishes nothing for herself and does everything insofar as it is helpful to the organisation and the society, which makes the leader holy and virtuous. It is having complete control of yourself in serving an organisation by keeping in mind the reason for which you were appointed to lead it and manage employees who work for it. It is like saying, 'The organisation is greater than me.' When you have gained this state of mind to serve the common good, you become beneficial to the people. That takes us to the eighth move and energy of *downward*, being earthly and pragmatic.

Downward—Being Earthly

> Sense shines with a double luster when it is set in humility. An able yet humble man is a jewel worth a kingdom.
>
> William Penn
>
> To be humble to superiors is duty, to equals courtesy, to inferiors nobleness.
>
> Benjamin Franklin

A leader is conscious about the organisation's history by moving backward, has a futuristic vision, influences via authority, manages emotion through the affective maturity, has the right attitude, is productive, and also transcends limitations. Now she needs to be grounded—*downward*—and humble so that she feels responsible towards the society and the environment. She must contribute to the growth and development of the society she lives in. She must care for and carry the people who suffer as the earth does.

A leader must be grounded, earthly, and pragmatic. Being pragmatic implies that the leader should stand shoulder to shoulder with her people/employees to understand their pain and struggles. This understanding makes an impact and difference in the lives of people.

In the entire structure and dynamics of *Business Moves*, this *downward* move and the energy of being humble and pragmatic is the ultimate outcome that a leader is expected to work on, and the test of leadership lies here.

This demands sincere efforts of a leader to take part in the lives of the people she leads. Effective leadership needs to gain experiential knowledge of employees' cultural background, their ways of life, their tastes, and their inner yearnings. By doing so, the leader would be able to know where to place an employee and what targets are to be assigned to her. In time of conflict, negotiation will be easy, and a resolution will be arrived at with ease. This is an experiential learning, not a learning that one normally has by reading certificates and the curriculum vitae of employees.

In the participation of the lives of employees and the experiential learning a leader gains, there are affective learning outcomes, knowledge outcomes, and behaviour outcomes.[278] Experiential learning for leaders is critical to be effective as well as efficient in the ways in which they lead people in an organisation. In his discussion about how international exposures for leaders make an impact in their behaviour, Kolb (1984) sees experiential learning as critical as it would provide leaders with cultural intelligence that is a moderating variable.

The experiential learning makes a leader humble to walk shoulder to shoulder with employees. This leads not only to the achievement of goals of the organisation but also positive change in the lives of employees.

Mother Teresa gave her life working for the less fortunate. One day, when Mother Teresa was in Calcutta, living in a small house with some orphan children, she realised that there was no food to give the children. So after a small prayer, she called all the children and said, 'Come, now let us go and beg.'[279] So they all went to beg on the streets. In the neighbourhood, there was a shopkeeper who disliked Mother Teresa. When Mother Teresa went to that shopkeeper and begged for some food, he looked at Mother Teresa angrily and spat on her hand. Mother Teresa gently wiped the saliva and said, 'Thank you for what you have given to me. Will you give something for my children?' The shopkeeper was shocked by the humility of Mother Teresa. The leader should also be humble in a way that humility makes a difference in the lives of other people and the society she lives in. Like Mother Teresa, the earth cares unconditionally and carries living beings in spite of all the destructions done to it. Leaders should be earthly and give unconditionally to the environment.

There was a former undersecretary of Defence who was invited to give a speech at a large conference, about a thousand people.[280] He was standing on the stage with his coffee in a Styrofoam cup, giving his prepare to march with his PowerPoint behind him. He took a sip of his coffee, and he smiled and looked down at the coffee. Then he went off script, and he said, 'You know, last year, I spoke at this exact same conference. Last year, I was still the undersecretary, and when I spoke here last year, they flew me here in business class. When I arrived at the airport, there was somebody waiting for me to take me to my hotel. They took me to my hotel. They had already checked me in, and they just took me up to my room. The next morning, there was someone waiting in the lobby to greet me. They drove me to this same venue. They took me through the back entrance and took me into the green room. They handed me coffee in a beautiful ceramic cup. But now I am no longer the undersecretary. I flew here by coach. I took a taxi to my hotel, and I checked myself in. When I came down the lobby this morning, I took another taxi to this venue. I came in the front door and found my way backstage. When I asked someone, "Do you have any coffee?" he pointed to the coffee machine in the corner. I poured myself coffee into this Styrofoam cup. The lesson is, the ceramic cup was never meant for me. It was meant for the position I held. I deserve a Styrofoam cup.' As you gain fame, as you gain fortune, as you gain position and seniority, people will treat you better. They will hold doors open for you. They will get you a cup of tea and coffee without you even asking for it. They will call you sir and ma'am, and they will give you stuff. None of that stuff is meant for you. That stuff is meant for the position you hold. It is meant for the level that you have achieved as a leader or success. But you will always deserve a Styrofoam cup. Remember that lesson of gratitude and humility. You can accept all the free stuff. You can enjoy them. But just be grateful for them and know that they are not for you. Always be humble and grounded.

This is a story of how a father humbled himself in order to leave behind a legacy which not only made his son proud but also made his son emulate that move.[281] During the Prohibition in the 1920s, Al Capone became the main enemy of the public because the Mafia was killing people, and he was getting them off. He ordered the murder of several people. His people would respond only with violence. Easy Eddie was his lawyer. He was so good at his job that no matter what charges were pressed on Al Capone or his people, none of them could be put in jail. He was so valuable that the Mafia gave him huge amounts of money, the best cars, and the best of everything. Easy Eddie had a son. Though he got lots of valuables from the Mafia, he was not happy. Easy Eddie thought that though he had given his son everything, everything money could buy, there was one thing he hadn't given his son. He did not set an example of a father which his son could be proud of. Easy Eddie came to the conclusion that the only way he could make his son proud was by helping the government and sending the Mafia to prison. In this way, he would earn a good name and make his son proud and happy of his legacy. He hence testified, and many of the biggest people in the Mafia were put in prison. He was completely aware that he would be killed for doing this. Just like he had expected, one day when he was riding in his car, another car came by, and several people with machine guns filled his body with bullets. He lay dead on the street. He paid a very high price in order to give his son a father whom he could be proud of. He proved that life is larger than money.

During World War II, there was a man in the United States Air Force.[282] He took off on his ship to fight against the Japanese. He saw about nine Japanese bombers coming towards USS *Lexington* in order to sink the boat, and there were thousands of people on the boat. He was alone, but he decided to stop them. So he single-handedly charged at the nine airplanes and was shooting and shooting and shooting, and he actually hit two of the airplanes, which fell into the ocean. Then he ran out of bullets, but they were still shooting at him and attacking him. He was so fearless that he was flying directly towards these different planes that were shooting at him, and he was knocking off their wings. Finally, after five of the nine airplanes sank, the other four thought that this man was completely crazy and got out of there. Hence, they all flew away. He was the first person in the US Air Force in World War II to get the US Congressional Medal of Honour, the highest award. That existed. His name was Butch O'Hare, and the airport in Chicago, O'Hare Airport, is named after him. He is considered as one of the greatest heroes of the American history because he was willing to sacrifice his own life for the higher cause of others. What makes this story so interesting is, Butch O'Hare was the son of Easy Eddie. The humility which Easy Eddie taught his son, Butch O'Hare, through his life is what enabled Butch O'Hare to fight back bravely.

Have we lived a life humble enough to be remembered? What are we giving our children? People work so hard for money. They give that money to their children, and then their children fight as enemies to see who gets it. Is that the legacy? Is that a fulfilling life? Is that what we want to leave to the world? Our values, our character, our humility, our grace, and our compassion of the love that flows through us are the greatest contributions we could make to our own life, to our families, and to the world. And when we have those values and we work and we build that foundation, we could have a wonderful, fulfilling, meaningful life beyond birth and beyond death. We could leave that as a legacy for the world! A legacy humble enough to be remembered.

A leader must be grounded on earth and act pragmatically that benefits people, the environment, and living beings. This I call being earthly. All the preceding seven movements we discussed so far must ultimately guide the leader of an organisation to contribute to the earth. Historical consciousness, vision for a future, authority, love, attitude, and expressions will remain merely as abstract ideas unless they lead to benefit the place and people where a leader lives. As seen earlier, profit is not all that matters in life; life is larger than money. What I give to the others will finally demonstrate the true meaning of being a leader. History does not remember the leaders who earned money and accumulated wealth. Instead, the leaders who lost everything in order to give to the earth are imprinted in the pages of history. Moneymaking is a by-product of being earthly, not the reverse. The country that loses sight of this uses and abuses the natural and human resources for making profit, and it finally ends in an irreparable crisis. Successful companies do not focus on profit but on values that keep the people and the earth above all else.

Mother Earth is the source of everything. The word *earth* comes from the Latin word *humus*, meaning 'humility'. In Eastern cultures, *humility* means 'modesty, and not conceited'.[283] In literal terms, the phrase 'humble leadership' means 'leading from the ground' or 'bottom-up leadership'.[284] The virtue of humility is essential for an effective leader.[285] Expressed humility is more workable and easier to develop when compared to the stable attribute of humility. Leaders with humility take that extra effort to lower their status and view the hierarchy in a bottom-up approach. Humble leaders are efficient in reducing the turnover intent of followers. When the leaders lead with a humble approach and behave humbly in their interactions, they encourage the followers better and also accomplish better job performance. When the humble leader is perceived by the followers as an expert and the leader also gives effective assistance to the followers during difficult times, the dedication and commitment of the followers will be enhanced. Humble leaders regulate emotions well and also manage the negative emotions like anger and stress.[286] Humble leaders have very high moral values, charisma, and courage. They act as role models, teaching their followers how to grow. A humble leader feels responsible and makes herself useful to the surroundings, to the people, and to the society. A humble leader is responsible to the organisation.

Humility is most often associated with religious personalities like Mother Teresa, Jesus, or the Dalai Lama.[287] It is because the concept of humility has sound religious overtones. Humility has been associated with individuals who are very selfless, spiritual, or religious. Very rarely is humility associated with professional success or intellectual aptitude. Humility is a powerful mindset, a psychological construct, an intellectual and philosophical virtue. Humility is a self-accurate, open-minded mindset about oneself which reminds one that it is not always about 'me'. In the pursuit of human excellence, humility warrants one to accept the world as it is. Humility does not imply thinking small about oneself. It implies thinking about yourself less in terms of how you are being judged, how you are coming across, what others say or think about you, or how you look. This mindset of humility is the foundation and inspiration for critical thinking. 'Intellectual humility does not imply spinelessness or submissiveness. It implies the lack of intellectual pretentiousness, boastfulness or conceit, combined with insight into the logical foundations, or lack of such foundations, of one's beliefs.'[288] Leaders need to acquire this kind of humility in order to survive in the smart machine age. Leaders should not be wasting time on the 'big Me' but instead focus more on team activities, like innovative thinking, critical thinking, and emotional engagement with a more collaborative attitude instead of a competing attitude. Humility would help to change from the attitude of 'big Me' to 'big Us.' Old cultural ways would be replaced with new cultural ways—team winning behaviour over individual winning attitude, transparency over playing cards close to the chest, best argument or idea over the highest rank, listening to learn over listening just to confirm, asking questions over merely telling, understanding that it is okay to not know over knowing everything, intellectual quotient coupled with emotional quotient over just intellectual quotient, learning to address mistakes as learning opportunities over merely addressing them as bad, collaborative spirit over competing spirit, and self-reflection over self-promotion.

Humility has been analysed as a behaviour, a character strength, a theory of mind, a personality trait, and an intellectual virtue in psychology.[289] Humility has both interpersonal and intrapersonal advantages and is also correlated with higher psychological and physical well-being. Humility helps to improve metacognitive abilities, relationship building, and leadership skills. Carol Dweck and her team have identified a positive relationship between intellectual humility and real achievement and also learning goals instead of performance goals. In other words, they have identified that humility improves learning. 'According to the psychologists June Price Tangney, Christopher Peterson and Martin E. P. Seligman, the psychological attributes of humility are: having an accurate, not over- or underestimated view of one's abilities and achievements, being able to acknowledge one's mistakes, imperfections, knowledge gaps and limitations, being open to new ideas, contradictory information and advice, keeping one's abilities, and accomplishments in perspective, having a low focus on self or a tendency to forget the self, appreciating the value of all things and the many different ways other people and things contribute to the world.'[290] Humility enables individuals to be open-minded. Humility implies accepting and acknowledging both the strengths and the weaknesses and, at the same time, keeping in perspective one's achievements and accomplishments. Humility also enables oneself to value other people and their strengths and, at the same time, understand their limitations. Humility is a way to prevent ego defensiveness, which is the extreme focus on oneself by attempting all possible ways to be smarter and better than others in order to be more successful. Humility shifts the attention from self-focus to outward focus. Innovation, collaboration, and teamwork fail to work when leaders get more worked up in being defensive and feeling more superior over others instead of being humble. Hence, leaders should begin embarking on a personal betterment plan in order to develop meaningful work and good relations with others. Leaders need to embrace humility by muting their ego, managing their emotions and thoughts, listening reflectively by ending automaticity, and forming emotional relationships with others. Leaders need to be humble in order to fulfil their complete human potential.

When individuals are humble, they tend to confess their limitations and admit that they are incapable of performing in isolation.[291] When working in a team, such a mindset is important as the others in the team are now more than willing to help. Humility also implies that you are willing to help others in the team with their work whenever there is a need. Hence, humility allows people of varying personalities to coordinate with each other. However, humility should never be used as an excuse to slack. Humility is not courtesy, hospitality, or a friendly and kind attitude.[292] Humility does not imply being indecisive or weak. It does not demand publicity. An acclaimed CEO of a large Hollywood studio in Los Angeles was humble enough to share his own drawbacks, failures, and blind spots and how they stimulated his learning to a group of students and young professionals. This was very impressive, and he portrayed his self-confidence to the group.

Humility is not exactly the opposite of pride.[293] Comprehending the true value of one's contribution is humility. Humility nurtures trust in relationships, and people would only want to follow leaders whom they can trust. Trust would play a very important role at times of crises and protect the organisation from brand damage. Humility is contagious, and the employees would want to follow the humble leader and accept weaknesses and appreciate others like the leader. Hence, the advantages of humility spread through the organisation. Humility also motivates creativity and innovation as the humble leader is always receptive to new ideas. The expression of humility by the leader is a practical way of enhancing the followers' creative engagement.[294] Humble leaders positively influence the innovative ability of the employees.[295] They create an inclusive learning environment within the organisation by having an open mind towards advice and new knowledge and high-risk tolerance, thereby providing the employees the autonomy required to work innovatively. Humble leadership triggers the intrinsic motivation of employees and influences the formation of the followership of the subordinates. Humble leaders also enable their employees to be proactive at work by giving them psychological freedom, empowerment, motivation, and recognition of their contribution to the organisation, which gives the employees a sense of meaning in their work.[296] These leaders bravely give up a part of their power so that their employees have the freedom to decide within the dimension of their job profile. This freedom motivates the employees to initiate tasks with determination. The power experienced by the employees because of the leader's humility enables them to speak up as they know that their leader would give attention to their voice and also endorse the same.[297] A leader's humility makes the followers realise how much they contribute towards the productivity of the organisation and how valuable their work is.[298] The humility also increases the competence of the followers as the leader's praise acts as an acknowledgement of their ability to achieve higher performance levels.

When leaders flaunt their accomplishments and greatness, they tend to get disconnected and disassociated with their team.[299] Great leaders earn more admiration and respect because of their exceptional personality and humility. Humble leaders appreciate and enhance the team's talents. Coercion and fear could only help to achieve short-term goals, but over the years, this would only result in a demotivated team. The team's entire potential could be exploited only by a humble leader who supports, guides, and values the team. Humble leaders share the success and limelight with the team. They understand that success can be achieved only by collective excellence. Humble leaders are collaborative, and they focus on not only the brilliant performers but also coach and guide everyone to excel.

Humble leaders are more like good parents.[300] They readily admit their vulnerabilities and enhance the mutual trust. They are encouraging, appreciative, and non-judgemental, all of which helps to develop self-esteem and self-confidence. Like parents, they also help their followers have self-realisation so that they can see themselves well. They are the best role models to look up to and be inspired, just like good parents. Humble leaders act as caregivers in the organisational environment. The humble leaders always motivate their followers to open up about their apprehensions and doubts and are always receptive to criticisms, which in turn build a deep sense of security among the followers. The followers feel very secure under a humble leader, develop a 'can do' attitude during difficult situations in the workspace, and feel safe to open up or attempt a new approach. Owens and Hekman (2012)[301] proposed several behavioural patterns of humble leaders. The behavioural patterns include showcasing and appreciating the contributions and strengths of the followers, acknowledging the mistakes and limitations, and being receptive of the followers' inputs, queries, and advice. The behaviour of the humble leaders led to several outcomes, like development of loyalty and trust, being more of the self as humility gives the psychological freedom to accept limitations and weaknesses, increased engagement and responsibility of the followers, and improvement of adaptability as humility welcomes constructive criticisms.

Leaders with humility agree that they gain from the expertise of others who are less powerful than them.[302] Humble leaders always seek the unique ideas and contributions of their employees serving them, thereby enabling a very interactive work environment, and the employees also feel empowered. These leaders attempt to increase the ownership of the employees and motivate them to implement their own ideas. Humble leaders do not just ask their employees to do a better job. Instead, they ask their employees how they can assist them to do their jobs in a better way. Employees who do the real work in the organisation most often know better about how to do a great job than the leader who just makes decisions and delegates. Hence, when the employees' ideas are respected and when their approaches for more effective work are motivated, they give more of themselves to the job. Leaders often miss to see the value added by the lower-level workers. Only when the leaders are humbler are they able to be respectful and also offer to help the employees do their jobs better and ultimately enhance their organisation. Humble leaders are better human beings.

Humility authenticates an individual's humanity, and hence, it is an essential trait of a leader.[303] Humble leaders need to inspire followership by showcasing not merely their achievements but their character. Their achievements should serve as a platform to bring the others together to achieve greater things. Humble leaders demonstrate humility at the work environment by moderating authority through enabling others to make decisions, to form their own objectives, and to set the goals for the team. Humble leaders have the courage to promote others to even positions higher than theirs, thereby grooming talent. They acknowledge others' work and own failures. When humble leaders celebrate the team first and self second, everyone tends to notice what the leader and the team have achieved. Humble leaders are more grateful than proud.

Humble leaders should spread humility throughout the organisation as it is humility which provides a more conducive and collaborative work environment where people work together without the feeling of being put down or being exploited.[304] Humble leaders should lead by example and always support the employees with manpower and other resources especially during crunch times. They should speak less and listen more to the employees. They need to make the employees voice their innovative ideas and delegate responsibilities to them. Humble leaders should stress on cooperation and working together among the employees in order to achieve the goals. If the employees need to work together, they need to be humble enough to acknowledge each other's limitations and be ready to both accept and offer help at the same time. Humble leaders should recruit humble employees. During the interview process, they should look for signs of humility. These signs include disregarding others arrogantly, taking credit for their achievements, not showcasing team skills, and being unable to talk about failures. Humble employees tend to talk more about others' involvement while solving problems and other challenges.

The leadership style of Jungkiu Choi, the head of Consumer Banking at Standard Chartered, is a great example of humble leadership.[305] When Jungkiu Choi moved to China from Singapore for his job, he learnt that he had to visit the branches personally and pressure the branch managers to reduce costs. The staff at the branches would spend a lot of time anxiously prepping for this visit. Jungkiu Choi decided to amend this process slightly. Without using his formal power, he began going to the branches without any formal notice. He also began his visit by offering breakfast to all the branch staff. Jungkiu then held 'huddles' and asked how he could assist the employees in enhancing their branches. Most of the staff at the branches was taken aback by this, and they did not know how to respond to this new behaviour. But this new process tamed the anxiety of the employees and also motivated innovative ideas. In just a year, Jungkiu Choi visited nearly eighty branches spread over twenty-five cities. He was very consistent and more than willing to assist the employees. This attitude eased out even the employees who were sceptical initially. The huddles were very helpful in identifying the 'pain points' that he could assist. A lot of innovative ideas were also shared during these huddles. One such idea, which was a tremendous success, was at the Shanghai branch. One of the Shanghai branches was located inside a shopping mall. During one of the huddles, the employees asked Jungkiu if they could operate the branch during the same hours as that of the shopping mall instead of the usual operating time. The employees wanted to check the productivity of the branch on weekends. Jungkiu agreed, and to his surprise, the branch's weekend income exceeded its complete weekday income. Hence, Jungkiu's humble leadership and his methods of interactive discussions paid off very well in terms of the company's performance. Customer satisfaction hiked by 54 per cent during the two-year tenure of Jungkiu's humble leadership. The customer complaints also declined by 29 per cent during the same time. The employee attrition ratio, which had been the largest among all of China's foreign banks, also decreased lower than the other foreign banks.

Rick Hensley, the vice president for information technology at Messer Construction, inducted humility in his recruitment process itself.[306] He has developed a 'personal humility index' which he employs during the interview process of recruitment. Rick looks for a lot of qualities, like self-awareness, the use of *we* and *team* instead of *I* and *me*, modesty, and the passion to enhance the employees at different levels of hierarchy. Rick insists that the employees should also be trustworthy and with strong core values of honesty and integrity.

Most of the great leaders are humble. Brad Anderson, CEO of Best Buy, said, 'Our customers are kings and queens, our employees are royalty, and headquarters employees are servant leaders.'[307] Jim Quinn, president of Tiffany & Co., said, 'There is only one star here, and it is Tiffany.' Phil Tomlinson, CEO of TSYS, said, 'Leaders serve employees, and employees serve clients.' These humble leaders obeyed simple principles like leading by example, taking care of their people, always staying close to the customers and employees, and doing what is right always. Humble leaders are passionate about working intricately into the fine details of the business. They are anxious only about hubris, complacency, and arrogance, not about competition or globalisation. They always want the attention to be on their company and not on themselves. They give credit to their staff. In order to be a humble leader, one should learn to share the blame and appreciate the contributions of others, should admit the faults made which results in supportive behaviour and better performance, should continuously request for constructive criticisms, should welcome diversity in the team and act respectfully towards them, and should lead by example.[308]

The following traits make a leader humble and grounded:

Be humble

Leaders need to have a lower estimate of their importance in spite of all the power and authority they command. A humble leader is easily approachable. She is perceived as friendly and open to constructive criticisms. The organisational structure is more flat than hierarchical when the leader is more grounded. In flatter organisations, problem-solving becomes easier as the problems are identified more quickly and solved faster as the layers are minimal. As the organisational members become part of the problem identification and solution process, they actively participate in implementing the solution. The members are happier to work under a humble leader, and this happiness converts to higher productivity and overall growth. Humble leaders connect to the earth and serve all on the earth.

Be pragmatic

Pragmatism means your life and your words are beneficial not only to you but also to the people around. Leaders need to be realistic and sensible with respect to practical implementations and should not restrict themselves to theory alone. They need to solve problems in a practical way that suits the present scenario given the current limitations and working conditions. Pragmatic solutions always work when compared to idealistic solutions. Pragmatic leaders can survive through any new organisational crisis as they have always come up with spontaneous realistic solutions, which are implementable in any given scenario. Pragmatic leaders go beyond their bookish knowledge. They stand the test of time. In the ever-changing business world, pragmatic leaders are the need of the hour to confront any business cycle.

Be other-centred

Leaders need to be selfless and more other-centred to develop a healthy organisation. A leader who constantly thinks about her peers and looks at problems from others' point of view becomes a very likeable leader. These selfless leaders would be looked upon by others in the organisation, and they would try to imbibe the same qualities. Hence, the quality of being other-centric spreads throughout the organisation. Being other-centric becomes the culture of the organisation. Thus, the organisation grows by leaps and bounds, embracing both the strengths and weaknesses of its members.

The leader should be sensitive to the sufferings of the people, sensitive to the environment, and sensitive to the society. Sheryl Sandberg, chief operating officer of Facebook, founded the non-profit *Lean In* to advocate for women in the business world. She has made the successful transition from government work at the Treasury Department to the tech industry at Google and Facebook.

Sylvia Metayer, CEO of Sodexo Corporate Services worldwide, says, 'I've been CEO for 18 months, so I'm learning. I'm learning that to be a CEO is to be a servant. My main job is to support our employees, and be a support to our clients and to our consumers. In supporting our employees, I think the most important thing—and it really comes as a consolidation of many trends—is how do you make people's work easier? It's why we focus a lot on the impact of automation robotics technology and the work that our people do. It's also very much about making them ready. The world is changing very fast, so we have to create career paths, and we have to support the training of our people so that they're ready for change. It's actually quite an endeavour, because it means shifting our organization from a very traditional model, which is very top-down, to one where we learn how to be collaborative.'[309]

Cheryl Bachelder, CEO of Popeyes Louisiana Kitchen, looked at her leadership as a service to others. She says, 'It was a conscious decision to create a new workplace [with rigorous measures in place] where people were treated with respect and dignity yet challenged to perform at the highest level.' Her philosophy is, 'We needed to serve the people who have invested the most in Popeyes.' This meant Bachelder and her team shined the spotlight on the restaurant owners, listening and responding to their needs. Self-serving leaders were filtered out as collaboration increased and people were valued.[310]

Leaders who do not contribute to the growth of the society and are worried only about the company profits do not make great leaders. A leader should not be for herself or for profit or for amassing wealth. A leader should care for people and ultimately die for people. Only then would every company turn out to be a company for the society.

Be authentic

The eight energies will make you authentic. Leaders who practise the moves and the energies will surely follow values and principles, even at the risk of themselves. Motivations, intentions, and inner movements of *backward (historical consciousness)*, *forward (vision)*, *leftward (love and flexibility)*, and *rightward (power and authority)* that a leader go through must be governed by values that benefit others more than oneself. A sense of self comes from the practice of values. That self should guide you in life and work. For that, you need to be true to say what you feel, not having a dichotomy between who you are and what you say and do. This is to stand for goodness, truth, and justice. What is good for the organisation stands above all else for an authentic leader. Equally, what benefits the employees in terms of their well-being and career growth get more focus than her own career advancement.

An authentic leader empowers others who work for/with you. Your eight energies will make your employees and others feel empowered and secure. An authentic leader speaks for others, and it is to side with the people who are on the margins or neglected in the company or the organisation. An authentic leader is not afraid to speak against injustice, and even she is ready to face suffering and accusations. This will make you build a strong team around you, make help the live integrated, grounded lives.[311]

Give selflessly

The ultimate goal of a leader is to die for her people. You should give selflessly. Your time, your energy, and your life are for the people you lead and guide. For this, you need to love your organisation, love passionately. This love is the possessive or appetitive one. Real love transcends self-care and self-interests. Of course, you have to love your family and devote time and energy for a happy and healthy life with your family. But as a leader of an organisation, you need to go beyond loving your family. You are a head of a family of people inside the organisation. Remember, you are not an employee there; you are a leader. In a sense, you own the company; therefore, you are responsible. People in the company must be able to see that you treat them as your family and care for them as your own. That is what love is.

Love gives. It does not like to receive. It is patient. It does not keep accounts of what is given and what is received. Love gives and gives selflessly. Selfless giving makes you who you are as a leader. The eight energies are meant to be given to others who really them. You are historically conscious (*backward*), you know how to envision (*forward*), you are mature and flexible (*leftward*), your power and authority is for service (*rightward*), you have an attitude of a leader (*inward*), you are productive and you perform (*outward*), you know how to transcend triviality and suffering (*upward*), and you live selflessly for the people on earth (*downward*). You are an energetic leader who is humble enough to surrender your energies to empower the people you lead and serve.

Part III
DYNAMICS OF MOVES AND ENERGIES

We need to understand the dynamics in the movements of energies. No excess of any of the locus of movements should be there. If so, it is to be seen as an abnormality. If you are concerned only about historical consciousness but not ready to think of the future and envision a future, then you will not promote any growth. This is equal to a child who does not want to move from breastfed milk to sold milk. This is like saying, 'I like this school, and I do not want to go college.' You need to make a move if you want to grow. You must move on. In another sense, too much fixation on the past will stall creativity. You are stuck in nostalgia. You are inordinately attached to the past glory. Staying in one locus of energy is an obsession. It is a sort of narcissism.

When you focus excessively on the vision of the future (*forward*) without being rooted in the past (*backward*), your world will remain purely in imagination, missing the lessons learnt in the past, and you will reinvent the wheel. In the same way, without flexibility and emotional maturity (*leftward*), one's authority (*rightward*) becomes autocratic, rigid, and hard-hearted, leading finally to an absence of sense of belonging to the institution. What a leader has within (*inward*) and the attitude with which she looks at life has to be seen and expressed (*outward*) concretely in behaviour. All these moves and energies—*backward, forward, rightward, leftward,* and *inward*—that remain in internal realms will be seen in behaviour, *outward*. That often leads to conflicts or challenges in real-time interactions and encounters with others. Here, a leader is called to transcend (*upward*) and go beyond pettiness to see a larger picture of realising the vision set for the institution. Finally, every move and use of energy must be useful and beneficial to the earth and the people (*downward*). The last move makes a leader humble at all levels of thinking and action.

Therefore, one needs to move back and forth. From backward to forward, from leftward to rightward, from inward to outward, and from upward to downward. All movements are connected to one another. One does not have any meaning isolated from the other. The first five movements are the foundational source from which the other three movements are born.

Organic Connect of Moves and Energies

A leader in using the energies functions like a dynamo. As known, a dynamo is an electrical generator. In it, mechanical energy is converted into electrical energy to produce direct current. Through Faraday's law of induction, rotating coils of wire and magnetic fields convert mechanical rotation into a pulsing direct electric current. In the moves and energies, a leader converts static energy into organic energy through connecting one to another, achieved best by a constant move. As a commutator in a dynamo is needed to produce direct current, a leader with the eight energetic moves connects with stationary energies and activates them within, which would result in behaviours.[312] This action of commutator is continuous to be in touch with all the eight moves. Each energy in each move helps a leader make a decision to achieve a goal set for the organisation and the people assigned to fulfil tasks towards the realisation of goals.

In the eight energies of eight moves, there is a blend of physical energy, cognitive energy, and affective energy and an organic connect between these energies, linking one to another, by which a leader should make a decision for an action. In the moves and energies—backward (historical consciousness), forward (vision for the future), rightward (power of authority), leftward (flexibility), inward (attitude), outward (expression), upward (transcendence), and downward (pragmatism)—there is a nature connectedness that gives a certain coherence between thinking, feeling, and behaviour in a leader.[313] This connect relates to the concept of biophilia, which explains about an innate orientation to be connected to nature.[314] To be related to nature as a human being is to reconnect with roots of existence. Similarly, in the interplay of moves and energies, there is a need to stay in the connect with all the moves and energies. Leadership means at once being historically conscious, future-oriented, able to use power and authority responsibly, flexible, able to have the right attitude, productive, able to transcend trivialities, and able to remain pragmatic and beneficial to all on earth.

Achieving organic unity in forming the character of a leader is possible through maintaining an equal measure of the eight energies. Leadership is made up of these interdependent energies that give an organic connectedness. It is a kind of organic form that Aristotle talks in his *Poetics* about narratives and actions in a drama. Every act must be seen as a complete whole in which many incidents are interconnected and withdrawal of any one incident will disjoint the whole.[315]

Organic unity is different from mechanic unity. Parts in mechanic unity are not connected organically; each part that does not affect any other major parts can be removed. Removing a part in a car does not affect the whole. But in organic unity, it is like a seed that falls into the earth and a plant sprouts. Nothing outside forces this action; instead, the force is from within. Similarly, the energies we have discussed move a leader from within.

Any attempt to disconnect from one move and energy results in the loss of identity of a leader. Having only some moves and energies and deficient in other moves and energies don't make a leader a real leader. Though it may look ideal, it is desired that a leader is competent in all the moves and energies to perform optimally. It is a self-organised affective ecosystem in which a leader enjoys a certain facility to make good use of the eight energies in equal measure to make decisions and evolve strategies to achieve the goals of her organisation. Each energy relates to another energy in cyclical fashion, carrying the strength of each energy to result in leadership behaviours.[316] Each energy rests in its capacity to affect the other energy and to be affected. The energies reinforce one another, and there is a reciprocal influence between energies. Being conscious of the past (*backward*) helps evolve a future plan (*forward*) so that mistakes are not repeated. Power and authority (*rightward*) receives love and flexibility (*leftward*) to realise its purpose. The nature and dynamics of expressions (*outward*) depend upon the attitude (*inward*). The six energies help a leader involve in different sets of activities in the process of leading an organisation where she is called to go beyond (*upward*) triviality and pettiness. All the seven energies ultimately must benefit the earth, nature, and its people (*downward*).

The relating and affecting produces a common vitality in the ways in which a leader behaves and gives birth to a certain sense of unity that makes a leadership relevant and efficient. A leader must learn to connect one move and energy to another move and energy constantly to experience the unity and realise it in concrete actions.

Deep Practice

The organic connect is a result of deep practice that builds the muscles of a leader. The best way for a leader of moves and energies is to undergo deep practice.[317] Moving between eight moves constantly and making good use of each energy in a move is essential to gather strength and wisdom to make decisions and lead a group to achieve goals. Deep practice helps you push hard beyond your comfort zone. When you make mistakes, you stop and reflect on errors to adjust and continue the process. You should not stay in an energy among the eight energies. You must move on. When you make mistakes, take time to reflect why you made that mistake and repeat the process. It is a very slow process, and how we learn is how we grow, and it's how we build our skill and optimise our neural paths. As Daniel Coyle says, it involves a neural insulator, a microscopic substance called myelin, which neurologists see as the holy grail of acquiring skill.[318] Every human skill, playing a game or music, is created by chains of nerve fibres carrying a tiny electrical impulse—basically, a signal traveling through a circuit. Myelin plays a key role in wrapping those nerve fibres the same way that rubber insulation wraps a copper wire, making the signal stronger and faster by preventing the electrical impulses from leaking out. By a regular and constant move between the eight moves, it will insulate by wrapping neural circuits, and then according to the signals, a leader will be able to feel, think, and act. This has to be repeated for years to become a leader of moves and energies. Leadership is a process and lifelong learning exercise, requiring practising and perfecting. In the process, a leader is bound to make mistakes, but what is important is to learn from the mistakes and build a character of leadership, like how we build a muscle through constant training in a gym or deliberate exercise.

This explains that leadership is not an innate talent but a deep practice. At the edge of one's abilities, a leader struggles, falls down, but gets up to reflect on why she fell, and readjusts to build a neural circuit.

1. In the deep practice, first a leader should chunk up, breaking the eight energies into composite chunks, and master them one by one. Every energy by a move has its own dynamics, and that has to be comprehended. The more you fire up an energy among the eight energies.
2. Secondly, you need to take two energies together to learn to absorb their elements. For example, backward and forward moves help you to see the past (history) and future (vision). In the eight energies, every two energies have a close connect between each other that would give a meaningful whole to practise leadership skills.
3. At every move, you need to slow down to assimilate the nature and character of each energy. This slowing down helps to see why and how the mistakes have happened. It helps to learn to

correct deficiencies. Spending every day for two hours on your mistakes makes a huge impact in developing leadership.
4. Repetition is key to build the skills needed for an efficient leader. Repetition helps you develop habits that form the core of leadership.
5. It is not sufficient to stay with few energies of the eight energies. The more energies you use, the better leader you become. Often, we find a leader who dwells on historical consciousness more than on other energies. That makes a leader have a narrow focus that fails to have a broad outlook.
6. It is important that you feel deeply the struggle you go through in the process of becoming a leader of energies. The pain of becoming a leader lies in the mistakes and failures. That has to be felt comprehensively.

The word *practice* comes from the Greek word *praktike*, feminine of *praktikos*, 'fit for or concerned with action, practical', and from the verb *prasso*, 'to achieve, bring about, effect, accomplish'. Leadership is a practice of moves and energies that forms a leader.

The practice would lead to a strong, energetic leader of moves and energies. She must make a difference in the lives of people. In doing so, she must follow a mantra of DINCO: *discernment*, *innovation*, *networking*, and *collaboration*.

Part IV
DINCO—A MANTRA FOR MOVES LEADERSHIP

The life we live after the pandemic—COVID-19—is different and unprecedented. Every company and organisation goes through disruptive transformation. In 2019, we thought we would have high unemployment levels, millions of businesses being closed, the cancellation or postponement of sporting events, and millions of infections and deaths all over the world. But we have seen dramatic changes by the use of digital technologies, reducing 'face-to-face interactions and safeguard customer and employee health and well-being. These digital technologies include consumer-facing applications such as grocery and food delivery services, business-to-business e-commerce applications, and applications such as videoconferencing that seem to have penetrated the consumer, business, and not-for-profit worlds. Searches for terms such as "contactless" increased 7x between November and late April,2 while the stocks of technology companies aligned with new-found customer health and safety concerns have skyrocketed.'[319]

You live in the post-COVID era. You cannot live and work as you did in the pre-COVID times. Things have changed; it is a metamorphosis. The world has shifted from a pipeline process to a platform model of businesses. Virtual competence determines your success. As a leader, first of all, you need to *discern* a future in the post-COVID world for your company and the people who depend on it. Secondly, you have to be *innovative* and creative to mitigate the challenges the world faces due to the pandemic. Thirdly, social and digital *networking* is a key to success. You need to stay connected while you stay distanced physically from others. Fourthly, *collaboration* with others in the field strengthens your resolve in leading an organisation. *Discernment, innovation, networking, and collaboration (DINCO) must be your mantra of leadership.*

Discernment

Human beings are driven by motives in daily life and at the time of making major decisions in life. What drives a man to start a business or a woman to choose a profession? Many things contribute to this. Or what drives a man who has been alcoholic for years to quit or an obese man to get thin? Many inner motives interact in a kind of movement that eventually drives the person to act. This is a dense complex of motives.

Discernment 'is the interactional and communicative process that takes place within a community of practice to reflect on habits, actions and communication patterns, and to bring to the surface that which is relevant but hidden, in order to determine the best course of action for a particular situation'.[320] It is a process by which 'judgements of conscience' are made, and it is an important component of the development process of morals.[321] Discernment can be combined with strategic decision-making by utilising these elements: (1) beginning the process of decision-making with a reflective inner disposition; (2) having patience in revealing the underlying essence of the decision problem; (3) collecting abundant information which is painstaking, followed by benchmarking, innovation, reconciling differences, and collaborative problem-solving; (4) prayer and reflection; (5) making decisions which are tentative and giving a lot of attention to results; and (6) re-evaluation.[322]

Discernment is a process of recognising these interior movements, consisting of desires, emotions, inclinations, intentions, feelings, and motivations, or what is called motions of the soul. Discernment involves becoming sensitive to these movements, reflecting on them, and understanding where they come from and where they will lead us.

These interior movements take on two configurations, which are called *consolation* and *desolation*. Both consolation and desolation can move the leader towards the vision of an organisation or pull away from it. Being true to the vision, with intentions of doing good to all, gives an experience of consolation, whereas not being true and not having intention of doing good brings a dry feeling of desolation. At times, such decisions may bring profit, but there would not be any sense of satisfaction. Decisions that do not come from the framework of *truth-goodness-beauty* might look successful, but they will lead finally to bankruptcy. Only the leaders who are in touch with their deeper self and its interior movements would be able to discern well and choose the right decision by ignoring the ego-gratifying options, which would make them feel guilty and desolate. At the same time, they should choose the right qualities needed to be developed, those that are truly meaningful and for the common good of the organisation. That would be beautiful and respectable.

In the process of discernment, there must be a constant check of inordinate attachment to the leader's ulterior motives that move one away from truth and goodness. Selfish interests may bring excitement initially but will leave behind an aftertaste of emptiness finally. On the other hand, the decisions after having discerned bring consolation, which brings a sustainable, calm energy. Consoling decisions would be fulfilling and in line with the moral values and the vision of the organisation, whereas decisions which cause desolation create a feeling of emptiness. These decisions need not always make one happy. For example, laying off decisions for organisational goals may not bring happiness but bring consolation and fulfilment, because it comes from being true and doing good. Discerning leaders are mature enough to resist decisions that lead to desolation and embrace ways of making decisions that bring consolation. Decisions taken after appropriate discernment sometimes may bring failures, but personally, leaders will experience consolation.

By discernment, leaders will be able to perceive the source of actions, thoughts, and feelings; help increase awareness of the connection between free will; understand the influence of good or bad in the thinking process; and help take the right decisions that reflect the vision and core values of an organisation. Ultimately, discerning culture creates the atmosphere of goodness at every level of organisation, in every activity done, and in every person involved in the functioning of the organisation.

For example, *Enron* failed because of the absence of discernment. There was no discernment in the board level. Deep self-interest and profit motive were the reasons for not checking on their decision-making process. As Jim Collins says in his book *How the Mighty Fall: And Why Some Companies Never Give In*, the organisation failed to be in touch with the interior movements which helps in decision-making and did not discerned them properly, which resulted in the fallout of Enron. Kenneth Lay, the founder of Enron, set the goal of the organisation as high stock prices above everything else, and the employees were forced to increase the return rates by borrowing more money and trading assets. Ethical business practices were ignored, and non-standard accounting techniques were practised. Employees from the best B-schools were hired and rewarded with incentives based only on profits and growth, which made the work environment very tolerant to unhealthy practices. Enron also dismissed the lowest 20 per cent of the performers with no second chance, thereby creating a culture of fear and mistrust. This system fuelled by rewards, punishments, and fear only resulted in illegal practices and debt, creating strategies in order to push profits. All warning signs were ignored, and Lay led the organisation into irreparable losses because of his personal greed for money.

One of the main reasons for the failure of development of leaders is the absence of practising personal discernment. Profit-making problems, unethical practices, and deception of customers with fake promises are all the outcomes of making decisions without discerning. Leaders who lack discernment would not be confident enough to face the competitors. They would not influence positive changes. The integrity of the leader is challenged as absence of discernment implies absence of truthful decisions and thereby absence of healthy results. When the integrity is questioned, the influence exerted would decline. Ultimately, if the leader is powerless to influence, leadership would be at stake.

Each discerning leader must take all others who work with him into confidence by involving them in the discernment process. Ideally, in any organisation, teams would have to collaborate and come up with important decisions. Collaborative discernment would need active participation of its team members, which is bound to result in differences with respect to the decision being made. It ensures freeing of disordered attachments and relations and makes sure that the rightful decisions taken realise the organisational vision when put into practice.

In order to have a good collaborative discernment, each person who takes part in the discernment should know the matter well. Complete quality information about the issue to be decided and the output that is expected from the process should be accessible to all the participating members. In this way, discernment cannot be merely used to justify either minor or major decisions. The content of the case will determine the participants of the collaborative discernment process. The participants should accept the reasons for and the conditions under which they participate in the discernment process. They should develop interior freedom, which means that they should put aside their own selfish interests and be liberated to pursue the truth in accordance with the organisational vision and values. This interior freedom would enable the development of unwarranted relationships with others with the goal of pursuing the common good of the organisation even when it involves personal abandonment.

The main purpose of collaborative discernment is to make a clear distinction between the right and the wrong in accordance with the organisational vision. This can be fulfilled only by merging the heart and the mind, which implies a shared sense of purpose, because what is at stake in the process directly affects everyone. Here, it involves emotional capacities (*eros*), rational capacities (*logos*), and moral capacities (*ethos*) of all those who are taking part in the discernment process. Hence, the participants need to have mutual knowledge of each other, which would result in mutual trust, thereby enabling active participation. There is an interior peace when the discernment is done right in agreement with the truth. It is necessary to reason out the pros and cons of making a certain decision against the horizon of the greater good of the organisation based on the conditions experienced by the participants of the discernment process. A good collaborative discernment depends on the participants' skill in employing their understanding to perceive that the greater good is based on the vision and the core values of the organisation.

The collaborative discernment process enables the transition from seeking to finding the truth. The examination of the interior movements of the participants enables the confirmation of the discernment process and helps to decide if the process should be continued and also how to go about it in accordance with the vision of the organisation. Continuous observation of the interior movements of the participants helps to maintain a memory of the process. In the collaborative discernment, each participant should actively listen to others (*active listening*) and speak intentionally (*intentional speaking*). When you listen to what others speak of, you should put yourself in that person's thought process and his intentions. In the same way, when you speak, you must be conscious of your intentions of saying what you are saying. What happens here is that all have actively entered into the thought process of others in discernment and have been deeply conscious of the intentions of what they spoke of.

In collaborative discernment, a method of deep conversation is used. It is a kind of dialogue within each person and between others in discernment. Deep conversation constitutes the essential core difference in the quality of the close and friendly dealings of those who share thoughts, keeping in mind the purpose or the vision of the organisation.

It improves our capacity to converse deeply with the purpose in mind. The conversation is an opportunity to present to others with simplicity and without making unnecessary speeches what one has perceived as interior movements or as the fruit of one's personal reflection on the point in question. On the other hand, our disposition to 'listen to the other person' respectfully, without contradicting the movements that the other person has felt interiorly, can produce a new interior movement in the person listening, giving rise to a fresh way of perceiving things. The custom of deep conversation, the habit of listening attentively to others, and knowing how to communicate one's own experience and ideas simply and clearly contribute to good collaborative discernment when the matter under consideration requires it.

Properties of deep conversation

1. *Intentional speaking.* The main characteristic of deep conversation is intentional speaking. The intention of the conversation is analysed and categorised as a personal motive or in line with the purpose of the organisation. Perceptions are built based on the thought process, which is stated as intentions, as it is the thoughts which manifest into words and then into actions. Hence, analysing the intentions becomes important. When the thinking is negative, it will create a negative perception, and positive thinking creates positive perception.
2. *Active listening.* Active listening involves taking part in the conversation by listening keenly and sincerely with full concentration and understanding to what the other person is saying and trying to find linkages with the intention. The listener should understand the reason for what he or she says.

There are steps in this conversation:

Step 1. It starts with a brief time of silence, or if you prefer, call it a prayer. This is to gather yourself to focus and become attentive to what is going on deep within you. This helps you develop proper dispositions to the whole process of discernment.

Step 2. Then the leader reads out the matter for discernment as discernment statements and reasons for and against.

Step 3. After spending a few moments in silence on the matter, each one shares his/her feelings—consolation or desolation—about the statements.

Step 4. After all the persons have shared what they felt about the statements, the whole group could spend some time allowing what they have heard from others and what you have said to sink into themselves. To facilitate this, the leader could summarise what the entire group shared about the statements. In the summary, the leader could identify convergences and divergences. This would possibly give a picture of what the group feels.

Step 5. The leader invites the members to share how they have been affected by what they have heard and may suggest possible 'effects', like these: What did you hear? Were you struck by a common theme? By something absent but which you expected to hear? Were you especially touched by a particular sharing? What emotions are you feeling now, in response to the first round? Did any insights occur to you? What were they? Where did you experience harmony with the others as they shared?

Step 6. Now there can be a true discussion, with the quick give and take typical of discussions, with people replying to each other quickly, agreeing, disagreeing, etc. The fact that the discussion is preceded by steps of active listening and intentional speaking from the heart should help the discussion be relatively free of manifestations of ego and preserve the spiritual qualities of attentiveness and sincerity.

These steps of deep conversation will result in a discerned decision. Leaders often grumble that their subordinates don't collaborate in their decision-making. Some take decisions unilaterally, and later, they complain that they make good decisions, but the execution is not effective and their second-level leaders are not efficient. This is simply because they did not have a proper discernment of the eight energies. Before they make decisions, they should go through a process of discernment of the eight moves and energies. More than simply making decisions, discernment is rooted in self-knowledge of individuals in the dynamic process of the moves and energies, their deep awareness of the core purpose of the organisation, and their conviction about their actions for the growth of the organisation. In discernment, there is a connect with what goes on within, the interior movements of the eight energies, which actually brings union of minds and hearts among the employees, leading to committed and loyal workforce. That will help the organisation achieve any goals. More than ever, in the post-COVID world, we require discerning leaders to steer through the losses and disruptions.

Innovation

Once the discernment gives light to see what is required and important, a leader must be innovative to create s unique, valued position that stands above the rest. Innovation helps a leader enter into the process of transforming an organisation, not the solutions of the past (*backward*) for the questions of the future (*forward*) but solutions that provide a new way to solve not only today's problems but also the ways by which a leader mitigates the challenges of the future. You need to be an innovation catalyst who could create prototypes, do experiments, and learn constantly from customers, as *Intuit* has done to transform itself.[323] It is to understand the pain point of those who work under you (pain storm) that can come from any one of the eight moves and energies. You need to know exactly what bothers an employee that undermines his/her performance where you listen to the inner feelings and orientations of that employee. Once you know the pain point, you should work on possible solutions to the point by which you make the employees happy. Working on the solutions could be helped by understanding all the eight energies. Based on the solutions, you create and build structures and systems that help you lead an organisation. Sustained innovations contribute to an organisation's growth, increasing its performance. You need to disrupt what you do now and embrace the model of the eight energies. Because you live in a new context, in order to increase performance, disruptive innovation fosters increased performance.[324]

This innovation must start from the pre-existing culture (*backward*) that would give an idea about what lies ahead *(forward)*. When you want to move ahead to realise the vision you have, you require proper energies of power (*rightward*) and emotional maturity (*leftward*). Then comes the attitude (*inward*) with which you look at the introduction of innovation to increase the performance of the organisation. The performance we talk about here must be concrete expressions (*outward*) of the company's core character. Every innovative strategy and allied activities will always meet with challenges and conflicts that you manage to transcend (*upward*), not just overcome the challenges. In fact, every time you manage to transcend, you go through inner conversion and transformation as a leader. That transformative experience is essential to contribute to the well-being of the earth (*downward*) and the people who are on the margins, the most disadvantaged. Innovation is a significant change you make in your company that demonstrates who you are and what you are capable of.

Networking

Innovative leadership with the use of eight energies is not sufficient. You need to network with others who are with the same energy level. It is about developing and using your networks in a way that builds relationships and strengthens alliances in the service of your organisation's work and goals. When you network with them, it builds on your shared vision. When the vision is realised, you need them to celebrate. Networks also depend on persons able to provide vision and leadership for collaborative mission. When properly conceived, networking provides a healthy balance between authority and local initiative. It strengthens local capacity and encourages subsidiarity while assuring a unified sense of mission from a central authority. Local views are more readily and speedily heard.

There are three forms of interdependent networking: operational, personal, and strategic.[325] You must master the ways in which you network with people with similar energies and kindred spirits, and they will infuse enthusiasm and the needed drive to move from one energy to another. Your operational network involves people useful to you for fulfilling your current work tasks and responsibilities. These are your daily contacts for routine activities. Some leaders do not reach beyond this network to become more successful leaders—keeping themselves trapped in technical and operational roles without achieving their full potential. It is operational networking that provides who you should align and who you should avoid. There must be a personal connect with other leaders in your area who are like-minded people outside your own organisation who can assist your personal development and boost your advancement. Your mutual interest or pastime can leverage your acquaintance for business success. These contacts provide further references, information, and often, developmental support. Strategically also, you need to connect with successful external people who will draw your attention to new business possibilities, new directions, and new stakeholders necessary to achieve the key objectives of your organisation. The key to a good strategy is the ability to use information effectively and gain resources from networks.

Networking must begin within your organisation first. You need to recognise people who use the eight energies in their work and align with them to achieve the goals you have set for the company. Regular interactions with them, both casually and formally, will gradually increase the connect and union of minds and hearts that serves in the projects you have rolled out. This would also show you in a better light as a leader, who will not make decisions autocratically but based on insights from transactions with like-minded individuals. Here, a deep sense of trust plays a key role in bringing all on board. And very quickly, all will remain focused on the goals to be achieved. In a subtle way, you will actually promote others, not yourself, in the networking style of leading a company. As they say, you will not build stars but constellations.

Collaboration

Networking helps you make connections, but collaboration is to put the networks to work to realise the goals of a project. As seen earlier, while you move between the eight energies to make yourself an energetic leader, you cannot work alone, and you require the strengths and expertise of others in your efforts of actualising your vision. Collaboration makes you and others in the company to come out of silos. Often, knowledge hoarding stunts the growth of a company; it is a kind of tribal mindset that places restrictions to access and advancement. When locked in silos, there will always be power struggles and enmity, ultimately leading to the decrease in productivity. Collaboration makes you humble, and it attracts others to join you in your resolve. A collaborative team will stay together in the entire process of realising a project. Even when there are blocks and obstacles, they will stand united to face them. In failure and success, the team will remain well knit. There will be trust within the company that keeps everyone at work remain focused. Any success comes not just because of capabilities and strategies but because of the emotional resilience of all those who are part of the company's objectives.

Collaboration is important for the performance of any team.[326] The coordinated effort of the team members would enhance the profitability of the team. Working individually would be less effective when compared to working together as a team. There is definitely a positive relationship between collaboration and team performance. In today's business environment, collaboration is more important than ever.[327] It takes strategic leadership to collaborate in any group. In order to optimise the power of collaboration, leaders need six important behaviours: (1) leaders must stop hoarding knowledge, (2) leaders must build a team of trust, (3) leaders must be warm and caring in their body language, (4) leaders must value diversity, (5) leaders must be empathetic towards their collaborating team, and (6) leaders must create an environment which resonates psychological safety.

In order to collaborate well in a team, leaders should encourage everyone to listen and not just talk.[328] Expansive questions needs to be asked, and there should be more focus on the listener. Empathy needs to be practised. Collaborative leaders also need to make people more comfortable with feedback, as good collaboration involves giving and receiving feedback. Good collaboration also involves switching between the tasks of leading and following smoothly. Collaboration needs to be facilitated by good communication without any abstractions and by win-win interactions.

Any leader must be able to pool the strengths of individuals and be able to collaborate. Similar to the collaboration and coordination between the eight business moves and energies, the leader needs to collaborate with others who have the energies and moves. For example, a person who knows and understands the company history (historical consciousness) should be a part of your team. One who is able to envision the future (vision), one who is flexible and is able to negotiate and resolve conflicts (leftward), one with authority (rightward), one with a good attitude (inward), one who can put things in performance (outward), one who can go beyond problems and think beyond (transcendence), and those who are contributing to the earth (downward) should collaborate with each other. Hence, collaboration is very essential to a leader. Interaction between these eight business moves would make a leader a leader. Having these eight kinds of people with each move in a team is important to have completeness. A leader who can understand the eight moves and energies and work with people who understand these eight moves and energies and also have a team of people who have these energies will have a sense of history and a sense of vision, understand the power of authority and power, know how to be flexible and emotionally intelligent, have the right attitude, perform in concrete actions, and not be bogged down with problems and can go beyond transcendence. Ultimately, any team or any leader should rally the energies of people to contribute to the earth and the people on earth to make a difference in the lives of people, particularly the people on the peripheries. Any leader of an organisation or a company must ultimately contribute to the well-being of humanity and maintenance of the earth. Interplay and interconnection of the eight moves and eight energies necessitate collaboration.

Conclusion

I believe strongly that the power of leadership lies in energies used by a leader, because to move physically, you need energy. Any transformation a leader aims in the world needs enormous energy, physical energy. Without energy, there is nothing a leader could do. In the same way, the eight energies and eight moves we have discussed in this book are not just mental energies that remain in thinking, in the cerebral realm. They are emotional energies and energies of the heart that help gather strength and focus to look at any issue a leader faces in life and at work.

Historical consciousness (backward move) is not just in the mind but is also emotional as it is an attachment to the happenings of the past that define the identity of a company. A leader must be emotionally attached to the past of the company. It is not the inordinate attachment but the ordinate attachment that keeps the leader sensitive to the history of the company. The vision for a future (forward move) is a feeling of yearning for a position that a leader wants to take the company to. It is a kind of longing to reach a stage where the purpose is achieved, and it is the leader's dreams for the company. Power and authority (rightward move) makes a person energised to serve the company. It is both a physical and emotional power that the leader wields in her performance of leading others to achieve the goals. Emotional intelligence and flexible approach to leadership (leftward move) are ways of understanding limitations of energy and handling situations. The energy of affective maturity in the leftward move helps a leader inject intelligence to emotions. Inner attitude (inward move) is formed by a series of experiences and lessons learnt from the experiences. This gives a leader a perspective to look at life in general and the work of leading people. Expressions (outward move) are concrete deeds, and they are performances, ideas in action, what a leader does really with all that she has and who she is. It is being and doing. When faced with conflicts and issues, the leader goes beyond the triviality (upward move); it is a spirit of transcendence. A leader should not be stuck with failures; she has to rise above them, for which the energy of transcendence is required. All the energies in the eight moves must end in contributing to the earth (downward move) and the people who live in it, especially the people who are marginalised. A leader cannot just remain satisfied with profits she makes for her company; instead, she should ask what contribution she has made to make lives of people better.

Therefore, the dynamo competence of leadership is a result of the organic connect and movement of the eight energies to give a leader an integrated energy to lead people to achieve the targets set for a company and the mission given to an organisation. Moving between the eight energies constantly is what makes a leader a meaningfully successful leader.

APPENDIX

Moves and Energies in the Great Speeches

In this section, I attempt to explore the great speeches of world leaders both in business and in politics to identify the moves and energies we have discussed so far, because if one believes in the moves and energies, they will be expressed in her own words before they are seen in actions.

The speech, I believe, exhibits the intent or the vision a leader has, and by that, she wants to rally the people towards realising the vision. When every leader makes speeches or gives orations, in every speech or oration, all these eight moves discussed are present. This is why great speeches stand the test of time.

Here are some great speeches of leaders where you will find all the eight moves and the eight energies.

Steve Jobs—Apple

The following are excerpts of Steve Jobs's famous speech delivered at Stanford on 14 June 2005.[329]

Backward—Historical Consciousness

In his speech, Steve Jobs narrates his birth story and is conscious of the beliefs his biological mom had. He conveys to the audience his consciousness about his past.

> My biological mother was a young, unwed college graduate student, and she decided to put me up for adoption. (p. 1)

Forward—Futuristic Vision

Steve Jobs believes that whatever skill one learns would be of some use in the future, and one needs to believe that the dots will always connect in the future. His lessons in calligraphy were useful ten years later when he was developing the first Macintosh computer.

> None of this had even a hope of any practical application in my life. But ten years later . . . we designed it all into the Mac. (p. 1)

Rightward—Authority

Steve Jobs exercises authority by the rightward move in two different instances in his speech. One is when he makes the most important decision of dropping out of college, and the other is when he decides to start all over again, even after being thrown out of his own company, which he had founded. Both these decisions played a very important role in his life.

> So I decided to drop out and trust that it would all work out OK. (p. 1)
>
> The turn of events at Apple had not changed that one bit. I had been rejected, but I was still in love. And so I decided to start over. (p. 2)

Leftward—Affective Maturity

Steve Jobs expresses emotional intelligence when he refers to death as an intellectual concept. He expresses the emotions of how he experienced death so closely and then overcame those emotions.

> Having lived through it, I can now say this to you with a bit more certainty than when death was a useful but purely intellectual concept. (p. 3)

Inward—Inner Attitude

In his speech, Steve Jobs mentions that it is very important to follow one's inner voice. In one's limited lifetime, one should have a unique attitude which resonates with the inner self.

> Don't let the noise of others' opinions drown out your own inner voice. And most important, have the courage to follow your heart and intuition. (p. 3)

Outward—Being Productive

Steve Jobs was very productive, and he was able to accomplish a lot at a very early age with his hard work and breakthrough innovation. Even after leaving his own company Apple, he started several companies which were pioneers in their own fields.

> Woz and I started Apple in my parents garage when I was 20 . . . During the next five years, I started a company named NeXT, another company named Pixar. (p. 2)

Upward—Transcending Boundaries

Steve Jobs, in his speech, insists to transcend almost everything, including pride, fear of failure or embarrassment, and external expectations, in order to follow the heart. In the face of death, everything else is trivial and petty, so one should always follow the heart.

> Because almost everything—all external expectations, all pride, all fear of embarrassment or failure—these things just fall away in the face of death, leaving only what is truly important. (p. 3)

Downward—Being Earthly

When Steve Jobs narrates the incident of having to quit his own company and being portrayed as a public failure, his humility surfaces. Steve Jobs humbles himself after all the success he enjoyed after he founded Apple and learns to enjoy the lightness of being a beginner again. Though being thrown out of his own company was awful, the humility he gained in the process helped him to start fresh. This humility gave him the freedom to enter the most creative phase of his life.

> I didn't see it then, but it turned out that getting fired from Apple was the best thing that could have ever happened to me. (p. 2)

Mark Zuckerberg—Facebook

The following are excerpts from Mark Zuckerberg's commencement address at Harvard on 25 May 2017.[330]

Backward—Historical Consciousness

Mark Zuckerberg begins his speech by remembering his past, his days at Harvard. He still refers to his admission into Harvard as the proudest moment for his parents so far, even though he has achieved so much now. He recalls all his memories of his lectures and, most importantly, meeting his wife at Harvard. These fond memories go a long way in his life.

> I swear getting into Harvard is still the thing my parents are most proud of me for . . . But my best memory from Harvard was meeting Priscilla.

Forward—Futuristic Vision

Mark Zuckerberg mentions about what the future holds in two instances in his speech. One is when he suggests what achievements this generation could achieve in the future and how they could start small. The other is when he mentions how the society should also change and have a better outlook to support the newer challenges.

> These achievements are within our reach. Let's do them all in a way that gives everyone in our society a role. Let's do big things, not only to create progress, but to create purpose . . . We should have a society that measures progress not just by economic metrics like GDP, but by how many of us have a role we find meaningful.

Rightward—Authority

One of the most crucial decisions which Mark Zuckerberg took with great authority was to refuse the sale of his company, though many were against his decision. He stood tall and alone, confident enough to take the company forward. That decision came with a lot of authority and power.

> A couple years in, some big companies wanted to buy us. I didn't want to sell. I wanted to see if we could connect more people.

Leftward—Affective Maturity

Mark Zuckerberg mentions about the emotional intelligence exhibited by one of his students who, though being undocumented, had nothing to worry about and was mature enough to look at the bigger picture. He had a greater sense of purpose at such a young age.

> Here's a young guy who has every reason to be cynical. He didn't know if the country he calls home—the only one he's known—would deny him his dream of going to college. But he wasn't feeling sorry for himself. He wasn't even thinking of himself. He has a greater sense of purpose, and he's going to bring people along with him.

Inward—Inner Attitude

In his speech, Mark Zuckerberg mentions that the core attitude of the current generation should be to create a sense of purpose for everyone, which in turn creates true happiness. He tries to imbibe this attitude in the millennials of this generation.

> I'm here to tell you finding your purpose isn't enough. The challenge for our generation is creating a world where everyone has a sense of purpose.

Outward—Being Productive

Mark Zuckerberg mentions how his innovative idea of connecting the Harvard community expanded to connecting the whole world. He was able to achieve what big technology companies couldn't do because of his breakthrough, innovative idea.

> I remember telling him I was excited to connect the Harvard community, but one day someone would connect the whole world.

Upward—Transcending Boundaries

In his speech, Mark Zuckerberg mentions that seeds of good ideas bloom only by transcending several mistakes, dejection from the society, and challenges. It is better to start something, face challenges, and then transcend them rather than not do anything at all.

In our society, we often don't do big things because we're so afraid of making mistakes that we ignore all the things wrong today if we do nothing. The reality is, anything we do will have issues in the future. But that can't keep us from starting.

Downward—Being Earthly

Mark Zuckerberg has humbled himself for the betterment of the society, and he takes upon himself to enable the common man to pursue his purpose as it comes with a cost. The common man would not be able to pursue his dreams without sufficient cushioning to fall back upon. He and his wife have begun the humble initiative called Chan Zuckerberg Initiative to support equal opportunities.

And yes, giving everyone the freedom to pursue purpose isn't free. People like me should pay for it . . . That's why Priscilla and I started the Chan Zuckerberg Initiative and committed our wealth to promoting equal opportunity.

Elon Musk—Tesla

The following are excerpts from Elon Musk's commencement speech, titled 'Magicians of the 21st Century', delivered at Caltech on 15 June 2012.[331]

Backward—Historical Consciousness

Elon Musk goes back nearly three hundred years in time to remind the audience how simple things we do today were breakthrough innovations in the past. It is the innovations of the past which have made the world closer.

If you go back say, 300 years, the things we take for granted today, you'd be burned at stake for. (p. 2)

Forward—Futuristic Vision

Elon Musk has his futuristic vision very clearly laid out, and he mentions that in his speech in three different instances. One is when he initially learnt the way forward was only by advancing world knowledge. Next is when he mentions about how he framed his path forward by looking at the problems the future holds for humanity. Finally, it is when he mentions SpaceX's future plans of developing a reusable transport system to Mars, which seems nearly impossible.

> If we can advance the knowledge of the world . . . the only way forward. (p. 2)
>
> I thought well, what are some of the other problems that are likely to most affect the future of humanity? (p. 3)
>
> Breakthrough that needs to occur which is to create a rapidly and completely reusable transport system to Mars . . . we're going to try to achieve with SpaceX. (p. 7)

Rightward—Authority

Elon Musk states making his career choice and choosing the path less travelled was a very powerful decision which changed his life forever.

> Participate in the Internet and be part of it. So, I decided to drop out. (p. 2)

Leftward—Affective Maturity

Elon Musk, though having failed three times in a row trying to launch rockets and also failing to run the computer software without bugs, was able to be emotionally mature even after draining so much of his money. His emotional intelligence helped him to go past all the failures and still try the fourth time and succeed.

The first launch, I was picking up bits of rocket near the launch site . . . eventually with the fourth flight in 2008, reach orbit. (p. 6)

Inward—Inner Attitude

Elon Musk stresses one of the three important attitudes one should have in three different instances of his speech. One attitude is to always be open to feedback and rework the prior assumptions made. He reminds that United States is a land of explorers, and one should never give up the exploring attitude. The attitude of attempting to create magic and imagining the impossible must be imbibed.

If we hadn't responded to what people said, then we probably would not have been successful. (p. 3)
I think the United States is really a distillation of the spirit of human exploration. (p. 5)
You guys are the magicians of the 21th century. (p. 8)

Outward—Being Productive

Elon Musk has made breakthrough innovations which no one ever thought before. He developed the PayPal software when he understood that people were excited about the email payment option. His other innovations were companies like SpaceX, Tesla, and SolarCity, which aimed for futuristic transport. The unbelievable innovation was the Dragon spacecraft, which returned safely back to earth from the space station.

I've done a few things here and there. One of which is PayPal. (p. 3)
'The latter is the basis for SpaceX and the former is the basis for Tesla and SolarCity.' (p. 4)

Upward—Transcending Boundaries

In order to make such breakthrough innovations, Elon Musk had to transcend several problems and criticisms. Everyone he spoke to advised him against his ideas. His friend even made him watch a series of videos of rockets blowing up. His success story is an example of how far one could transcend boundaries to reach where you want in life.

> One friend made me watch a bunch of videos of rockets blowing up . . . and then, failed three times. (p. 5)

Downward—Being Earthly

Elon Musk was a pragmatic, humble leader who made sure that his life and his work was useful not only to the people in his current generation but also for the future generations. He acknowledges the generosity of Mother Earth for having borne humans for so long.

> Earth has been around for 4 billion years, but civilization in terms of having writing has been about 10,000 years, and that's being generous. (p. 6)

Jeff Bezos—Amazon

The following are the transcripts of Jeff Bezos's commencement speech delivered at Princeton on 30 May 2010.[332]

Backward—Historical Consciousness

Jeff Bezos begins his speech with an interesting incident from the past. He recollects his childhood days he spent with his grandparents and the important lesson he learnt from his grandfather, which formed the basis of his core principles.

> He gently and calmly said, 'Jeff, one day you'll understand that it's harder to be kind than clever.'

Forward—Futuristic Vision

Jeff Bezos explains the kind of inventions the future will witness. Amazing and extraordinary inventions like engineering lives itself are in store for the future.

> Your smarts will come in handy because you will travel in a land of marvels.

Rightward—Authority

The most authoritative and life-changing decision of Jeff Bezos was to quit a great job and follow his passion. He is what he is today because of that choice he made. Life is all about taking courage to authoritatively make such powerful decisions.

> I took the less safe path to follow my passion, and I'm proud of that choice.

Leftward—Affective Maturity

Jeff Bezos mentions how mature and emotionally intelligent his wife was when he wanted to quit his job and pursue his start-up. Though they had just begun their life together and with most start-ups failing, his wife, MacKenzie, was mature enough to support his start-up idea.

> I'd always wanted to be an inventor, and she wanted me to follow my passion.

Inward—Inner Attitude

Jeff Bezos suggests that learning the difference between choices and gifts is very important in order to develop the right attitude. One may be gifted with talents and knowledge, but the choices one makes is what decides the journey of life. The right attitude to make the right choices is very important instead of being overwhelmed with the gifts we have.

> You can seduce yourself with your gifts if you're not careful, and if you do, it'll probably be to the detriment of your choices.

Outward—Being Productive

Jeff Bezos had always had innovative ideas and had also successfully implemented his ideas since his childhood. Realising the potential of the rapidly growing web usage, he innovatively thought of an online bookstore with millions of books. His innovative idea took him places as he was able to successfully implement it.

> I got the idea to start Amazon 16 years ago . . . As a young boy, I'd been a garage inventor.

Upward—Transcending Boundaries

Jeff Bezos encourages the audience to transcend boundaries and make wise choices in life. He mentions that one should transcend criticisms, rejections, and troubles and live life contentedly without any regrets. He feels it is better to make mistakes and go beyond instead of staying guarded without doing anything.

> Will you choose a life of ease, or a life of service and adventure?

Downward—Being Earthly

Jeff Bezos encourages the audience to be humble in spite of having so many gifts and talents. It is how we put our gifts to use which is more important than being proud of the gifts. The important lesson he learnt as a child was that kindness is the most important virtue.

> And will you take pride in your gifts or pride in your choices?

REFERENCES

Aswathappa, K. (1997, 2002). *Human Resource and Personnel Management.* New Delhi: Tata McGraw-Hill Publishing Company Limited.

Boxall, Peter et al. (2007). *Oxford Handbook of Human Resource Management.* Oxford: Oxford University Press.

Collins, Jim, and Jerry I. Porras (1994, 2002). *Built to Last: Successful Habits of Visionary Companies.* New York: Collins Business Essentials.

Delery, J., and D. Doty (1996). 'Modes of Theorising in Strategic Human Resource Management: Tests of Universalistic, Contingency, and Configurational Performance Predictions'. *Academy of Management Journal* 39/4: 802–835.

Eilbert, H. (1959). 'The Development of Personnel Management in the United States'. *Business History Review* 33/5: 115–30.

Evans, P. et al. (2002). *The Global Challenge: Frameworks for International Human Resource Management.* New York: McGraw-Hill.

Farnham, D. (1921). *America vs. Europe in Industry.* New York: Ronald Press.

Kaufman, Bruce E. (2007). 'The Development of HRM in Historical and International Perspective'. In Peter Boxall et al. (eds). *The Oxford Handbook of Human Resource Management*, 19–47. Oxford: Oxford University Press.

Kellerman, B. (2012). *The End of Leadership.* Harper Business.

Kelly, M. (2012). *Owning Our Future: The Emerging Ownership Revolution*. Berret-Koehler.

Kolb, D. A. (1984). *Experiential Learning: Experience as the Source of Learning and Development*. Englewood Cliffs, NJ: Prentice-Hall.

Macduffie, J. P., and J. F. Krafcik (1992). 'Integrating Technology and Human Resources for High Performance Manufacturing: Evidence from the High Performance Auto-Industry'. In T. Kochan and M. Useem (eds). *Transforming Organisations*. New York: Oxford University Press.

Mahoney, T., and J. Deckop (1986). 'Evolution of Concept and Practice in Personnel Administration/Human Resource Management [PA/HRM]'. *Journal of Management* 12: 223–41.

Ostroff, C. (1995). 'Human Resource Management: Ideas and Trends in Personnel'. *CCH Incorporated* (June) 21: 356.

Ovans, A. (2012). 'When No One's in Charge'. *Harvard Business Review* (May 2012), 112–113.

Pfeffer, J. (1994). *Competitive Advantage through People: Unleashing the Power of the Work Force*. Boston, MA: Harvard Business School Press.

—— (1999). *The Human Equation: Building Profits by Putting People First*. Boston, MA: Harvard Business School Press.

Rao, T. V. (2006, 1999). *HRD Audit: Evaluating the Human Resource Function for Business Improvement*. New Delhi/Thousand Oaks/London: Response Books.

Rego, A. et al. (2014). *The Virtues of Leadership: Contemporary Challenges for Global Managers*. Oxford: Oxford University Press.

Ross, C. (2012). *The Leaderless Revolution: How Ordinary People Will Take Power and Change Politics in the 21st Century*. Blue Rider Press.

Schultz, P. W. (2002). 'Inclusion with Nature: The Psychology of Human-Nature Relations'. In P. W. Schmuck and W. P. Schultz (eds). *Psychology of Sustainable Development*, 62–78. Norwell, MA: Kluwer Academic.

Spencer, E. (1984). *Management and Labour in Imperial Germany*. New Brunswick, NJ: Rutgers University Press.

Strauss, E. (2001). 'HRM in the United States: Correcting Some British Impressions'. *International Journal of Human Resource Management* (September) 12: 873–97.

Welbourne, T., and A. Andrews (1996). 'Predicting Performance of Initial Public Offering Firms: Should HRM Be the Equation?' *Academy of Management Journal* 39: 839–919.

Yeung, A. K., and Bob Berman (1997). 'Adding Value through Human Resources: Reorienting Human Resource Measurement to Drive Business Performance.' *Human Resource Management* 36/3: 321–335.

ENDNOTES

Introduction

1. 'Carmakers Turn to Expats to Steer Their Business in India', Knowledge@Wharton (7 February 2013).
2. To substantiate this, he provides two examples: the Brazilian city of Porto Alegre in which participatory budgeting process has achieved tangible growth in education and economy and the New Orleans Restoration Project in which four thousand city residents scattered across the country came back in a virtual 'community congress' and evolved a Unified New Orleans Plan. For more details, read Ross (2012).
3. See *Harvard Business Review* (March 2014), 105–109.
4. Anthropology is a study of human persons: her thinking, feeling, and behaviour. Broadly speaking, anthropology deals with culture and society. It tries to understand and comprehend the ways in which people organise themselves as individuals and as different communities. To learn about the basics of anthropology, read Marvin Harris, *Culture, People, Nature: An Introduction to General Anthropology* (Allyn & Bacon, 1997); Clifford Geertz, After the Fact: Two Countries, Four Decades, One Anthropologist (Cambridge, MA: Harvard University Press, 1995); Clifford Geertz, *The Interpretation of Cultures* (New York: Basic Books, 1973); Marvin Harris, *Culture, People, Nature: An Introduction to General* Anthropology (7th edn, Boston: Allyn & Bacon, 1997).
5. The word *anthropos* refers to 'human person'. It is one of the social sciences. People who appear for Indian Administrative Services (IAS) are given anthropology as one of the papers. This is to mean that an IAS officer should understand people and cultures.
6. The method originated in the fieldwork of social anthropologists, especially Bronisław Malinowski and his students in Britain, the students of Franz Boas in the US, and in the urban research of the Chicago School of Sociology. See

K. M. DeWalt, B. R. DeWalt, and C. B. Wayland, 'Participant Observation', in H. R. Bernard, ed., Handbook of Methods in Cultural Anthropology (Walnut Creek, CA: Alta Mira Press), 259–299.

[7] See Nancy J. Adler, and Susan Bartholomew, 'Academic and Professional Communities of Discourse: Generating Knowledge on Transnational Human Resource Management', *Journal of International Business Studies*, 23 (1992), 551ff.

[8] K. H. Roberts, 'On Looking at an Elephant: An Evaluation of Cross-Cultural Research Related to Organizations', in Malcolm Warner, ed., *Comparative Management: Critical Perspectives on Business and Management*, 1 (Routledge, 2001).

[9] See a detailed study on studying organisations and their behaviour. See P. M. Blau, 'Organizations: Theories', in D. L. Sills, ed., *International Encyclopedia of Social Sciences* (Macmillan, NY, 1968).

[10] ABB company after the merger in 1987—Brown Boveri from Switzerland and the Swedish firm ASEA—the professionals and executives placed focus on communication skills that helped to rally the human resources to achieve the set objectives. They were able to achieve them in spite of a large network of processes, projects, and partners mostly due to the HR skills of its executives. Read K. Bareham, and C. Heimer, *ABB: The Dancing Giant* (FT/Pitman, 1998).

[11] See the case study of ABB company in Paul Banfield and Rebecca Kay, *Introduction to Human Resource Management* (Oxford: Oxford University Press, 2008), 27–28.

[12] See Banfield and Kay, *Introduction to Human Resource Management*, 27–28.

[13] See Thomas L. Friedman, *Hot, Flat, and Crowded: Why the World Needs a Green Revolution—and How We Can Renew Our Global Future* (London: Penguin, 2008).

[14] For a very good discussion on this theme, read Alex Nicholls, ed., *Social Entrepreneurship: New Models of Sustainable Social Change* (Oxford: Oxford University Press, 2008).

[15] Quoted in Banfield and Kay, *Introduction to Human Resource Management*, 4.

[16] Manuel London, ed., *Evolving Practices in Human Resource Management: Responses to a Changing World of Work* (San Francisco: Jossey-Bass, 1999), 176.

[17] Stephen Gibb, *Human Resource Development: Process, Practices and Perspectives* (Hampshire, UK, and New York: Palgrave Macmillan, 2008 [2002]), 29ff.

[18] See Gary Hamel, *The Future of Management* (Boston: Harvard Business School Press, 2007), 4–14.

[19] The Chattered Management Institute has published its twenty-five-page report that is downloadable. See http://www.managers.org.uk.

[20] See *The Guardian* (14 March 2008), 9.

[21] K. Aswathappa, *Human Resource and Personnel Management* (New Delhi: Tata

McGraw-Hill Publishing Company Limited, 2000), 5.

22 For detailed study of training and development in HRM, see G. M. Piskurich et al., eds, *The ASTD Handbook of Training Design and Delivery* (New York: McGraw-Hill, 2000).
23 See Gibb, *Human Resource Development*, 6–8.
24 See Hamel, *Future of Management*, 55–57.
25 Ibid. 23.
26 I am using the work of Matt Ridley heavily to explain that in the history of innovation in the use of energy, we have experienced a huge improvement in human life and dramatic changes in the society. See Matt Ridley, *How Innovation Works* (London: 4th Estate, 2020), 13–49.
27 Vaclav Smil, *Energy and Civilisation: A History* (Cambridge, MA: MIT Press, 2017), 1.
28 Cited in Smil, *Energy and Civilisation*, 2. See Ostwald Wilhelm, *Der energetische Imperativ* (Leipzing: Akademische Verlagesslschaft).
29 George Orwell, *The Road to Wigan Pier* (London: Victor Gollancz, 1937), 18.
30 Leslie White, 'Energy and Evolution of Culture', *American Anthropologist*, 45:335–356.
31 Ridley, *How Innovation Works*, 13–49.
32 Ibid. 25.
33 L. T. C Rolt, *Thomas Newcomen: The Prehistory of the Steam Engine* (David and Charles/Mcdonald, 1963). And see also Ken Smith, *Turbinia: The Story of Parsons and His Ocean Greyhound* (Tyne Bridge Publishing, 2009).
34 Ridley, *How Innovation Works*, 36–41.
35 World Economic Forum, 'Energy Vision', http://www3.weforum.org/docs/WEF_EN_EnergyEconomicGrowth_IndustryAgenda_2012.pdf, accessed 10 May 2021.
36 M. H. Hansell. *Animal Architecture* (Oxford: Oxford University Press, 2005); T. Sanz, J. Call, and C. Boesch, eds., *Tools Use in Animals: Cognition and Ecology* (Cambridge: Cambridge University Press, 2013).
37 S. Manikutty, ed., *The Essence of Leadership: Explorations from Literature* (New Delhi: Bloomsbury, 2015), 2.
38 See Erich Fromm, *The Art of Loving* (New York: Bantom Book, 1972), 6ff for similar approach to the human condition from a perspective of psychoanalysis.
39 I am using the simplified idea of a dynamo to suit the purpose here. The dynamo theory is divided into kinematic theory and fully self-consistent theory; kinematic theory concerns situations in which the velocity field is given, and fully self-consistent theory uses MHD equations to deduce the magnetic and velocity fields. Specific treatment is given to the conditions of symmetry and brute force in dynamos, and descriptions of alpha-squared and alpha-omega dynamos are given, as well as one for galactic dynamos. The Maximally efficient generation

approach and the WKBJ approach are set forth, and some applications are proposed. The methods discussed are of use in the analysis of slow, fast, and turbulent dynamos and permit the examination of dynamos in the context of stability theory. For a scientific look at the theory of dynamo, see P. H. Roberts and A. M. Soward, 'Dynamo Theory', *Annual Review of Fluid Mechanics*, 24 (A92-45082 19-34) (Palo Alto, CA: Annual Reviews Inc., 1992), 459–512.

40 For a detailed discussion on competence, see http://www.surveyorsboard.com.au/pdfdocs/WhatIsCompetence.pdf.
41 D. K. Rigby, J. Sutherland, and H. Takeuchi, 'Embracing Agile', *Harvard Business Review* (May 2016), 40–48, 50.
42 D. Rigby, S. Elk, and S. Berez, *Doing Agile Right* (Harvard: Harvard Business Review Press, 2020), 93–110.

Backward—Historical Consciousness

43 Refer to https://www.dictionary.com/browse/history.
44 'Timeless Leadership', *Harvard Business Review* (March 2008), 45ff.
45 J. J. Seaman and G. D. Smith, 'Your Company's History as a Leadership Tool', *Harvard Business Review*, 90/12 (2012), 44–52.
46 Ibid. 5.
47 Mayo, 'The Value of Leaders Learning from History', *Harvard Business Review* (2007), https://hbr.org/2007/12/what-i-learned.
48 Giuliano Maielli, 'Counterfactuals, Superfactuals and the Problematic Relationship between Business Management and the Past', *Management & Organizational History*, 2/4 (2007), 275–294.
49 Section on career, *The Times* (3 April 2008), 5.
50 R. Suddaby, W. M. Foster, and C. Quinn Trank, 'Rhetorical History as a Source of Competitive Advantage', in *The Globalization of Strategy Research* (Emerald Group Publishing Limited, 2010), 147–173.
51 R. Suddaby, W. M. Foster, and C. Quinn Trank, 'Remembering: Rhetorical History as Identity Work', in *The Oxford Handbook of Organizational Identity* (2016), 297–316.
52 M. Mordhorst, A. Popp, R. Suddaby, and D. Wadhwani, 'Uses of the Past: History and Memory in Organizations and Organizing', *Organization Studies*, 36 (2015), 1277–1280.
53 D. A. Gioia, M. Schultz, and K. G. Corley, 'Organizational Identity, Image, and Adaptive Instability', *Academy of Management Review*, 25/1 (2000), 63–81; P. H. Hansen, 'Organizational Culture and Organizational Change: The Transformation of Savings Banks in Denmark, 1965–1990', *Enterprise & Society*, 8/4 (2007), 920–953; M. Anteby and V. Molnar, 'Collective Memory Meets Organizational Identity: Remembering to Forget in a Firm's Rhetorical History',

Academy of Management Journal, 55/3 (2012), 515–540; M. Mordhorst, 'Arla and Danish National Identity—Business History as Cultural History', *Business History*, 56/1 (2014), 116–133.

54 M. Rowlinson, C. Booth, P. Clark, A. Delahaye, and S. Procter, 'Social Remembering and Organizational Memory', *Organization Studies*, 31/1 (2010), 69–87.

55 Suddaby, Foster, and Quinn Trank, 'Rhetorical History as a Source of Competitive Advantage', 147–173; M. Schultz and T. Hernes, 'A Temporal Perspective on Organizational Identity', *Organization Science*, 24/1 (2013), 1–21.

56 A. Popp and R. Holt, 'The Presence of Entrepreneurial Opportunity', *Business History*, 55/1 (2013a), 9–28; A. Popp and R. Holt, 'Entrepreneurship and Being: The Case of the Shaws', *Entrepreneurship & Regional Development*, 25/1–2 (2013b), 52–68.

57 M. Khaire and R. D. Wadhwani, 'Changing Landscapes: The Construction of Meaning and Value in a New Market Category—Modern Indian Art', *Academy of Management Journal*, 53/6 (2010), 1281–1304.

58 P. H. Hansen, 'Networks, Narratives, and New Markets: The Rise and Decline of Danish Modern Furniture Design, 1930–1970', *Business History Review*, 80/3 (2006), 449–483; P. H. Hansen, 'Cobranding Product and Nation: Danish Modern Furniture and Denmark in the United States, 1940–1970', in *Trademarks, Brands, and Competitiveness* (Routledge, 2010), 95–120.

59 D. Kirsch, M. Moeen, and R. D. Wadhwani, 'Historicism and Industry Emergence: Industry Knowledge from Pre-Emergence to Stylized Fact', in *Organizations in Time: History, Theory, Methods*, 217 (2014).

60 T. Schieder, 'The Role of Historical Consciousness in Political Action', *History and Theory*, 17/4 (1978), 1–18.

61 J. Rüsen, 'Historical Consciousness: Narrative Structure, Moral Function, and Ontogenetic Development', in P. Seixas, ed., *Theorizing Historical Consciousness* (Toronto, Canada: University of Toronto Press, 2004).

62 S. Ahonen, 'Historical Consciousness: A Viable Paradigm for History Education?' *Journal of Curriculum Studies*, 37/6 (2005), 697–707.

63 Rüsen, 'Historical Consciousness', 699.

64 Schieder, 'Role of Historical Consciousness in Political Action', 1.

65 A. Glencross, 'Historical Consciousness in International Relations Theory: A Hidden Disciplinary Dialogue', conference paper presented in Millennium Conference, University of Aberdeen, 1.

66 W. Lorenz, F. Coussée, and G. Verschelden, 'Historical Consciousness in Youth Work and Adult Education', *Social Work & Society*, 8/1 (2010), https://www.socwork.net/sws/article/view/21/60, 32–45.

67 A. Kieser, 'Why Organization Theory Needs Historical Analyses—and How This Should Be Performed', *Organization Science*, 5/4 (1994), 608–620.

68 R. Suddaby, 'Toward a Historical Consciousness: Following the Historic Turn in Management Thought', *M@n@gement*, 19/1 (2016), 46–60.
69 Ibid. 58.
70 M. Rowlinson and J. Hassard, 'The Invention of Corporate Culture: A History of the Histories of Cadbury', *Human Relations*, 46/3 (1993), 299–326; M. Ericson, 'Exploring the Future, Exploiting the Past', *Journal of Management History*, 12/2 (2006), 121–136; W. M. Foster, R. Suddaby, A. Minkus, and E. Wiebe, 'History as Social Memory Assets: The Example of Tim Hortons', *Management & Organizational History*, 6/1 (2011), 101–120; Anteby and Molnar, 'Collective Memory Meets Organizational Identity', 515–540.
71 P. H. Hansen, 'Business History: A Cultural and Narrative Approach', *Business History Review*, 86/4 (2012), 693–717; M. Mordhorst, 'From Counterfactual History to Counter-Narrative History', *Management & Organizational History*, 3/1 (2008), 5–26; Mordhorst, 'Arla and Danish National Identity', 116–133; R. Kroeze and S. Keulen, 'Leading a Multinational Is History in Practice: The Use of Invented Traditions and Narratives at AkzoNobel, Shell, Philips and ABN AMRO', *Business History*, 55/8 (2013), 1265–1287.
72 Suddaby, Foster, and Quinn Trank, 'Remembering: Rhetorical History as Identity Work', 297–316.
73 R. D. Wadhwani, and M. Bucheli, 'The Future of the Past in Management and Organization Studies', in *Organizations in Time: History, Theory, Methods* (2014), 3–32.
74 R. Koselleck, *Futures Past: On the Semantics of Historical Time* (New York: Columbia University Press, 2004).
75 C. Lubinski, 'From "History as Told" to "History as Experienced": Contextualizing the Uses of the Past', *Organization Studies*, 39/12 (2018), 1785–1809.
76 G. H. Frímannsson, 'Moral and Historical Consciousness', *Historical Encounters: A Journal of Historical Consciousness, Historical Cultures, and History Education*, 4/1 (2017), 14–22.
77 Seaman and Smith, 'Your Company's History as a Leadership Tool', 44–52.
78 Ibid.
79 Ibid. 6.
80 Ibid.
81 Ibid.
82 Ibid.
83 Ibid. 5.
84 The original Starbucks was founded jointly by English teacher Jerry Baldwin, history teacher Zev Siegel, and writer Gordon Bowker in Seattle, Washington, in 1971. The original Starbucks location was at 2000 Western Avenue from 1971–1976. Initially, they purchased green coffee beans from another outlet (Peet's),

but later, they began buying directly from coffee growers. Entrepreneur Howard Schultz joined the company in 1982 and, after a trip to Milan, advised that the company sell coffee and espresso drinks as well as beans. The owners rejected this idea, believing that getting into the beverage business would distract the company from its primary focus. To them, coffee was something to be prepared in the home. Certain that there was much money to be made selling drinks to on-the-go Americans, Schultz started the Il Giornale coffee bar chain in 1985. Read Howard Schultz and Dori Jones Yang, *Pour Your Heart into It: How Starbucks Built a Company One Cup at a Time* (New York: Hyperion, 1997). See *Time* (21 April 2008), 41ff about the comeback story. In 1987, the original owners of Starbucks sold the Starbucks chain to Schultz's Il Giornale, which rebranded the Il Giornale outlets as Starbucks and quickly began to expand. Starbucks opened its first locations outside Seattle at Waterfront Station in Vancouver, British Columbia, Canada (which now has more locations than anywhere in the world).

Forward—Vision

85 George Stroup is one of my very good friends from whom I learnt a lot on entrepreneurial leadership. I did my doctorate with him in 1999–2003 and have frequented to the shops often. During our times in pubs, he shared a lot about his business. He is a dreamer, but he knows as well how to translate the dreams into reality. He later went to London School of Economics to read first for MBA and later for law. I will be using some of that material in the book I am writing on entrepreneurship.

86 Hamel, *Future of Management*, 249.

87 T. Kenny, 'From Vision to Reality through Values', *Management Development Review*, 7/3 (1994), 17–20, https://search.proquest.com/docview/225229988?accountid=39490.

88 R. Ashkenas and B. Manville, 'You Don't Have to Be CEO to Be a Visionary Leader', *Harvard Business Review* (2019), https://hbr.org/2019/04/you-dont-have-to-be-ceo-to-be-a-visionary-leader.

89 Seaman and Smith, 'Your Company's History as a Leadership Tool', 44–52.

90 Ashkenas and Manville, 'You Don't Have to Be CEO to Be a Visionary Leader', 3.

91 Seaman and Smith, 'Your Company's History as a Leadership Tool', 44–52.

92 F. Westley and H. Mintzberg, 'Visionary Leadership and Strategic Management', *Strategic Management Journal*, 10/S1 (1989), 17–32.

93 Seaman and Smith, 'Your Company's History as a Leadership Tool', 44–52.

94 S. Kantabutra and G. C. Avery, 'Follower Effects in the Visionary Leadership Process', *Journal of Business & Economics Research (JBER)*, 4/5 (2011).

95 C. M. Taylor, C. J. Cornelius, and K. Colvin, 'Visionary Leadership and Its

Relationship to Organizational Effectiveness', *Leadership & Organization Development Journal*, 35/6 (2014), 566–583.

[96] S. Jeffrey, '10 Attributes of Visionary Leaders' (2017), https://www.business2community.com/leadership/10-attributes-visionary-leaders-01781989.

[97] M. J. Stoner-Zemel, 'Visionary Leadership, Management, and High Performing Work Units: An Analysis of Workers' Perceptions', unpublished doctoral dissertation, University of Massachusetts, Amherst, MA, 1988).

[98] D. E. Berlew, 'Leadership and Organizational Excitement', *California Management Review*, 17/2 (1974), 21–30.

[99] Westley and Mintzberg, 'Visionary Leadership and Strategic Management', 17–32.

[100] M. Smolenyak and A. Majumdar, 'What Is Leadership?' *The Journal for Quality and Participation*, 15/4 (1992), 28, https://search.proquest.com/docview/219162945?accountid=39490.

[101] D. Lavinsky, 'Are You a Visionary Business Leader?' *Forbes* (2013), https://www.forbes.com/sites/davelavinsky/2013/04/26/are-you-a-visionary-business-leader/#177815237bbf.

[102] 'Ten Qualities Shared by Visionary Business Leaders', AllBusiness, https://www.allbusiness.com/ten-qualities-shared-by-visionary-business-leaders-4113289-1.html.

[103] Westley and Mintzberg, 'Visionary Leadership and Strategic Management', 17–32.

[104] Ibid.
[105] Ibid.
[106] Ibid.
[107] Ibid.
[108] Ibid.
[109] Banfield and Kay, *Introduction to Human Resource Management*, 217.
[110] Ibid. 47.
[111] For a detailed discussion on features of effective HR planning, see Banfield and Kay, *Introduction to Human Resource Management*, 219.

Rightward—Authority and Power

[112] Refer to https://www.scribd.com/doc/24544182/the-Word-Authority-Derives-From-the-Latin-Word-Auctoritas for more details.

[113] Read the essay of Nancy Gibbs, 'Cool Running', *Time* (17 January 2008), http://www.time.com/time/magazine/article/0,9171,1704675,00.html, accessed 14 April 2008.

[114] Fiona Bowie, *Anthropology of Religion* (Oxford: Blackwell, 2005), 37ff.

[115] Thomas Bertels, ed., *Rath & Strong's Six Sigma Leadership Handbook* (Hoboken,

NJ: John Wiley & Sons, 2003), 4.
116 A. J. Grimes, 'Authority, Power, Influence and Social Control: A Theoretical Synthesis', *Academy of Management Review*, 3/4 (1978), 724–735.
117 T. Gautschi, 'Don't Confuse Authority, Power, and Politics', *Design News*, 52/9 (1997), 202, https://search.proquest.com/docview/235251579?accountid=39490.
118 P. Aghion and J. Tirole, 'Formal and Real Authority in Organizations', *Journal of Political Economy*, 105/1 (1997), 1–29.
119 R. M. Emerson, 'Power-Dependence Relations', *American Sociological Review* (1962), 31–41.
120 C. W. Mills, *The Sociological Imagination* (Oxford University Press, 1959), 36.
121 American Management Association, 'The Five Attributes of Authority', https://www.amanet.org/articles/the-five-attributes-of-authority/.
122 Karel S. San Juan, 'Re-Imagining Power in Leadership: Reflection, Integration, and Servant-Leadership', *The International Journal of Servant-Leadership*, 1/1 (2005), 187–209, https://search.proquest.com/docview/2221116501?accountid=39490.
123 A. C. Filley and A. J. Grimes, 'The Bases of Power in Decision Processes', *Academy of Management Proceedings*, 1967/1 (1967), 133–160.
124 J. R. P. French and B. Raven, 'The Bases of Social Power', in D. Cartwright, ed., *Studies of Social Power* (Ann Arbor, MI: University of Michigan, Institute for Social Research, 1959), 150–167.
125 F. C. Lunenburg, 'Power and Leadership: An Influence Process', *International Journal of Management, Business, and Administration*, 15/1 (2012), 1–9.
126 H. Aguinis, M. S. Nesler, B. M. Quigley, and J. T. Tedeschi, 'Perceptions of Power: A Cognitive Perspective', *Social Behavior and Personality: An International Journal*, 22/4 (1994), 377–384.
127 D. A. Gioia and H. P. Sims Jr, 'Perceptions of Managerial Power as a Consequence of Managerial Behavior and Reputation', *Journal of Management*, 9/1 (1983), 7–24.
128 D. J. Brass and M. E. Burkhardt, 'Potential Power and Power Use: An Investigation of Structure and Behavior', *Academy of Management Journal*, 36/3 (1993), 441–470.
129 S. M. Farmer and H. Aguinis, 'Accounting for Subordinate Perceptions of Supervisor Power: An Identity-Dependence Model', *Journal of Applied Psychology*, 90/6 (2005), 1069.
130 C. Chris, 'The 30 Most Powerful People in International Business', International Business Degree Guide (2017), https://www.internationalbusinessguide.org/powerful-people-international-business/.
131 Ibid.
132 Ibid.
133 Ibid.
134 J. B. Anderson, 'Persuasive Leadership', *Executive Excellence*, 6/12 (1989), 10,

https://search.proquest.com/docview/204529657?accountid=39490.
135 M. Sanborn, 'Are You a Leader or a Manager?' *American Agent & Broker*, 68/12 (1996), 43–47, https://search.proquest.com/docview/194943482?accountid=39490.
136 C. Weedon, *Feminist Practice and Post-Structuralist Theory* (Oxford: Basil Blackwell, 1987), 108. Read for a detailed discussion on discourse by Michael Foucault, *Archaeology of Knowledge* (New York: Pantheon, 1972) and 'Two Lectures', in Colin Gordon, ed., *Power/Knowledge: Selected Interviews* (New York: Pantheon, 1980).
137 Weedon, *Feminist Practice and Post-Structuralist Theory*, 113.
138 See http://www.bmw.com/com/en/insights/corporation/bmwgroup/content.html.
139 Read Kevin Frieberg and Jackie Freiberg, *NUTS and GUTS*, http://in.rediff.com/money/2005/apr/12guest2.htm, accessed 16 April 2008.
140 Visit http://www.tybro.com/html/words_of_power-_healing.html?gclid=CPfa48Xu4ZICFQZZMAodBifp5g (accessed 17 April 2008).
141 Https://www.theguardian.com/world/2020/may/31/jacinda-ardern-political-leaders-can-be-both-empathetic-and-strong (accessed 3 January 2021).
142 Lane Cooper, trans., *The Rhetoric of Aristotle* (New York: Appleton-Century-Crofts, 1932/1960). Also see H. Wichelns, 'The Literary Criticism of Oratory', in D. C. Bryant, ed., *The Rhetorical Idiom: Essays in Rhetoric, Oratory, Language, and Drama* (Ithaca, NY: Cornell University Press, 1925; repr. 1958), 5–42.
143 *Logos* (Greek λόγος) is used in philosophy mainly. Its origin is from the verb legō (λέγω): 'to count, tell, say, or speak'. The primary meaning of *logos* is 'something said; by implication a subject, topic of discourse, or reasoning'. Secondary meanings are 'logic' and 'reasoning'. See Henry Liddell and Robert Scott, *A Greek-English Lexicon* (9th edn, Oxford: Clarendon Press, 1996).
144 Cited in A. Rego et al., *The Virtues of Leadership: Contemporary Challenges for Global Managers* (Oxford: Oxford University Press, 2012), 69.
145 Francesca Gino of Harvard Business School and Adam Grant of Wharton School have done research on the power of gratitude to conclude that gratitude is a key quality of a successful leader. Read Francesco Gino, 'Be Grateful More Often', *Harvard Business Review* (26 November 2013). And see also Adam M. Grant and Francesco Gino, 'A Little Thanks Goes a Long Way: Explaining Why Gratitude Expressions Motivate Prosocial Behaviour', *Journal of Personality and Social Psychology*, 98/6 (2010), 946–955.

Leftward—Affective Maturity

146 E. J. Alpenfels, 'The Anthropology and Social Significance of the Human Hand', *Artificial Limbs*, 2/2 (1955), 4–21.
147 Read Randy Pausch and Jeffrey Zaslow, *The Last Lecture* (New York: Hyperion,

2008). Alternatively, visit Randy's website at http://download.srv.cs.cmu. edu/~pausch/news/index.html.
148   C. Lutz and G. M. White, 'The Anthropology of Emotions', *Annual Review of Anthropology*, 15/1 (1986), 405–436.
149   P. Salovey and J. D. Mayer, 'Emotional Intelligence', *Imagination, Cognition and Personality*, 9/3 (1990), 185–211.
150   Daniel Goleman, *Emotional Intelligence* (New York: Bantam Books, 1995).
151   K. Wiens and D. Rowell, 'How to Embrace Change Using Emotional Intelligence?' *Harvard Business Review* (2018), https://hbr.org/2018/12/how-to-embrace-change-using-emotional-intelligence.
152   Ibid.
153   M. T. Dasborough and N. M. Ashkanasy, 'Emotion and Attribution of Intentionality in Leader-Member Relationships', *The Leadership Quarterly*, 13/5 (2002), 615–634, https://doi.org/10.1016/S1048-9843(02)00147-9.
154   J. M. George, 'Emotions and Leadership: The Role of Emotional Intelligence', *Human Relations*, 53/8 (2000), 1027–1055.
155   Salovey and Mayer, 'Emotional Intelligence', 189.
156   J. McClellan, K. Levitt, and G. DiClementi, 'Emotional Intelligence and Positive Organizational Leadership: A Conceptual Model for Positive Emotional Influence', *Journal of Behavioral and Applied Management*, 17/3 (2017), 197, 2626.
157   Ibid.
158   D. Goleman and R. E. Boyatzis, 'Emotional Intelligence Has 12 Elements: Which Do You Need to Work On?' *Harvard Business Review* (2017), https://hbr.org/2017/02/emotional-intelligence-has-12-elements-which-do-you-need-to-work-on.
159   Denis Diderot, a French philosopher, in his *Philosophical Thoughts*, argues a case for a fine blend of reason with feeling. Read P. A. Kurt Ballstadt, *Diderot: Natural Philosopher* (Oxford: Voltaire Foundation, 2008).
160   Jerry Porras et al., *Success Built to Last* (Harlow, England: Wharton School Publishing, 2007), 39.
161   McClellan, Levitt, and DiClementi, 'Emotional Intelligence and Positive Organizational Leadership'.
162   M. Brusman, 'Leadership Development through Emotional Intelligence and Meditation', *Talent Development*, 68/9 (2014), 70–71, https://search.proquest.com/docview/1635069568?accountid=39490.
163   R. Akila and N. Thangavel, 'Impact of Team Leaders' Emotional Intelligence Competence on Teams' Emotional Intelligence', *International Journal on Leadership*, 1/1 (2013), 7.
164   K. Dearborn, 'Studies in Emotional Intelligence Redefine Our Approach to Leadership Development', *Public Personnel Management*, 31/4 (2002), 523–530.
165   S. Holt and S. Jones, 'Emotional Intelligence and Organizational Performance:

Implications for Performance Consultants and Educators', *Performance Improvement*, 44/10 (2005), 15–21.

166. H. Vasudevan and N. Mahadi, 'Emotional Intelligence, Commitment and Climate in Organizations: Bridging Contribution and Practical Implication', *Review of Integrative Business and Economics Research*, 6 (2017), 202.
167. A. E. Gordon, *Emotional Intelligence as an Antecedent of Leader-Member Exchange Relationships and Leader Effectiveness* (Order No. 3277253), ABI/INFORM Collection (304740876), https://search.proquest.com/docview/304740876?accountid=39490.
168. L. Gardner and C. Stough, 'Examining the Relationship between Leadership and Emotional Intelligence in Senior Level Managers', *Leadership & Organization Development Journal*, 23/2 (2002), 68–78.
169. 'How 5 Emotionally Intelligent CEOs Handle Their Power', Pagely blog, https://pagely.com/blog/emotionally-intelligent-ceos/.
170. Ibid.
171. Ibid.
172. Ibid.
173. J. Bowlby, *Attachment and Loss*, 1 (2nd edn, New York: Basic Books, 1999).
174. There are many works that discuss inordinate attachments. The origin of the term comes from the *Spiritual Exercises* of St Ignatius of Loyola. For helpful discussion related to our purpose here, see John English, *In Choosing Life: Significance of Personal Life in Decision Making* (New York: Paulist Press, 1978).
175. Read stories of personal transformation at http://www.personaltransformation.com/transform.html (accessed 23 April 2008).
176. Fritz Perls, 'Four Lectures', in J. Fagan and I. L. Shepherd, eds, *GesaltTherapy Now* (New York: Harper Colophon, 1970).
177. See Charles Guignon, *Being Authentic* (London: Routledge, 2004), 147–160.
178. Ibid. 147–163.
179. My sources for the idea of conversations come from what Gadamer talks about open and free conversation. See Hans-Georg Gadamer, *Truth and Method*, trans., J. Weinsheimer and D. G. Marshall (2nd edn, New York: Cross Road, 1989), 110–122.

Inward—Inner Attitude

180. R. E. Petty and P. Brinol, 'Attitude Change', in *Advanced Social Psychology: The State of the Science* (2010), 1, 217–259.
181. T. K. Altmann, 'Attitude: A Concept Analysis', *Nursing Forum*, 43/3 (Malden, USA: Blackwell Publishing Inc., 2008), 144–150.
182. I. Ajzen and M. Fishbein, 'Attitude-Behavior Relations: A Theoretical Analysis and Review of Empirical Research', *Psychological Bulletin*, 84/5 (1977), 888.

183 Ibid. 889.
184 M. Valcour, 'Motivating People Starts with Having the Right Attitude', *Harvard Business Review* (2017), https://hbr.org/2017/03/motivating-people-starts-with-having-the-right-attitude.
185 B. Heath Ansley, *The 'Right Attitude': What Is It and Can It Be Taught?* (2007) (Order No. MR26426), ABI/INFORM Collection (304719487), https://search.proquest.com/docview/304719487?accountid=39490.
186 Ibid.
187 B. Bartlein, 'Management: Hire for Attitude, Train for Skill', *Commercial Law Bulletin*, 17/6 (2002), 20, https://search.proquest.com/docview/201110747?accountid=39490.
188 Quoted in Porras et al., *Success Built to Last*, 50. Read also Maya Angelou, *I Know Why the Caged Bird Sings* (New York, NY: Random House, 1969).
189 R. Worrall, 'It's All about Attitude', *NZ Business*, 13/3 (1999), 43, https://search.proquest.com/docview/204564772?accountid=39490.
190 Cf. Martin Fishbein, 'An Investigation about Beliefs about an Object and the Attitude toward that Object', *Human Relations*, 16 (August 1963), 233–239.
191 E. Holly Buttner, Kevin B. Lowe, and Lenora Billings-Harris, 'The Influence of Organizational Diversity Orientation and Leader Attitude on Diversity Activities', *Journal of Managerial Issues*, 22 (September 2006). You can alternatively visit http://www.allbusiness.com/management/3911473-1.html.
192 B. George, P. Sims, A. N. McLean, and D. Mayer, 'Discovering Your Authentic Leadership', Harvard Business Review (2007), https://hbr.org/2007/02/discovering-your-authentic-leadership.
193 J. E. Henderson, 'Leader Authenticity: A Renewed Call for Research', *Journal of Leadership, Accountability and Ethics*, 12/2 (2015), 103–118, https://search.proquest.com/docview/1726786564?accountid=39490.
194 Ibid. 103.
195 M. Marič and M. Ferjan, 'Authentic Leaders and Their Employees' Power', *Scientific Papers of the University of Pardubice, Series D. Faculty of Economics and Administration*, 16 (2010), 200–212, https://search.proquest.com/docview/2265542482?accountid=39490.
196 S. N. Khan, 'Impact of Authentic Leaders on Organization Performance', *International Journal of Business and Management*, 5/12 (2010), 167–172.
197 Ibid.
198 F. Beddoes-Jones and S. Swailes, 'Authentic Leadership: Development of a New Three Pillar Model', *Strategic HR Review*, 14/3 (2015), 94–99, http://dx.doi.org/10.1108/SHR-04-2015-0032.
199 C. Vlachoutsicos, 'What Being an "Authentic Leader" Really Means', *Harvard Business Review* (2012), https://hbr.org/2012/12/what-being-an-authentic-leader-really-means.

200   C. Bielaszka-DuVernay, 'DNC Day1: Michelle Obama and Authentic Leadership', *Harvard Business Review* (2008), https://hbr.org/2008/08/michelle-obama.
201   Khan, 'Impact of Authentic Leaders on Organization Performance', 167–172.
202   Ibid.
203   Ibid.
204   Ibid.
205   Peter Goldie, *On Personality* (London: Routledge, 2004), 27–51. In addition, see J. Rusten, I. C. Cunningham, and A. D. Knox, eds/trans., *Characters* (Cambridge, MA: Harvard University Press, 1993), 95–97.
206   John Cottingham, *On the Meaning of Life* (London: Routledge, 2003), 103.
207   Aristotle links great character to virtue. His major emphasis is on having right feelings. Being right is also sometimes construed as appropriate behaviour. But what I mean here for leadership is that a leader of an organisation should be morally right to view the world as beautiful, do good things, and be truthful. Read Aristotle, *Nicomachean Ethics*, trans., Terence Irwin (Indianapolis: Hackett, 1985).
208   Cottingham, *On the Meaning of Life*, 60.
209   As quoted in Cottingham, *On the Meaning of Life*, 100.
210   Rego et al., *Virtues of Leadership*, 137.
211   Read Pierre Hadot, *Philosophy as a Way of Life* (Oxford, UK, and Cambridge, USA: Blackwell Publishers, 1995).
212   These lines I thump off while sipping my Irish cream coffee at Coffee Day in IIT-Madras (4.34 p.m., on 27 August 2008). I observe, in front of me, a girl and three boys trying to impress one another. It seems they are arguing over a lecture. None of them is ready to see sense in others' argument. Their faces show certain anxiety and unease. But suddenly, one boy leaves the place for some other work. After he had left, the boy and the girl sitting in front of me become totally relaxed, or what I prefer to call at ease. There is a grace in the ways they look at each other, and they do not argue. They share what they feel about the same issue. Why this difference? They love each other. They accept themselves as they are. This applies to leadership. You need to love the people whom you lead and accept them as they are. This comes from one's acceptance of the truth I am talking about—the gap.

Outward: Expressions and Productivity

213   K. M. Sherony, *Leader Emotional Expression and Leader-Member Exchange* (2002) (Order No. 3099851), ABI/INFORM Collection (305538217), https://search.proquest.com/docview/305538217?accountid=39490.
214   Ibid. 16.
215   L. Ritzenhöfer, P. Brosi, M. Spörrle, and I. M. Welpe, 'Leader Pride and Gratitude

Differentially Impact Follower Trust', *Journal of Managerial Psychology*, 32/6 (2017), 445–459, http://dx.doi.org/10.1108/JMP-08-2016-0235.

216 L. Ritzenhöfer, P. Brosi, M. Spörrle, I. M. Welpe, 'Satisfied with the Job, but Not with the Boss: Leaders' Expressions of Gratitude and Pride Differentially Signal Leader Selfishness, Resulting in Differing Levels of Followers' Satisfaction', *Journal of Business Ethics*, 158/4 (2019), 1185–1202, http://dx.doi.org/10.1007/s10551-017-3746-5.

217 M. B. Eberly, *Follower Reactions to Leader Emotions: A Cognitive and Affective Path to Leadership Effectiveness* (2011) (Order No. 3501532), ABI/INFORM Collection (937199940), https://search.proquest.com/docview/937199940?accountid=39490.

218 P. A. Stewart, B. M. Waller, and J. N. Schubert, 'Presidential Speechmaking Style: Emotional Response to Micro-Expressions of Facial Affect', *Motivation and Emotion*, 33/2 (2009), 125–135, http://dx.doi.org/10.1007/s11031-009-9129-1.

219 The Arbinger Institute, *The Outward Mindset: How to Change Lives and Transform Organisations* (Oakland, CA: Berrett-Koehler, 2016).

220 K. E. Russell, *Examinations of Leader Effect Behavior within Successful Fortune 100 Companies* (2006) (Order No. 3237802), ABI/INFORM Collection (304909595), https://search.proquest.com/docview/304909595?accountid=39490.

221 I. D. Brooks, *The Impact of Leader Behaviors on Employee Efficacy Perceptions and Performance* (2010) (Order No. 3452385), ABI/INFORM Collection (864672633), https://search.proquest.com/docview/864672633?accountid=39490.

222 T. M. Amabile, E. A. Schatzel, G. B. Moneta, and S. J. Kramer, 'Leader Behaviors and the Work Environment for Creativity: Perceived Leader Support', *Leadership Quarterly*, 15/1 (2004), 5–32, https://search.proquest.com/docview/200773952?accountid=39490.

223 G. J. Lynch, *Effective Leadership Behavior: Competing Values and Objective Outcomes in Selected Municipal Departments* (2000) (Order No. 9974982), ABI/INFORM Collection (304651103), https://search.proquest.com/docview/304651103?accountid=39490.

224 G. Yukl, A. Gordon, and T. Taber, 'A Hierarchical Taxonomy of Leadership Behavior: Integrating a Half Century of Behavior Research', *Journal of Leadership & Organizational Studies*, 9/1 (2002), 15–32, https://search.proquest.com/docview/203142703?accountid=39490.

225 A. Şen and E. Eren, 'Innovative Leadership for the Twenty-First Century', *Procedia-Social and Behavioral Sciences*, 41(2012), 1–14.

226 Ibid. 1.

227 D. P. Young and N. M. Dixon, *Helping Leaders Take Effective Action* (Greensboro, NC: Center for Creative Leadership, 1996), 1.

228 A. R. Jassawalla and H. C. Sashittal, 'Strategies of Effective New Product Team Leaders', *California Management Review*, 42/2 (2000), 34–51.

229 B. Yeganeh and D. Good, 'Micro-Actions', *Leadership Excellence*, 29/3 (2012), 15, https://search.proquest.com/docview/1010048909?accountid=39490.
230 'The Games: Up in the Air', *Time* (2 August 1976). Also read Nadia Comaneci, *Letters to a Young Gymnast* (Basic Books, 2004).
231 R. J. Sternberg, ed., *Handbook of Creativity* (Cambridge: Cambridge University Press, 1999).
232 T. M. Amabile et al., 'Assessing the Work Environment for Creativity', *Academy of Management Review*, 39/5 (1996), 1154–1184.
233 K. Graham-Leviss, 'The 5 Skills That Innovative Leaders Have in Common', *Harvard Business Review* (2016), https://hbr.org/2016/12/the-5-skills-that-innovative-leaders-have-in-common.
234 Hamel, *Future of Management*, 102.
235 J. Zenger and J. Folkman, 'Research: 10 Traits of Innovative Leaders', *Harvard Business Review* (2014), https://hbr.org/2014/12/research-10-traits-of-innovative-leaders.
236 J. Dyer, H. Gregersen, and C. M. Christensen, 'Innovative Companies Demand Innovative Leaders', *Harvard Business Review* (2011), https://hbr.org/2011/08/innovative-companies-demand-in.
237 Ibid.
238 Ibid.
239 Masaaki Sato, *The Toyota Leaders: An Executive Guide* (New York: Vertical Inc., 2008), 62ff.
240 Ibid. 63.
241 J. Womack, 'A Productive Leader Seeks Success', *Training*, 51/1 (2014), 8, https://search.proquest.com/docview/1500947424?accountid=39490.
242 For more on the type of leadership by Toyota, read Sato, *Toyota Leaders*.
243 Mehrabian and Ferris, 'Inference of Attitude from Nonverbal Communication in Two Channels', *The Journal of Counselling Psychology*, 31 (1967), 248–252.
244 R. Baumeister and M. R. Leary, 'The Need to Belong: Desire for Interpersonal Attachments as a Fundamental Human Motivation, *Psychological Bulletin* 117 (1995), 497–529.
245 Netflix, in its recruitment philosophy, speaks about some core values, and among them are courage to say what you think and do what you believe. This is how the company has been rated one of the best companies for its innovative way of recruiting employees. Read Matt Burgess, *Reed Hastings: Building Netflix*. London: Weidenfeld & Nicolson, 2020).
246 Refer to https://www.vocabulary.com › dictionary › transcendence for more details.

247 P. Korzynski, 'Overcoming Leadership Limitations: A Theoretical Study of Leadership Behaviors and Methods', *Management and Business Administration. Central Europe*, 127/4 (2014), 26–38.

248 J. J. Z. Gardiner and E. L. Walker, 'Transcendent Leadership: Theory and Practice of an Emergent Metaphor', *The International Journal of Servant-Leadership*, 5/1 (2009), 243–267, https://search.proquest.com/docview/2220142072?accountid=39490.

249 Ibid. 243.

250 J. Cottingham, *In Search of the Soul* (Princeton and Oxford: Princeton University Press, 2020), 118.

251 C. Jung, *Collected Works*, trans., G. Adler and R. F. C. Hull, 20 vols (rev. edn, London: Routledge, 1967), 77.

252 G. M. Hopkins, *Poems and Prose*, ed., W. H. Gardner (Harmonds-Worth: Penguin, 1953).

253 F. Nietzssche, *Untimely Meditations* (Cambridge: Cambridge University Press, 1997).

254 Cited in Cottingham, *In Search of the Soul*, 119.

255 Ibid.

256 http://news.stanford.edu/news/2005/june15/jobs-061505.html (accessed 24 May 2009).

257 J. J. Z. Gardiner, 'Transcendent Leadership: Pathway to Global Sustainability', First Working Collaboratively for Sustainability International Conference, Seattle University, Seattle (2009), http://integralleadershipreview.com/1928-transcendent-leadership-pathway-to-global-sustainability/.

258 Ibid.

259 Ibid.

260 Ibid.

261 Ibid.

262 Ibid.

263 Ibid.

264 Ibid.

265 K. S. San Juan, *The Spiritual Formation of Leaders Based on the Ignatian Tradition* (2007), 90 (Order No. 3267125), ABI/INFORM Collection (304748643), https://search.proquest.com/docview/304748643?accountid=39490.

266 W. Baker, 'Breakthrough Leadership: Believe, Belong, Contribute, & Transcend', *Organization Development Journal*, 19/4 (2001), 80.

267 R. Vanagas and V. R. Adomas, 'The Dichotomy of Self-Actualization and Self-Transcendence', *Verslo Sistemos Ir Ekonomika*, 4/2 (2014), https://search.proquest.com/docview/1628901217?accountid=39490.

268 C. Carter, *What Is the Experience of Leaders Who Transcend Organizational Paradox? A Phenomenological Inquiry* (2007) (Order No. 3264338), ABI/INFORM Collection (304753856), https://search.proquest.com/docview/304753856?accountid=39490.
269 K. Barron and S. Y. Chou, 'Toward a Spirituality Mode of Firm Sustainability Strategic Planning Processes', *Society and Business Review*, 12/1 (2017), 46–62.
270 Rego et al., *Virtues of Leadership*, 134.
271 G. Stebbins, 'Six Keys to Transcendent Leadership', *Forbes* (2017), https://www.forbes.com/sites/forbescoachescouncil/2017/05/11/six-keys-to-transcendent-leadership/#212b4dac7e2d.
272 M. Crossan and D. Mazutis, 'Transcendent Leadership', *Business Horizons*, 51/2 (2008), 131–139.
273 Ibid.
274 Rego et al., *Virtues of Leadership*, 116.
275 J. Collins, 'Level 5 Leadership: The Triumph of Humility and Fierce Resolve', *Harvard Business Review*, 79/1 (January 2001), 67–76.
276 In *The Spiritual Exercises* by St Ignatius of Loyola, this idea of attachment is extensively dealt with. When a person wants to make a decision to follow a way of life, he or she must be detached from inordinate attachments that would stand in the way of making proper decisions, p. 310.
277 N. C. Howard, M. R. McMinn, L. D. Bissell, S. R. Faries, and J. B. VanMeter, 'Spiritual Directors and Clinical Psychologists: A Comparison of Mental Health and Spiritual Values', *Journal of Psychology and Theology*, 28/4 (2000), 308–320.

Downward—Being Earthly

278 Rego et al., *Virtues of Leadership*, 172.
279 Refer to this page for more details: https://datatorch.com/life/Mother_Teresa_gets_Saliva_from_Shop_Keeper, 1.
280 Adapted from the story narrated by Simon Sinek, https://www.youtube.com/watch?v=uHGLtO69ADo.
281 Adapted from the story 'How Did Al Capone's Lawyer Save America?' from http://www.george-morosan.com/mafia-lawyer-easy-eddies-inspiring-legacy-radhanath-swami-goalcast/.
282 Ibid.
283 J. Li, Q. Z. Liang, and Z. Z. Zhang, 'The Effect of Humble Leader Behavior, Leader Expertise, and Organizational Identification on Employee Turnover Intention', *Journal of Applied Business Research (JABR)*, 32/4 (2016), 1145–1156.
284 B. P. Owens and D. R. Hekman, 'Modeling How to Grow: An Inductive Examination of Humble Leader Behaviors, Contingencies, and Outcomes, *Academy of Management Journal*, 55/4 (2012), 787–818.

285 Ibid.
286 Ibid.
287 E. D. Hess, 'Humble Leaders', *Leadership Excellence*, 24/5 (2007), 10, https://search.proquest.com/docview/204625007?accountid=39490.
288 Ibid. 55.
289 Ibid.
290 Ibid. 57.
291 J. Baldoni, 'Use Humility to Improve Performance', *Harvard Business Review* (2009a), https://hbr.org/2009/11/use-humility-to-improve-perfor.
292 J. Dame, and J. Gedmin, 'Six Principles for Developing Humility as a Leader', *Harvard Business Review* (2013), https://hbr.org/2013/09/six-principles-for-developing.
293 S. Coops, 'The Humble Leader', *Training Journal* (2017), 32–34, https://search.proquest.com/docview/2226344808?accountid=39490.
294 L. Yuan, L. Zhang, and T. Yanhong, 'When a Leader Is Seen as Too Humble', *Leadership & Organization Development Journal*, 39/4 (2018), 468–481, http://dx.doi.org/10.1108/LODJ-03-2017-0056.
295 F. Zhou, and Y. J. Wu, 'How Humble Leadership Fosters Employee Innovation Behavior', *Leadership & Organization Development Journal*, 39/3 (2018), 375–387, http://dx.doi.org/10.1108/LODJ-07-2017-0181.
296 Y. Chen, B. Liu, L. Zhang, and Q. Shanshan, 'Can Leader "Humility" Spark Employee "Proactivity"? The Mediating Role of Psychological Empowerment', *Leadership & Organization Development Journal*, 39/3 (2018), 326–339, http://dx.doi.org/10.1108/LODJ-10-2017-0307.
297 X. Lin, X. Zhen, H. H. M. Tse, W. Wu, and C. Ma, 'Why and When Employees Like to Speak Up More under Humble Leaders: The Roles of Personal Sense of Power and Power Distance', *Journal of Business Ethics*, 158/4 (2019), 937–950, http://dx.doi.org/10.1007/s10551-017-3704-2.
298 B. Beal, 'Leaders' Courage in Showing Humility', *Human Resource Management International Digest*, 25/2 (2017), 28–30, http://dx.doi.org/10.1108/HRMID-01-2017-0004.
299 P. Keijzer, '5 Reasons Why Humility Is an Essential Leadership Trait', Business2Community (2018), https://www.business2community.com/leadership/5-reasons-humility-essential-leadership-trait-02026513.
300 K. Bharanitharan, X. C. Zhen, S. Bahmannia, and K. B. Lowe, 'Is Leader Humility a Friend or Foe, or Both? An Attachment Theory Lens on Leader Humility and Its Contradictory Outcomes', *Journal of Business Ethic* (2018), 1–15, http://dx.doi.org/10.1007/s10551-018-3925-z.
301 Owens and Hekman, 'Modeling How to Grow', 787–818.
302 D. Cable, 'How Humble Leadership Really Works', *Harvard Business Review* (2018), https://hbr.org/2018/04/how-humble-leadership-really-works.

303 J. Baldoni, 'Humility as a Leadership Trait', *Harvard Business Review* (2009b), https://hbr.org/2009/09/humility-as-a-leadership-trait.
304 Ibid.
305 Ibid.
306 Ibid.
307 Hess, 'Humble Leaders', 10.
308 Ibid.
309 Marcel Schwantes, 'The World's Top 10 CEOs', https://www.inc.com/marcel-schwantes/heres-a-top-10-list-of-the-worlds-best-ceos-but-they-lead-in-a-totally-unique-wa.html, accessed 27 May 2021.
310 Cheryl Bachelder, *Dare to Serve: How to Drive Superior Results by Serving Others* (Berrett-Koehler Publishers, 2018).
311 *Authentic Leadership: Emotional Intelligence Series* (Boston: Harvard Business Review Press, 2018), 8.
312 John Meurig Thomas, *Michael Faraday and the Royal Institution: The Genius of Man and Place* (Bristol: Hilger, 1991).

Organic Connect of Moves and Energies

313 Nature connectedness is explained well in P. W. Schultz, 'Inclusion with Nature: The Psychology of Human-Nature Relations', in P. W. Schmuck and W. P. Schultz, eds, *Psychology of Sustainable Development* (Norwell, MA: Kluwer Academic, 2002), 62–78.
314 E. O. Wilson, *Biophilia* (Cambridge, MA: Harvard University Press, 1984).
315 Aristotle, *Poetics*, trans., with an introduction and notes, M. Heath (London: Penguin, 1996).
316 Eric J. Cunningham, 'Nature Interrupted: Affect and Ecology in the Wake of Volcanic Eruption in Japan', *Conservation and Society*, 16/1 (2018), 41–51.
317 Daniel Colyle, *The Talent Code: Greatness Isn't Born. It's Grown. Here's How* (New York: Bantam Books, 2009), 12–53.
318 Ibid. 32.
319 G. C. Kane, J. Copulsky, A. N. Philips, and R. Nanda, 'A Case of Acute Transformation', Deloitte Insights, https://www2.deloitte.com/us/en/insights/topics/digital-transformation/digital-transformation-COVID-19.html, accessed 29 May 2021.
320 J. Barentsen, 'Embodied Realism as Interpretive Framework for Spirituality, Discernment and Leadership', in *Leading in a VUCA World* (Springer Cham, 2019), 119–138, 133.
321 C. Bernacchio, 'Pope Francis on Conscience, Gradualness, and Discernment: Adapting Amoris Laetitia for Business Ethics', *Business Ethics Quarterly*, 29/4 (2019), 437–460.

322 A. L. Delbecq, E. Liebert, J. Mostyn, P. C. Nutt, and G. Walter, 'Discernment and Strategic Decision Making: Reflections for a Spirituality of Organizational Leadership', in *Research in Ethical Issues in Organizations* (2003), https://doi.org/10.1016/S1529-2096(03)05008-9.

323 Roger L. Martin, 'Innovation Catalysts', in *Innovation* (Boston, MA: Harvard Business Review Books, 2013), 1–10.

324 C. Christensen and M. Raynor, *Innovator's Solution: Creating and Sustaining Successful Growth* (Boston, MA: Harvard Business Review Press, 2003).

325 H. Ibarra and M. Hunter, 'How Leaders Create and Use Networks', *Harvard Business Review* (January 2007).

326 J. M. Assbeihat, 'The Impact of Collaboration among Members on Team's Performance', *Management and Administrative Sciences Review*, 5/5 (2016), 248–259.

327 C. K. Goman, 'Six Crucial Behaviors of Collaborative Leaders: Optimizing the Power of Collaboration', *Leadership Excellence*, 34/9 (2017), 15–16.

328 F. Gino, 'Cracking the Code of Sustained Collaboration', *Harvard Business Review*, 97/6 (2019), 72–81.

329 Adapted from Steve Jobs's speech, https://www.researchgate.net/publication/301899412_Steve_Jobs_Speech.

330 Adapted from Mark Zuckerberg's commencement address at Harvard, https://news.harvard.edu/gazette/story/2017/05/mark-zuckerbergs-speech-as-written-for-harvards-class-of-2017/.

331 Adapted from Elon Musk's commencement speech 'Magicians of the 21st Century' at Caltech, https://singjupost.com/elon-musks-commencement-speech-at-caltech-full-transcript/.

332 Adapted from Jeff Bezos's commencement speech delivered at Princeton University, https://www.princeton.edu/news/2010/05/30/2010-baccalaureate-remarks.

INDEX

A

agencies:
  constructive 55-6
  destructive 55-6
anthropology xiv, 3-6, 8, 11, 21, 46, 187, 197
Apple 2, 120, 171, 173
appropriateness 7, 75-6
Aristotle (philosopher) 69, 71, 200, 206
attachments:
  emotional 36, 64, 85
  inordinate 85, 129
  ordinate 85
attitude x-xii, 10, 14, 25, 31-2, 47, 75, 87-91, 130, 132, 141, 151-2, 167, 176, 198-9
  inner x, 87
authenticity 86, 92
authority vii, x, xiii, 25, 29-32, 42, 57-65, 67, 69-73, 87, 102, 104, 117, 147, 149, 164, 172, 175, 178, 181, 194-5
  formal 61
  line 63
  staff 63
awareness 39-40, 73, 77, 158

B

balance xii, 8, 32, 35, 51, 75, 78, 164
Banerjee, Arunav 1
behaviour xi, 4-5, 10, 39, 47, 58, 61-3, 66, 70, 75-7, 80, 84-8, 94, 101-2, 104-5, 166
Branson, Richard 63, 82
Bresch, Heather 40

C

Carlzon, Jan 52-3
change agent 45, 56, 63
Churchill, Winston 50
collaboration vii, xv, 27-8, 156, 166
commitment xiii, 15-16, 70-1, 198
communication xiv, 3, 5-6, 8, 28, 41, 65, 103, 115
competence vii, xi, 2-3, 7, 10-11, 15-16, 21, 25, 29, 63, 76, 80, 89, 197
competency ix, 1, 8, 14, 17, 54, 56, 78
Confederation of Indian Industry (CII) 16
courage 60, 71, 84
creativity 51, 77, 140, 202
crises:
  economic 7
  energy 7

criticisms, constructive 76

D

developments, historical 38-9
discernment vii, 55-7, 154, 156, 158-60
discourses 65-8
  ownership 67
  positive 67-8
dynamo 24, 189-90
dynamo competence 3, 11, 25, 63, 75, 78, 86, 89
dynamo power 24
dynamo theory 24

E

empathy 69-70, 78, 94, 103
energies:
  earthliness x-xi, 25, 30, 32, 145, 151
  futuristic vision x, 25, 29-30, 32, 53, 57, 73, 87, 172, 175, 178, 181
  inner attitude x, 87
  productiveness x, 6, 15, 25, 30, 56, 64, 76, 81
  transcendence x-xi, 25, 30, 32, 118, 121, 126, 151, 167, 202
  use of authority vii, x, xiii, 25, 29-32, 42, 57-65, 67, 69-73, 87, 102, 104, 117, 147, 149, 164, 172, 175, 178, 181, 194-5
ethos 69, 71, 159
expressions xi, 22, 32, 66, 77, 86
exteriority 60

F

flexibility x-xi, 13, 80, 147, 151
fragility 21, 72
futuristic vision x, 25, 29-30, 32, 53, 57, 73, 87, 172, 175, 178, 181

G

Gandhi, Mahatma 50, 86
goodness 72

H

historical consciousness vii, xi, 25, 29, 32-3, 35, 37-42, 45, 58, 73, 87, 147, 171, 174, 177, 180, 190-2
  defined 38
HR leaders 53, 57-8, 63-4, 67, 71, 90
HR professionals 7-8, 15, 18
HRM leadership 10
human behaviour 3, 5
human resource development (HRD) ix, xii, 14, 16
human resource management (HRM) xii, 3-6, 8-10, 12, 14-17, 54
human resource planning (HRP) 10, 54
human resources ix, 1-6, 8-13, 16-18, 25, 33, 45, 56, 183-4
humanity 9, 18, 22
humility x, 136-40, 205

I

Iacocca, Lee 52
innovation vii, 13, 18, 42, 47-8, 51, 107-11, 154, 156, 163
intelligence, emotional 13, 31-2, 73, 75-82, 168, 197-8
interiority 60

J

Jobs, Steve 2, 52, 171
Jong-Yong, Yun 2

K

King, Martin Luther 50
Kyung-Bae, Suh 62

L

Land, Edwin 52
leaders:
  agile 27
  competent ix, 8, 10-11, 21, 29-30, 45
  dynamo 26-7
  effective 53
  efficient 9, 73
  good 62, 88
  intelligent 80-3
  mature 73, 85
  persuasive 65
  productive xii
  transformative 85
  visionary 49-52
leadership:
  autocratic 70
  balanced xii
  dynamo 26, 28
  effective ix, 77, 79-81
  energy 8
  innovative 18, 105, 201
  mature 79
  model of xiii, 2
  passionate 79
  real 72, 84
leadership competence 3, 6, 17-18, 78-9
  pillars of 3, 6, 93
leadership style:
  bricoleur 52
  creator 52
  diviner 53
  idealist 52
  proselytizer 52
leadership: visionary 49-50, 52, 194
learning: locus of 32, 42
legitimations 59-60
letachment 77
Lévesque, René 52
limitations 22, 71, 84, 117-18, 126, 132, 203

logos 66, 69, 71, 159, 196
love x-xii, 3, 23, 54, 73-4, 79, 147-8

M

management xii, xiv, 3, 5-6, 8-9, 11-12, 14, 16-17, 24, 39, 45, 183-4, 188-90, 193-5, 199, 202
maturity 8, 74, 76, 78, 86-7, 101-2, 104, 112, 132, 149
  affective 73, 86-7
  emotional x, 25, 30-2, 73
McCullough, David 33
McKay, David 63
Miller, Alexey B. 2
mindset 49, 87, 90
moneymaking 7
Mother Teresa 79
motivation 13, 16, 50, 60, 83, 88, 140, 201
moves:
  backward x, xiii, 25, 29-30, 33, 46, 53, 57, 64, 73, 87
  downward x-xi, 25, 29-30, 32
  forward x, 15, 25, 29-30, 41, 46, 48, 53, 57, 64, 73, 84, 87
  inward x, 25, 29-31, 87, 89
  leftward x, 25, 29-31, 73, 75, 78, 86
  outward vii, x-xi, 25, 29-30, 32, 100, 103-4, 112, 148, 150, 152, 164, 167, 173, 176, 179, 182, 200
  rightward x, 25, 29-30, 57-8, 72, 87
  upward x-xi, 25, 29, 32
Musk, Elon 81-2, 177

N

Nadella, Satya 83
Nooyi, Indra 82

O

observation, discernment, and designing (ODD) 55

211

P

Pascal, Blaise 73
pathos 69, 71
Pausch, Randy 74
perception 50, 61-2, 84, 104, 194-5
performance 2, 6, 9, 11, 15-17, 28, 31, 45, 49, 72, 87, 91, 104, 127-8, 144, 164, 169, 184-5, 199, 201, 207
persuasion 6, 10, 65, 71, 87
Pistorius, Oscar 57
power vii, ix-xi, 3, 12-13, 20-1, 25, 30, 33, 35, 57-65, 68-9, 72, 81, 87, 147, 168, 184, 194-5, 199
  authoritative 58
  coercive 61
  expert 61
  legitimate 61-3
  organisational 61
  personal 61
  position of 6, 31, 64, 79
  referent 61
  reward 61-2
pragmatism x, 25, 145, 151
Procter & Gamble 18
productiveness x, 6, 15, 25, 30, 56, 64, 76, 81
productivity vii, 6, 15, 76, 81, 100, 111, 200

R

realisation x, 21, 23, 26, 52, 58, 84-5
reformation 84-5
Rüsen, Jörn 38

S

School of Inspired Leadership Innovation Board 1
Schultz, Howard 45
self-awareness 23, 78, 93, 95
separateness 23-4
spirituality xv
stakeholders 47-8, 60, 71-2, 127
Starbucks 45, 68, 193
structure, organisational 39, 53, 62
success 7, 12, 14-15, 18, 21, 32, 45, 49, 53-4, 56, 66-7, 77, 81-2, 88-9, 166, 197, 202

T

thinking: collective 70
Toyota 18
trust 13, 80-1
truth 26, 34-5, 73, 99, 114, 160, 198
Turnbull, Lucy 62

U

Usmanov, Alisher 62

V

values 20, 34-5, 37, 41, 44, 47, 50, 56, 63, 80, 87-8, 131, 137, 193, 202
vision vii, x, 30, 32, 36-7, 46-56, 58, 64-5, 67-8, 71, 87-8, 102, 104, 106, 122, 132, 147, 151, 153, 164, 167, 193
visioning 48-9
vulnerability 21, 84

www.ingramcontent.com/pod-product-compliance
Lightning Source LLC
Chambersburg PA
CBHW030920180526
45163CB00002B/412